ROUTLEDGE LIBRARY EDITIONS: LIBRARY AND INFORMATION SCIENCE

Volume 1

A CHANGING WORLD

A CHANGING WORLD

Proceedings of the North American Serials Interest Group, Inc.

Edited by
SUZANNE MCMAHON, MIRIAM PALM AND
PAM DUNN

Routledge
Taylor & Francis Group

LONDON AND NEW YORK

First published in 1991 by The Haworth Press, Inc.

This edition first published in 2020
by Routledge
2 Park Square, Milton Park, Abingdon, Oxon OX14 4RN

and by Routledge
52 Vanderbilt Avenue, New York, NY 10017

Routledge is an imprint of the Taylor & Francis Group, an informa business

© 1991 The Haworth Press, Inc.

All rights reserved. No part of this book may be reprinted or reproduced or utilised in any form or by any electronic, mechanical, or other means, now known or hereafter invented, including photocopying and recording, or in any information storage or retrieval system, without permission in writing from the publishers.

Trademark notice: Product or corporate names may be trademarks or registered trademarks, and are used only for identification and explanation without intent to infringe.

British Library Cataloguing in Publication Data
A catalogue record for this book is available from the British Library

ISBN: 978-0-367-34616-4 (Set)
ISBN: 978-0-429-34352-0 (Set) (ebk)
ISBN: 978-0-367-37096-1 (Volume 1) (hbk)
ISBN: 978-0-367-37125-8 (Volume 1) (pbk)
ISBN: 978-0-429-35273-7 (Volume 1) (ebk)

Publisher's Note
The publisher has gone to great lengths to ensure the quality of this reprint but points out that some imperfections in the original copies may be apparent.

Disclaimer
The publisher has made every effort to trace copyright holders and would welcome correspondence from those they have been unable to trace.

A CHANGING WORLD:
Proceedings of the
NORTH AMERICAN SERIALS INTEREST GROUP, Inc.

6th Annual Conference
June 14-17, 1991
Trinity University
San Antonio, Texas

Suzanne McMahon
Miriam Palm
Pam Dunn
Editors

The Haworth Press, Inc.
New York • London

A Changing World: Proceedings of the North American Serials Interest Group, Inc. has also been published as *The Serials Librarian*, Volume 21, Numbers 2/3 1991.

© 1991 by The Haworth Press, Inc. All rights reserved. No part of this work may be reproduced or utilized in any form or by any means, electronic or mechanical, including photocopying, microfilm and recording, or by any other information storage and retrieval system, without permission in writing from the publisher. Printed in the United States of America.

The Haworth Press, Inc., 10 Alice Street, Binghamton, NY 13904-1580
EUROSPAN/Haworth, 3 Henrietta Street, London WC2E 8LU England

Library of Congress Cataloging-in-Publication Data

A Changing world: proceedings of the North American Serials Interest Group, Inc. / Suzanne McMahon, Miriam Palm, Pam Dunn, editors.
    p. cm.
  "The North American Serials Interest Group held its Sixth Annual Conference at Trinity University, San Antonio, Texas, June 14-17, 1991" – Introd.
  "Has also been published as The Serials librarian, volume 21, numbers 2/3, 1991" – T.p. verso.
  Includes index.
  ISBN 1-56024-263-9. – ISBN 1-56024-298-1 (pbk.)
  1. Serials control systems – Congresses. 2. Libraries – Special collections – Serial publications – Congresses. 3. Serial publications – Congresses. I. McMahon, Suzanne. II. Palm, Miriam. III. Dunn, Pam. IV. North American Serials Interest Group. Conference (6th: 1991: San Antonio, Tex.)
Z692.S5048 1992
025.3'432 – dc20
                                                            91-39991
                                                                       CIP

A Changing World: Proceedings of the North American Serials Interest Group, Inc.

CONTENTS

Introduction	1
Announcement: NASIG Conference Grant Awards	3

PLENARY SESSION 1 – CHANGING TECHNOLOGIES

The Impact of Electronic and Networking Technologies on the Delivery of Scholarly Information *Timothy B. King*	5
Electronic Serials: Realistic or Unrealistic Solution to the Journal "Crisis?" *Anne B. Piternick*	15

PLENARY SESSION 2 – CHANGING INFORMATION WORLDWIDE

Globalization of Research, Scholarly Information, and Patents – Ten Year Trends *Francis Narin*	33
Europe 1992 – Implications for Scholarly Publishing and Distribution *John F. Riddick*	45
Zastroika, Perestroika, Rasstroika, Dostroika, and Us *Edward Kasinec*	59

Scholarly Information and Serials in Latin America:
   Shifting Political Sands   69
      Margarita Almada de Ascencio
      Sylvia Pérez de Almada

PLENARY SESSION 3 – STRATEGIES AND RESPONSES

Automated Library Systems: What Next?   87
      Carol Pitts Hawks

Embracing the Electronic Journal: One Library's Plan   97
      Gail McMillan

Information Technologies and the Transformation
   of Libraries and Librarianship   109
      Charles B. Lowry

Wrap-Up Session   133
      Dan Tonkery

WORKSHOP SESSION REPORTS

Case Study: Starting a New Medical Journal   139
      Barbara A. Carlson

Marketing a New Social Science/Humanities Journal
   to Libraries, Then and Now   143
      Isabel Czech

SUPER-OPAC: Records for Articles and Chapters
   in Your Catalog   147
      Birdie MacLennan

Periodicals Receiving Units and Public Service Areas:
   A Productive Combination   149
      Phoebe Timberlake

The Continuations Saga: Converting Non-Periodical Serials   153
      Judith M. Shelton

Interfacing Automated Environments: Linking the Integrated
  Library Systems 157
    Christie T. Degener

Conversion to Automated Serials Control Systems:
  From the Drawing Board to the Front Lines 161
    Marla Edelman

Replacement Issues: Where Do You Find Them
  and at What Cost? 165
    Lawrence R. Keating II

How Vendors Assess Service Charges and a Publisher's
  View of Discounts to Vendors 169
    Kathleen Meneely

Case Study: Managing the Established Sci-Tech Journal 173
    Brenda Dingley

Case Study: A Society Journal Published by a Commercial
  Publisher 177
    Mary K. Castle

Multiple Version Cataloging and Preservation Microfilming
  for Brittle Issues of Serials 181
    Geraldine F. Pionessa

The Impact of Electronic Journals on Traditional Library
  Services 185
    Linda Hulbert

Journal Contents Online: Patron Use and Implications
  for Reference Service 189
    Lisa A. Macklin

An Introduction to the Structure of ANSI X12 and a Tutorial
  on X12 Mapping for Serials Related Transactions 193
    Joseph Barker

Job Descriptions Vis-à-Vis Job Applications: A Match Often
  Not Made in Heaven 197
    Rita Broadway

Serials Claims: Three Perspectives, Library/Publisher/Vendor 201
    Louise Diodato

Acquiring and Cataloging the Elusive Latin American Serial 205
    Lisa Peterson

Sixth Annual NASIG Conference Registrants, Trinity
   University, June 1991   209

Index   225

Introduction

The North American Serials Interest Group (NASIG) held its Sixth Annual Conference at Trinity University, San Antonio, Texas, from June 14-17, 1991. The Program Committee chose "A Changing World" as the theme of this year's conference.

In our changing world the Cold War era is a memory. The bipolar dominance of the U.S. and the U.S.S.R. is giving way to a new configuration of power. The Pacific Rim is on the ascendant. EC-92 is almost a reality and mail-order catalogs are selling pieces of the Berlin Wall. The Slavic behemoth wrestles to throw off lethargy and enter the market economy. The U.S. is facing straitened means and a piper who must be paid to the tune of over 3 trillion dollars.

Just as the invention of movable type and its application to commercial printing in fifteenth century Europe sent waves throughout the western world that shook the halls of power, so the technological marvels of these last decades of the twentieth century have touched off a revolution that has spanned the globe, propelled us beyond its gravitational pull, and set us on a course for who knows where — only a seer could predict with certainty.

How do institutions like libraries, the print-oriented beneficiaries of post-war prosperity, enter the computer wonderland that beckons with wild promises of unimaginable speed, inconceivable storage capacity, and universal access. With our shrinking bankbook how will we pay our entrance fees?

Speakers at this years plenary sessions offered insight, inspiration and practical experience arranged under three major headings: "Changing technologies," "Changing Information Worldwide," and "Strategies and Responses." Conference participants also had the opportunity to choose among eighteen workshops addressing the practical aspects of serials work. Papers of the main speakers, a

© 1991 by The Haworth Press, Inc. All rights reserved.

transcript of the wrap-up session, and summaries of all the workshops are included in this volume.

The Seventh Annual NASIG Conference will be held at University of Illinois, Chicago Campus, June 18-21, 1992.

We wish to thank Pat Rice and Mary Beth Clack for guiding us through the editorial process and Dena Hutto for preparing the index. We also gratefully acknowledge the assistance of Lisa Carlson in preparing the typescript.

S.M.

Announcement: NASIG Conference Grant Awards

The North American Serials Interest Group (NASIG) is an independent organization bringing together many segments of the serials information chain to study and explore common interests, problems, and ideas. NASIG is currently seeking candidates for grants to attend the Seventh Annual Conference to be held at the University of Illinois at Chicago, June 18-21, 1992. Through the granting of these awards, NASIG desires to encourage participation in this information chain by students who are interested in some aspect of serials work upon completion of their professional degree.

GUIDELINES

SCOPE OF AWARD: Recipients are expected to attend the entire conference and submit a brief written report to NASIG. Expenses for travel, registration, meals and lodging will be paid by NASIG.

ELIGIBILITY: Students who are currently enrolled in any ALA accredited library school, who do not already have an ALA accredited degree, and who have expressed an interest in serials and/or technical services work, are eligible. Applicants *must* be full or part-time students at the time of application. In order to accept an award, a recipient *must not* be employed in a position requiring an ALA accredited degree, nor be on leave from such a position, at the time of acceptance of the grant. Applicants must be a citizens of, or have permanent resident status in, the United States, Canada, or Mexico. Equal consideration will be given to all qualified applicants, with preference given to those graduating the year of the conference.

APPLICATION PROCEDURE: Application forms will be available after February 1, 1992, in ALA accredited library schools and from Harriet Kersey, Chair, Library Science Student Grant Committee. Application forms should be sent to: Harriet Kersey, Head, Serials Cataloging, Georgia Tech Library, Atlanta, Georgia 30332-0900. Telephone number: (404) 894-4523.

APPLICATION DEADLINE: March 1, 1992. Applications postmarked after this date will not be considered.

AWARD NOTIFICATION: Award recipients will be notified by April 15, 1992. A maximum of six grants may be awarded for 1992.

PLENARY SESSION 1 – CHANGING TECHNOLOGIES

The Impact of Electronic and Networking Technologies on the Delivery of Scholarly Information

Timothy B. King

Let me start with some unqualified predictions concerning the impact of electronic and networking technologies on the delivery of scholarly information: between now and the end of 1991 nothing will change noticeably. Fifteen years from now, in the year 2006, we will look back and say, "Good Lord, how much things have changed." Further, whatever the situation in the year 2006, information will be accessed and delivered in a more individualized manner than it is now. We will also be able to search for information in an interactive, multimedia format, and that information will be delivered to us more quickly than it is now, even in real time. We will use information in new ways that we haven't even thought of yet.

Timothy B. King is Vice President, Planning & Development, John Wiley & Sons, 605 Third Avenue, 5th Floor, New York, NY 10158-0012.

© 1991 by The Haworth Press, Inc. All rights reserved.

Just as radio offered possibilities unimagined by the newspaperman, and just as television offered possibilities unimagined by the radioman, so the electronic network medium will provide opportunities for accessing and using information which so far have not been imagined by the print mind.

I also predict that in the year 2006, even though there will be extraordinary electronic networks out there doing extraordinary things, the print medium will continue to exist along with the electronic medium—just as newspapers, radios, and televisions all coexist. What will change is the role of each. The electronic networks will grow; they will expand; for some activities, they will be preferred to the print medium, but they will not eliminate the print medium. We are facing evolution, not revolution. We will work with the new medium while continuing to use the existing media.

Well, that's about all I'm sure of—from here on it's informed speculation! If you want several hundred pages of informed speculation, I recommend a British Library Research publication entitled *Information UK 2000* published by Bowker/Saur in the fall of last year.

Let us now look more closely at the impact of electronic and networking technologies on what I would define as the four phases or aspects of scholarly communication:

- finding out what's going on, but not yet published
- staying current with what has just been published
- searching the literature
- collaborating on research at a distance

I think it is important to consider these aspects separately, rather than merging them all together and extrapolating (erroneously) the impact of technology on one of them to all the others. For instance, just because researchers use e-mail frequently for informal communications does not mean that e-mail will become the publishing medium of preference for formal publication.

So let's look at the first phase—finding out what is going on right now in the world of research. The technologies used currently include telephone, FAX, e-mail, electronic bulletin boards, mail, and, of course, personal encounters at meetings, symposia and seminars.

The use of e-mail, voice mail, electronic bulletin boards, transmission of scanned images, as well as FAX and phone will continue to increase. Electronic conferencing, the transmission of scanned images, televideo conferencing, and electronic newsletters will all grow in popularity. Mail and telex use will decrease; attendance at scholarly meetings could conceivably decrease, though I doubt that it will.

In addition, editors and journal reviewers (who are aware of what has been completed and submitted for publication) will continue in these rules to stay abreast of what's new in research. Increasingly, articles will be sent to editors and reviewers over the networks with the expectation that reviews and comments will be returned over the same network. However, it may be the latter half of the 1990s before complex illustrations and halftones can be sent efficiently over the networks and before most researchers have workstations that can handle complex graphics. The memory capacity for the workstation of the editor of a journal, for example, will have to be especially large, as multiple versions of every article submitted will have to be stored.

Despite the use of electronic networks, I'm not convinced that the reviewing process will be dramatically speeded up, beyond the five or six days saved by transmitting an article electronically rather than mailing it. Once the novelty of working on an electronically transmitted article has worn off, I doubt that scholars will get around to reviewing submitted articles any faster than they do now. On the contrary, knowing that they can transmit their completed reviews instantaneously could well result in them putting off the review process for a few extra days.

Apart from this gradual transition for traditional reviewing, a new reviewing category seems to be emerging: the review of items submitted to moderated electronic bulletin boards, innovative electronic journals, and to discipline databases such as the one on the Human Genome maintained at Johns Hopkins. Review of these electronic articles will probably increase rapidly, although they will still represent only a small portion of all articles reviewed, at least until the latter half of this decade.

Now let's look at the next phase of information gathering, which is finding out what has been published recently. Maintaining current awareness by browsing the most recent issues of journals in one's field will remain a common method, as long as the paper issue arrives before current awareness databases can be updated and made available. This method will probably start to decline in popularity as researchers find they can get the information they need in a timely manner at their electronic workstations without having to make a trip to the library.

The electronic networking technologies which will be responsible for this change are already being used by the secondary publishing services such as Current Contents and the A and I services. Over half the revenue for many U.S. secondary publishers comes from electronic forms of distribution, whether from hosts such as BRS and Dialog, from tape sales to university and corporate networks, or from CD's and floppy discs. I expect this trend to continue, with heavily used services being mounted on institutional networks with site licenses and updated via regular tape shipments or by transmissions over the network.

These institutional networks will one day be able to overlay their own standard access and usage software on to the databases, so that their users need to learn only one set of search protocols. Less frequently used services will be accessed via the database hosts on a fee-per-use or subscription basis. CD versions of these services will be used where internal networks are not highly developed. As confidence in the reliability and durability of the electronic editions of these services continues to grow, the demand for the print editions will decline.

Having reviewed the abstracts, the researcher will want copies of articles of interest for his or her files. The process of obtaining copies of the articles will be increasingly electronics-based and will eliminate labor costs involved in locating an article, photocopying it, and then returning it to its original location.

The basic technology already exists for this electronics-based access, under the name of "custom publishing" machines. Xerox has its DocuTech copier; McGraw-Hill/Donnelly have their Primis system; Adonis has its system of mainly off-the-shelf components; UMI has its proprietary equipment for document reproduction.

All these systems depend on electronic storage of articles. Some systems—for instance Adonis and Xerox's DocuTech—use a bitmapped image of the typeset page, usually stored on optical disk. The straight-forward ASCII file is the usual form for on-line databases, but a complex, digital PostScript file can produce an image of the typeset page, with illustrations, when connected to the appropriate output device. The McGraw-Hill/Donnelly system uses PostScript.

Many organizations are already planning to deliver articles using these technologies. The Colorado Alliance of Research Libraries is basing its UnCover document delivery service on the electronics-based access and storage technology currently used for "custom publishing." And a group of about fifteen research libraries, organized at the March 1991 meeting of the Coalition for Networked Information, is investigating the possibility of using the Xerox DocuTech technology for on-campus distribution of articles.

The speed at which electronics-based document delivery develops depends on — and this should surprise no one — demand, standards, copyrights and economics. But a number of companies, and Faxon is one of them, believe that this is a business with enormous growth potential over the next five to six years.

If demand is great, then publishers themselves may provide the electronic master copies to the electronic document deliverers. Initially (in two to five years), the master copies would be non-searchable bit-mapped images of the typeset page; the complex, digital PostScript files, which could produce a fully searchable image of the typeset page, would not be available right away. It will take at least two additional years before typesetting suppliers will all have the capability of producing PostScript files and before publishers can find economical ways of getting all figures and illustrations, particularly halftones, in a digital form. Researchers' workstations, campus networks and the national networks will all need upgrading. Currently only a few can handle these complex graphic transmissions.

By the time publishers are able to provide electronic master copies of journal issues for document deliverers, the networks will have the enormous capacity needed to transmit these materials quickly and economically. At that point, I would guess five to seven years from now, journal publishers will offer their journals in the same way that the A and I services like ISI and H.W. Wilson currently offer their publications — in print form, as well as on tape, magnetic disk, optical disk, or online.

From this point on, I believe we are going to see some very interesting things. In particular, research papers will have motion simulations or video, with sound. We are going to see the reverse of what we have now. Presently the online version of a journal refers to the print version for the figures and illustrations. Seven to ten years from now, it will be the print version which refers to the electronic one for moving illustrations and sound. At that point the electronic version will be the definitive one — the one that must be archived.

During the intervening years, will some journals be published only in electronic format? The answer must be "yes," as nearly thirty exist already, according to Ann Okerson's research. However, the contents will generally be restricted to papers by authors who write primarily for electronic journals and who do not expect their articles to be widely archived.

One other electronic publishing alternative I would like to mention is the subject specific electronic database. The two best known examples are the Human Genome project at Johns Hopkins and the *c. elegans* project at the University of Arizona at Tucson. Both projects are working to develop an electronic database that holds *all* scientific information relating to a given subject, which will be kept current by continually adding new information as it becomes available. Researchers in the field can search the database directly and their contributions are or will be posted in an unreviewed section of the database. Following peer review and acceptance, the contributions will be transferred to the archival section of the database.

The concept is attractive, but difficult and expensive to implement. Large amounts of current and historical information and data have to be keyed in; existing databases have to be incorporated; and hypertext links have to be established along with graphics to handle illustrations. Updating and management of the database must be ongoing. I have no idea if such subject specific databases will develop widely, but you may be sure that publishers will be watching the experimental ones closely to determine the resources needed to establish and run them, the usage made of them, and their acceptance for archival purposes.

Let me move now to the third phase the researcher goes through—the retrospective search of the literature. Here, we are going to see the slowest changes; none of the currently existing material is in usable electronic format, and the cost of scanning it comprehensively would be very expensive. Unlike microforms, comprehensive scanning would not result in major space savings (microforms already have been used successfully for this purpose). So, I believe the comprehensive historical literature search still will begin with an examination of A and I publications and the citation indexes (increasingly in electronic format). The researcher will then request a copy of the articles desired and receive them in the conventional way. Comprehensive electronic retrospective searching of full-text articles is a long way off—if it will ever be possible.

There are two possible exceptions to this rash prediction; first, the subject specific databases I mentioned earlier. The concept for such databases includes the back loading of all relevant articles, so a full historical search can be made electronically.

Second, it is conceivable that the larger document deliverers, such as the British Library at Boston Spa, the Colorado Alliance CARL, or Faxon (if it grows as large as it hopes), might create an electronic database of all the articles they scan. Over the years, they would accumulate a database of articles significant enough to have been requested at least once. With the right optical character recognition and search software, such a database could be searched historically. It's an interesting possibility, but frankly don't hold your breath!

Moving on to the fourth phase of the process, the research itself, we find a major development from the electronic and network technologies—collaborative research at a distance. The networks enable the exchange of information (text, data, images) virtually instantaneously. This exchange permits the simultaneous development and discussion of research results in several locations, leading to joint conclusions and a collaborative final report.

The nature of the research published also will change with the emergence of electronic and networking technology. It will become possible for research results to appear in multi-media format, including sound and motion. (Wiley publishes research on cell motility which is meaningful only if you can see the cell's motion on video.) I believe that this development will offer us new areas for research just as film has offered a new medium of artistic expression compared with the written word.

What does all this mean for librarians and publishers? Let me summarize.

Phase 1: Learning what's going on and staying up to date. This area of exchange will grow in magnitude and complexity as the networks grow in capacity and speed. Electronic conferencing and electronic newsletters will continue to increase in number. Librarians, I believe, will be considering what portions, if any, of these electronic communications they should archive.

Publishers need to become connected to the networks and, eventually, to install in their editors' offices large capacity e-mail memories to cope with the submission of articles via e-mail.

Phase 2: Current awareness. Publishers are going to be looking for ways to make the electronic masters of their journals' contents available on subscription, for the abstract and index publishers as well as for the document deliverers — whether they are commercial like CARL or Faxon, or institutional such as research libraries. Publishers will be developing generic output formats to fit our customers needs. Increasingly, librarians will be mounting current awareness services electronically and deciding whether to keep the print subscription.

Librarians also will have to think about their own role in the areas of print and electronic document delivery. How much electronic redistribution on local institutional networks can they support? Will they charge fees to cover the extended level of service they supply? Will some of these functions be absorbed by fee-for-service entities such as commercial document deliverers, on-campus print shops, or campus bookstores? Librarians also will have to consider who is to archive the experimental electronic journals and how. Publishers will be less concerned with these issues. I doubt if most publishers will become heavily involved in electronic journals until electronic display quality matches that of the print medium, and institutions have workstations capable of reproducing print quality electronic displays. Abstracting and indexing services already publish many titles in electronic format; their experience migrating from print format could be helpful to librarians and publishers, who now anticipate a similar move toward electronic publications in other areas.

Both publishers and librarians also should keep an eye on the subject specific databases. These databases could remain isolated projects—or they could become widespread. It's impossible to say at this point.

Phase 3: Historical Searching. I would be surprised to see extensive retrospective electronic conversion of full text journal articles in the foreseeable future. This means that historical searches will continue to be done using the A and I services and the citation indexes. Libraries will remain as the primary source for copies of the desired articles.

Some libraries may substitute electronic scanning for microform purchases, making electronic document retrieval increasingly easier. Companies like UMI and Research Publications may enter this new market.

Phase 4: Cooperative research and the development of multimedia electronic articles. There will be a very slow increase in the number of articles that have motion or sound components requiring the use of electronic formats. Some print journals (like Wiley's journal on cell motility) publish occasional multiformat issues if articles have these sound and motion components. The number of these articles will increase as high-capacity workstations and networks facilitate this type of research. Librarians will be asked to archive all the components of such multi-media journals.

As the number of these articles increases, both publishers and librarians will be pushed into handling the fully electronic journal. By then, the fully electronic journal will be as well designed and easy to use as today's print journals. In fact, electronic journals will be as superior to the print journal as the word processor is to the typewriter, or as electronic spreadsheets are to the calculator. However, we won't see much of this before the year 2000.

Electronic Serials: Realistic or Unrealistic Solution to the Journal "Crisis?"

Anne B. Piternick

The husband of one of my friends bought an old farmhouse in Italy a couple of years ago and began to restore it. He is an academic jet-setter: lives in England, is a visiting scholar three months of the year at MIT, and regularly travels to Japan, Italy, and other places to lecture, attend conferences, and act as consultant. Once he had made a room of his Italian farmhouse habitable, he installed a FAX machine. Immediately, he could be in touch with his colleagues in Europe, America, and Japan. He could exchange drafts of papers, make arrangements for meetings, plan conferences, edit proofs, and otherwise communicate with his book editors. His wife complains that he installed the FAX machine in the master bedroom; she does not like being wakened in the middle of the night as the machine beeps and cranks out communications from across the world. But on the whole, he has easily absorbed this technology into his lifestyle.

The same thing has happened elsewhere. FAX is now endemic on my university campus. Campus mail is considered too slow for many communications; it is hard to reach people on the phone, and increasingly one finds oneself talking to an answering machine. Support staff do not want to spend time running across campus with documents, so they use FAX instead.

Apart from the speed of transmission, why is FAX so popular? It is convenient to use, especially if you do not have to operate the

---

Anne B. Piternick is Professor, School of Library, Archival & Information Studies, University of British Columbia, Vancouver, B.C., Canada, V6T 1Z1.

© 1991 by The Haworth Press, Inc. All rights reserved.

machine yourself. FAX, like mail, is most often sent from departmental office to departmental office; a machine for personal use is not required. Using FAX does not require a change in work patterns: one can still write memos or letters. "What you see is what you get." Everything arrives unchanged—letterhead, drawings, handwriting—although it is all in black and white.

Electronic messaging has not caught on so readily. Using e-mail requires some computer literacy and access to equipment which is more complicated than a FAX machine. In addition, the colleagues with whom one wishes to communicate must also must have access to the network. Many people, particularly in the humanities and some areas of the social sciences, still do not have personal computers in their offices or even at home. Those who have computers do not necessarily have modems. Scholars in these fields tend to work independently and are not constantly in touch with colleagues. This year, for the first time, our campus directory lists network addresses. Looking through the directory, I would say that only twenty-five to thirty percent of the entries for academic staff show network addresses, but at least network addresses are now included, which may draw attention to the network and encourage others to use the messaging system.

Other studies have shown that electronic messaging is not always enthusiastically embraced by those who have access to it. Rice and Case, in a study made in the early 1980s, found that "people do not necessarily attribute greater benefits to using computer-based messaging as they gain experience."[1] They also found that e-mail did not altogether replace other means of communication with colleagues, but instead it was adopted as another medium to use when convenient. Heavy telephone users continued to be heavy telephone users and made comparatively little use of e-mail. I myself send e-mail messages to a colleague in Ottawa who prefers to phone me back.

Hiltz and Johnson, in a later study, found that frequency of use is not necessarily linked to subjective satisfaction or perceived benefits. Employees might continue to use an internal e-mail system even if they did not perceive any value in it, because they felt they were required to use the system.[2]

What does all this have to do with electronic serials? The way in which people react to technological developments and adapt to changes depends very much on human factors — behavioral and psychological. Experience has shown that similar human factors also influence the acceptance of electronic serials.

Electronic messaging systems have made possible the development of various types of scholarly communications which bear some resemblance to their counterparts in printed form. For example, scholars from many disciplines, members of the "invisible college," systematically exchange preprints and unpublished seminar papers, expecting comments and criticisms from colleagues. Librarians generally categorize these communications as "gray literature" but in some cases may collect them and catalog them as serials. The electronic counterpart of this "gray literature" — using file servers and messaging systems instead of photocopy machines and the mail — usually operates as a closed system with restricted access, but from all accounts operates successfully.

Another type of electronic communication is the computer conference. Computer conferences use electronic messaging to set up systems for the exchange of information among experts or others interested in a particular topic. Subscribers are free to submit items and to read the contributions of others. In many ways, computer conferences resemble printed "notes and queries" publications. The contents may include reports, original short contributions, discussions, queries and answers, or suggestions from other subscribers. Using the electronic network, however, the whole process is speeded up; contributions are posted without having to wait for cumulation into an "issue." Content may be monitored to some degree, but contributions are not refereed in the traditional sense.

The costs of subscribing to computer conferences are ultimately absorbed by the institution, in the same way that the university library pays institutional subscriptions to serials in printed format. From the library's point of view, however, conferences are even "grayer" than the conventional preprint exchange systems. The qualities which make these conferences popular with their users also make them almost impossible to control from a bibliographic point of view. Their scope is usually very flexible: if a group of subscribers gets too large, one conference may split into smaller conferences identified with sub-topics. Similarly, if a topic becomes exhausted or loses subscribers, a conference can be discontinued without formality.

PACS-L membership can be a mixed blessing. The messaging system at my institution does not list messages by title or sender. When I sign on each morning to the campus computer, I am told that I have messages waiting. The screen does not display a contents list to tell what the messages are, or where they are coming from. Items from the newsletter are mixed in with messages (urgent of otherwise) from colleagues everywhere. I have to display all the messages to find out what I have received and must decide quickly whether to download, print, save, or delete. The messages come thick and fast — message overload can be a problem. I was recently away for a week, and when I got back I had eighty messages waiting; mostly PACS-L contributions. I can appreciate the fact that some people decide not to subscribe because of the amount of material they will receive. Next time I go away for vacation, I shall cancel my membership until I return.

The electronic newsletter, published as regular or irregular "issues," is closer to the bibliographic concept of a serial than the preprint exchange or conference. One popular example is *Public-Access Computer System News,* an irregular electronic serial with ISSN and volume and issue numbers. The issues, accessed through PACS-L, contain brief news items, short enough to read on-line. An increasing number of newsletters, conferences, and other electronic serials are now accessible on Bitnet, and the Council on Library Resources has produced a directory of these electronic "publications."

Generally, experiments with electronic serials have indicated that informal, unrefereed serials are likely to be popular and to succeed. The number of informal serials accessible right now on Bitnet dealing with Library and Information Science is evidence of this. The focused subject scope and the calibre of many of the contributors make these serials attractive to people who might not otherwise feel inclined to sign on to the network. All people with valid comments may contribute; there is no "class system" which might discourage junior staff or non-professionals.

If informal conferences and electronic newsletters can be successful, why not formal, refereed electronic journals? Technologically, at least, it does not seem to be a very big step from one to the other. Charles Bailey has clearly outlined the steps to be taken and the procedures necessary to produce an electronic journal.[3] But technology is not the only factor operating here. Others in the past have perceived problems with the scientific journal system, and have made attempts to find alternatives based on the technology then available. Before turning our attention to electronic journals, it will be instructive to look at some of these earlier experiments with scientific journal publishing and to consider why they failed.

In 1960 Unesco commissioned the report "Alternatives to the Scientific Periodical." The report outlined perceived deficiencies of the scientific periodical, including the failure to publish papers promptly and the restrictions placed on length of articles. In case we feel that the rising cost of serials has only recently become a concern, the report pointed to the high cost of journal subscriptions "as a factor in the failure of libraries and abstract services to maintain complete coverage of any field." It also remarked on the "excessive costs to scientific societies that publish journals," and the volunteer work of editing and managing journals, which it criticized as "wasteful of scientists' time."[4]

Several years ago I reviewed the alternatives to the scientific journal that have been tried.[5] A review of my findings has been published; what follows is a brief synopsis.

1. *Dissemination of separates.* The Society of Automotive Engineers began to publish separates in 1965, which can be ordered individually, or purchased as bound volumes or microfiche sets. I suspect most libraries purchase the complete collection of papers; ours certainly does. No cost savings here.

2. *Selective dissemination of separates.* In 1968 the American Mathematical Society set up the Mathematical Offprint Service, which distributed individual articles based on user profiles. The individual article service never reached its minimum target of subscribers, although the citation service continued. Other similar experiments ended in failure. The ability to have articles of interest automatically downloaded to one's electronic mailbox as soon as they are made available on a database has been suggested as one potential benefit of electronic journals. But these experiences with dissemination of separates show that, while many people may ap-

preciate current awareness services, they still prefer to choose for themselves which articles to read or retain.

3. *Publication of synopses.* Various organizations tried this approach, and a few journals still publish in synopsis format, with copies of the full papers available on demand, in paper, microform or reduced print format. Most of these experiments failed, however, because of lack of support from authors. One survey of synopsis publishing concluded that "a synopsis journal will have difficulty in recruiting sufficient enthusiastic authors to maintain itself permanently."[6] Another study found that articles published in synoptic form were not highly cited, nor were they well covered in abstracting and indexing services.[7]

4. *Publication in miniprint or microform.* Miniprint is eye-legible, or at least can be read without special equipment other than a magnifying glass. Obviously miniprint has not been generally adopted as a means of reducing the size and costs of journals; however, it is usually rated as preferable to microforms. Cady has recently published an interesting study of microfilm, referring to it as the "new technology" of the past, which has failed to live up to its promise.[8] Although it has been successfully used as a storage method for back issues of journals, it has not found favor as an alternate format for publishing current issues. A recent comparison of output from an experimental electronic journal found that computer-output microfiche was judged the least acceptable format.[9] The Geological Society of America (GSA) tried out a synopsis-plus-microfiche publishing system in 1979, but abandoned it in 1981. In the words of the President of the GSA:

> Most authors didn't want to write for microfiche, and most readers didn't want to read articles in that format. As a result, the Bulletin rapidly decreased in size and deteriorated as resistant authors sent their articles elsewhere for publication.[10]

What can one learn from all this? It appears that readers will not accept formats they consider "unfriendly" or that are not universally available. And authors are not willing to write for journals in such formats. It is also worth noting that almost all the alternatives I reviewed did not involve cost savings for libraries, although they may have been cheaper for individual subscribers.

There have been comprehensive experiments to examine the possibility of publishing electronic journals which would more closely correspond to the traditional scholarly journal model. The first of these, the EIES (Electronic Information Exchange System), was launched at the New Jersey Institute of Technology at the end of the 1970s. The directors of the project wrote:

> The original plans for this electronic journal on mental workload called for it to be advertised, refereed, edited, copyrighted, and mass distributed — just as are traditional journals.[11]

This component of the experiment was, however, not successful, and the reasons for failure were found to be primarily motivational. Prestigious authors in the field agreed to submit articles in electronic form to the new journal *Mental Workload,* but did not live up to their promises. They submitted few papers, did not meet their deadlines, and reported difficulty in using the electronic system, finding it more "frustrating" and less "productive" than did other groups using EIES. Sixty-five percent of these authors said they made limited use of EIES because "other professional activities must take higher priority." In the words of the project directors: "How do you motivate people to take the risk of expending effort to write and review for an electronic journal which has no established prestige-granting rating in the scientific community?"[12]

EIES did, however, produce some successful products: a current awareness and headline service; a totally unrefereed journal serving for preprint distribution and feedback from other EIES members; and a "journal" which in many ways resembled an electronic conference such as PACS-L. The informal scored heavily over the formal in acceptability.

One problem experienced by EIES was that the project could not accept participants from Britain. The British Post Office refused to permit EIES to transmit its products over TELENET, because such transmission would violate an agreement with Western Union International. A group in Britain did, however, set up an electronic journal experiment known as BLEND (Birmingham Loughborough Electronic Network Development), a cooperative project of the Universities of Birmingham and Loughborough.[13] This three-year experiment, which ended in 1984, recruited between forty and fifty members. Each member agreed to submit at least one full-length paper and one shorter note per year for the duration of the experiment. These contributions were to appear in an electronic journal entitled *Computer Human Factors*. Learning from the EIES experience, BLEND did not require these authors to submit articles electronically; manuscripts could be keyed by BLEND staff or scanned from typescript. BLEND also permitted authors to submit their papers to traditional printed journals three months after the articles had been deposited in the BLEND electronic archive. Even so, after four years only two issues of *Computer Human Factors* had been produced, each containing editorials, a discussion section, and four refereed papers. An additional twenty-one unrefereed papers were circulated on a system called "Poster Papers," set up to draw comments on preprints.

Despite all claims that an electronic journal would speed up publication by permitting access to papers as soon as they had been accepted into an electronic archive, the EIES experiment demonstrated that participants preferred the release of papers according to a predictable schedule.

> It appears that both the authors and the editorial board need predictable deadlines which provide a motivation for them to schedule a definite time within a week to finish their work (that time, of course, is usually right before the deadline). . . . In addition, at least some readers like the predictability of a new issue every Monday morning, waiting online.[14]

One also might conjecture that, in a fully-operating system, priority of publication would be a problem if papers were made available on-line as soon as their release had been approved. Similarly, the risk of not being among the first to read an important paper, because one had missed the moment of its release, also might count in favor of regular issues.

Since EIES had found that readers prefer regular issues which appear predictably, BLEND published its electronic journal and a newsletter on a regular schedule. But the BLEND experiment also showed that "electronic access creates a new publishing problem: the possibility of publishing papers too quickly for the author to incorporate any second thoughts." Further, "the electronic format permits letters to editor and discussion of papers in the same issue as the subject being discussed."[15] Interestingly enough, the editor of the *Journal of the American Society for Information Science* recently issued an apology for publishing letters about a paper in the same issue as the paper itself, because of objections raised.[16]

Even without the requirement of submitting manuscripts electronically, and with the concession of a regular publication schedule, many members still did not come through with papers. They pleaded lack of time, although there was no lack of computer conferencing. Several members prepared a joint paper through conferencing, but concluded their group lacked the leadership to follow through with the project. As with EIES, human factors played an important role:

> On-line authorship seems not to be immediately attractive; there are not enough incentives in the form of obvious and visible results, nor is there enough motivation to start. On-line searching, reading, and access may be more tempting, but without input there will be no content available . . .
>
> There also seems to be no evidence that on-line networks reduce the human delays in getting down to work (refereeing or editing, for example), even if time is saved once work has begun. It would appear that the lack of visible reminder and the need for log-on procedures, however simplified, may actually serve as disincentives which could even increase the total time involved.[17]

Further electronic journal experiments have followed EIES and BLEND. A University of Calgary project examined the problems experienced by users when inputting papers, compared acceptability of various outputs, and looked at costs. The conclusion reached was that, overall, the electronic journal did not demonstrate cost savings over the conventional journal.[18] An attempt was made in

France to produce a publication entitled *Journal of Applied Mathematics* in electronic form. The project succeeded in creating a highly sophisticated desktop publishing package which could cope with mathematical expressions, and this product was commercialized. However, the journal itself was not a success, and the reasons have a familiar ring: "Authors felt that their work would not get wide readership, and they resisted technical innovation."[19]

An experiment to produce chemical journals from machine-readable manuscripts had to be abandoned, because "there was too great a disparity of diskette and manuscript formats, especially for the high proportion of graphics, tables, equations and special characters."[20] This disparity of format was also noted by the American Chemical Society, which in the spring of 1987 surveyed authors who had published in ACS journals. Ninety-three percent of the authors prepared their manuscripts on computers or word processors, but there was much disparity in the software packages they used. "Authors employed over 50 different software packages to prepare mathematical equations"; "41 different packages for drawing chemical structures"; and "81 graphic drawing software tools, an astonishing number."[21] No doubt standardization and compatibility of software will be a problem for electronic journals in the sciences.

So far this paper has looked at some experiments to replace traditional journals and examined why those experiments were not successful. Beyond these experiments, other concerns have been raised about the migration to an electronic journal system.

1. Discomfort with an electronic medium is one problem that may gradually go away as more and more people grow up using computers or become accustomed to using them for word processing. The problem of ready access to equipment is also likely to remedy itself—at least in the developed world.[22] However, access may remain a concern in disciplines where contributions from and visibility to participants from less developed countries are important.

2. Network access raises questions of politics, reliability, and cost in some countries. Transborder data flow problems may disrupt access to databases. The EIES project encountered this difficulty

when the British Postal Service barred access to British participants. The editor of *Mental Workload,* writing on this matter, stated that "unless an electronic journal is accessible outside the USA telephone network it is almost an immoral medium; insofar as it generates information of high quality, which is systematically unavailable to very large proportions of the scientific community."[23] Even where network access is not a problem, reliability of service can be a factor. A recent issue of *On-line Review* contained a report of the Eusidic 1990 Monitoring Week, which noted a big improvement in the reliability of public data networks in northern Europe. Failure rates were 14.41 percent for Britain, 9.05 percent for Sweden, 14.55 percent for Finland and 9.08 percent for Norway. In Southern Europe, however, Spain showed a failure rate of 28.78 percent and Italy a failure rate of 34.3 percent.[24] Telecommunication costs also may influence access in some countries. EUROLOG (The European On Line User Group) recently reported that the cost of telecommunications links to the U.S. to conduct 100 on line searches averaged 144 ECUs from Portugal, 167 from Germany, 314 from Spain, 331 from Italy, and 421 from Greece.[25]

3. Access to an electronic system implies bibliographic as well as network access. The *PACS Review* appears in some library holdings lists, and you can request articles from it on interlibrary loan. Such an arrangement is a partial answer to the problem of bibliographic access, but for complete access articles in electronic journals also must be included in abstracting and indexing (A and I) databases. This seems to be a "chicken-and-egg" situation. A critical mass of high-quality electronic journals is necessary before most A and I services will begin to index them, but such critical mass will not be achieved until authors can be persuaded to contribute to such journals. And having their contributions indexed (and their names listed) in A and I databases is one incentive which might induce authors to publish electronically.

4. Linked to concerns about bibliographic access is the lack of a standard format for citing items in electronic databases.[26] What is a "page" of electronic text? Will electronic text have to be restructured to permit referencing, for example by numbering paragraphs instead of pages? Authors are concerned that, without accepted

standards, their electronic contributions may not be properly cited. Articles may be cited without an adequate network address; cited as "personal communications" (i.e., unpublished); or — worst of all — not cited at all.

5. There is a lack of appropriate formats for screen reading. The BLEND project paid special attention to providing appropriate layouts and functions for reading on screen and moving from place to place in a document.[27] Hypertext structures may help here. It is also possible that authors will be asked to provide abstracts or synopses, and to apply formats using modular structures with clearly identifiable sections.[28] Attention must be paid to output formats. Many people will want to print out articles, even if they normally read most of the content of newsletters on line.[29] Some libraries now print out whole issues of electronic serials to make them readily available to users. It is worth noting that the *PACS Review* is compatible with WordPerfect, which will produce paged output.

6. Authors are concerned because they do not have control over what will appear on the computer screen in the same way they control what appears on the printed page. Formats and search software which make it easy to scan portions of an online text may also make authors nervous about publishing in this form. Carol Tenopir noted that authors and publishers are concerned about online functions like "KWIC" on DIALOG, that make it possible to read segments or isolated paragraphs of articles out-of-context, without ever viewing the whole document. They considered such functions "a threat to the integrity of writing and to the author's meaning."[30]

7. There are concerns about security and the integrity of text. Authors are worried about losing files, about alteration of their submissions by others, about intrusions by viruses, and so on. They are also concerned that database articles they have read and cited could be altered at some point in the future without leaving any trace of the original text. Related issues are copyright and ownership of material stored in databases.

8. Permanence is also a concern. I like to show my students our library copy of Daines Barrington's original communication describing his encounter with the young Mozart, published in 1770 in the *Philosophical Transactions of the Royal Society*.[31] Will scholars in the future have access to the contributions made today to an elec-

tronic journal? Who will take on the responsibility for archiving these materials? How will the archived files be stored? On disk? On tape? In memory banks? Will changes in search software be considered, so that out-of-date software is retained for archival files, or files revised to make them compatible with new software?[32] As I write, durability of CD-ROMs and other digital media is a hot topic on PACS-L. Archivists and conservationists are heavily involved with these problems; depository libraries are looking at legal deposit requirements. The fact that subscriptions to CD-ROM databases do not necessarily carry rights of ownership to a disk and its contents has brought this problem to the fore.

9. Some descriptions of an electronic system for scholarly communication mention monitoring as a component; for example, Rogers and Hurt refer to "citation and usage logs."[33] Authors are justifiably nervous about citation counts being used to decide whether an item should be retained in the system. Recent analyses published in *Science* on the "uncitedness" of research papers revealed that 98 percent of papers in the arts and humanities were never cited in the four years after publication; the figure for the social sciences was 74.7 percent and for engineering 72.3 percent.[34] Even if monitoring were based on the number of times an item was accessed online, rather than on the number of times it was cited, still there could be cause for concern. An item might not be retrieved because of indexing failures, misspelling of the author's name, or similar inputting errors. Graham Cornish, writing about copyright and document supply and with the experience of the ADONIS project in mind, notes:

> New technology may allow closer monitoring of copyright material but can also bring the danger of economic censorship. . . . This can be a very useful management tool for the publisher and librarian, but it will also have the potential for editors to decide which articles should be retained in future discs, which topics are currently popular and which material should not, therefore, be accepted for publication because it is not heavily used and so, potentially, not a revenue-earner.[35]

CONCLUSION

I have tried in this paper to present some of the human factors which are likely to influence adoption of an electronic journal system. In conclusion, I think I can do no better than to quote May Katzen. Dr. Katzen wrote, in 1986, on electronic publishing for the humanities, and introduced her topic by commenting thus on the adoptions of innovations:

1. New techniques and technologies are introduced within an already existing context, social, economic, and intellectual, within which has developed a nexus of institutional and organizational structures, social roles, and norms.
2. An existing social context exerts powerful forces of inertia, tending towards the maintenance of familiar traditions.
3. Innovations, however revolutionary their ultimate potential may be, tend, in the first instance, to be used and interpreted in the light of familiar, traditional ways of doing things.
4. The introduction of an innovation must, ipso facto, involve some disturbance of existing patterns. Hence, innovations are likely to be taken up readily if they offer better, easier, cheaper, more efficient, and more effective ways of doing what has already been done before.
5. Some new technologies offer the possibility of improving existing ways of doing things. Others, which may be regarded as genuine new media, make it possible to do what could not be done or even envisaged before. [A new medium] is more likely to lead to a new distribution of functions between different media rather than to the total displacement or elimination of the old by the new.[36]

I interpret all this to mean that, however much sense an electronic journal system may make in technological and perhaps economic terms, the human factors involved indicate that its adoption is likely to be slow, and may never be complete. In my opinion, we cannot look to it as a realistic solution to the journal "crisis."

NOTES

1. Ronald E. Rice and Donald Case, "Electronic Message Systems in the University: A Description of Use and Utility," *Journal of Communication* 31, no. 1 (Winter 1983): 131-152.

2. Starr Roxanne Hiltz and Kenneth Johnson, "Measuring Acceptance of Computer-Mediated Communication Systems," *Journal of the American Society for Information Science* 40, no. 6 (November 1989): 386-397. A major review of the various forms of computer-mediated communication and its human and social impacts has been published by Howard Rosenbaum and Gregory B. Newby, "An Emerging Form of Human Communication: Computer Networking," *Proceedings of the ASIS Annual Meeting* 27 (1990): 300-325.

3. Charles W. Bailey, Jr., "Electronic (Online) Publishing in Action . . . The Public-Access Computer Systems Review and Other Electronic Serials," *Online* 15, no. 1 (January 1991): 28-35.

4. Ralph H. Phelps and John P. Herlin, "Alternatives to the Scientific Periodical: A Report and Bibliography," *Unesco Bulletin for Libraries* 14 (March-April 1960): 61-75.

5. Anne B. Piternick, "Attempts to Find Alternatives to the Scientific Journal: A Brief Review," *Journal of Academic Librarianship* 15, no. 5 (1989): 260-266.

6. J.F.B. Rowland, "Synopsis Journals As Seen By Their Authors," *Journal of Documentation* 37, no. 2 (June 1981): 69-76.

7. Dirk G. van der Heij et al., "Comparative Analysis of the Penetrative Capacity of Synopses and of Full Papers Unrelated to the Synopses Published in the Same Broad-scope Agricultural Journal," *Journal of Information Science,* 16 (1990): 155-164.

8. Susan A. Cady, "The Electronic Revolution in Libraries: Microfilm Deja Vu?" *College & Research Libraries* 51, no. 4 (July 1990): 374-386.

9. Oldrich L. Standera, "Electronic Publishing: Some Notes on Reader Response and Costs," *Scholarly Publishing* 16 (July 1985): 291-305.

10. H.R. Gould, "GSA—A Legacy and a New Era," *Geological Society of American Bulletin* 93 (January 1982): 2.

11. Murray Turoff and Starr Roxanne Hiltz, "The Electronic Journal: A Progress Report," *Journal of the American Society for Information Science* 33, no. 4 (July 1982): 195-202.

12. Turoff and Hiltz, p. 198.

13. Priscilla Oakeshott, "The 'BLEND' Experiment in Electronic Publishing," *Scholarly Publishing* 17, no. 1 (October 1985): 25-36.

14. Turoff and Hiltz, p. 200.

15. Oakeshott, p. 32.

16. Donald H. Kraft, "Editorial Note: A Clarification of the Policy on Printing Letters to the Editor," *Journal of the American Society for Information Science* 42, no. 2 (1991): 77.

17. Oakeshott, p. 35.
18. Standera, pp. 291-305
19. F.A. Mastroddi, "Experiments in Electronic Publishing and Document Delivery: Results of the EEC's DOCDEL Programme," *Interlending and Document Supply* 16, no. 4 (1988): 121-128.
20. Mastroddi, p. 125.
21. Marianne C. Brogan and Lorrin R. Garson, "Requirements for and Challenges Associated with Submission of Machine-Readable Manuscripts," *Journal of Chemical and Computing Science* 30, no. 3 (1990): 271-277.
22. Ronald H. Epp and JoAn S. Segal, "The ACLS Survey and Academic Library Service," *College & Research Libraries News* 48, no. 2 (February 1987): 63-69. The survey was conducted on behalf of the American Council of Learned Societies; the survey population was 5,385 members of eight humanities and social science societies affiliated with the Council. Epp and Segal noted that "over 50% of the respondents report that they or their research assistants routinely use computers of some kind. . . . About 70% of the computer users have their own PCs, and 46% of these use their computers at home for scholarly work."
23. Cited in Turoff and Hiltz, p. 200.
24. "Telecommunication news," *Online Review* 14, no. 5 (1990): 351. This report notes: "It's good news, too, that Soviet computer users will soon be able to access databases and online services throughout the world via their own high-speed data link."
25. "Online User Groups Query 'Arbitrary Data Charges,'" *Library Association Record* 93, no. 4 (April 1991): 174. An announcement of a report entitled "Barriers to the Free Flow of Books by a Working Group of European Librarians and Publishers" notes that "books ordering by standard computerized systems is helping to reduce costs for the book trade. Unfortunately these systems stop at national frontiers because of the prohibitive costs of international telecoms tariffs." The note appeared in *Information Market* No. 63 (November 1990-January 1991): 9.
26. Gisle Hannemyr and Even Flood, "Scholarly References to Machine-Readable Documents," *Information Technology and Libraries* 4, no. 1 ((March 1985): 61-64.
27. See also Cliff McKnight, "Workstations for Academic Applications," *Aslib Proceedings* 42, no. 10 (October 1990): 263-269.
28. Arie A. Manten, "Possible Future Relevance of Publishing Primary Scholarly Information in the Form of Synopses," *Journal of Information Science* 1 (1980): 293-296.
29. Paula Hane, "Paper: The Security Blanket of the Electronic Age," *Database* 14, no. 1 (February 1991): 6-7.
30. Carol Tenopir, "Searching Full-Text Databases," *Library Journal* 113 (May 1, 1988): 60-61.
31. Daines Barrington, "Account of a Very Remarkable Musician," *Philosophical Transactions of the Royal Society* 60 (1770): 54-64.

32. Margaret A. Cribbs, "The Invisible Drip . . . How Data Seeps Away in Various Ways," *Online* 11, no. 2 (March 1987): 15-26; Paula Kaufman and Angie LeClerq, "Archiving Electronic Journals: Who's Responsible for What?" *Information Issues* 2, no. 1 (Fall 1990): unpaged.

33. Sharon J. Rogers and Charlene S. Hurt, "How Scholarly Communication Should Work in the 21st Century," *The Chronicle of Higher Education* (October 18, 1989): A56. (This article was reprinted as a guest editorial in *College & Research Libraries* 51, no. 1 (January 1990): 5-6,8.)

34. David P. Hamilton, "Research Papers: Who's Uncited Now?" *Science* 251, no. 4989 (4 January 1991): 25. It must be stated that the figures for uncitedness have been challenged. There is apparently unpublished evidence to indicate that the citation rates published in the Science article are too low—at least in some fields.

35. Graham Cornish, "The Conflict Between Copyright and Document Supply: Real or Imagined?" *IFLA Journal* 16, no. 4 (1990): 414-421.

36. May Katzen, "Electronic Publishing in the Humanities." *Scholarly Publishing* 18 (October 1986): 5-16.

PLENARY SESSION 2 – CHANGING INFORMATION WORLDWIDE

Globalization of Research, Scholarly Information, and Patents – Ten Year Trends

Francis Narin

INTRODUCTION

The recent article in the "Science Times" section of the *New York Times,* entitled "In the Realm of Technology, Japan Looms Ever Larger," illustrated with a marvelous map of the world the trends in globalization of research and scholarly information, and patents over the last ten years: in all those fields Japan has become much larger and, especially in technology, is now the second largest player in the world.[1]

In technology today, and perhaps in science in the future, we are

---

Francis Narin is President, CHI Research, Inc., 10 White Horse Pike, Haddon Heights, NJ 08035.

clearly headed toward a tri-polar world, with one pole in North America dominated by the United States, a second pole in Europe dominated by the European Community (EC) countries, and a third pole in Southeast Asia dominated by Japan. Offsetting this polarization, to some degree, has been a steady increase in international cooperation. However, the dominant trend in globalization over the last ten years has been the growth of the Japanese share of technology and science, the shrinkage of the U.S. share, and the relative stability of Europe.

The rest of this paper will summarize some Science and Technology Indicators underlying these statements, and will show how the current trends are in general accord with long-term waves of scientific, technological and economic strength, waves that have been occurring for a century or more.

SCIENCE, TECHNOLOGY AND ECONOMIC INDICATORS

The recent *New York Times* article was based on counts of patents by company country, that is, patents were attributed to a given country if the company was headquartered in that country. This count is accurate for the Japanese, since virtually all of the patents of Japanese companies are invented in Japan; but it tends to overestimate the technological strength of a country like the Netherlands, which is given credit for all of the patents of Shell and of Philips, both of which have extensive research activity outside of the Netherlands.

The first point I will make in this paper is that the idea of tracking national performance through bibliometrics — that is, by counting publications (and now patents) — is quite an old idea. The first known example of bibliometric research is reported in an elegant paper published by Cole and Eales in 1917.[2] Figure 1, redrawn from their original paper, shows the rise in comparative anatomy publications, including the founding of the first journals in the 1660s, the rise in publication following the end of the Napoleonic Wars, and the final sustained emergence of serial publications in the early 1800s. Coles and Eales not only presented their data with clarity, but also discussed the myriad problems involved in this kind

FIGURE 1

6434 COMPARATIVE ANATOMY PUBLICATIONS BETWEEN 1550 AND 1860
(adapted from Cole & Eales, 1917)

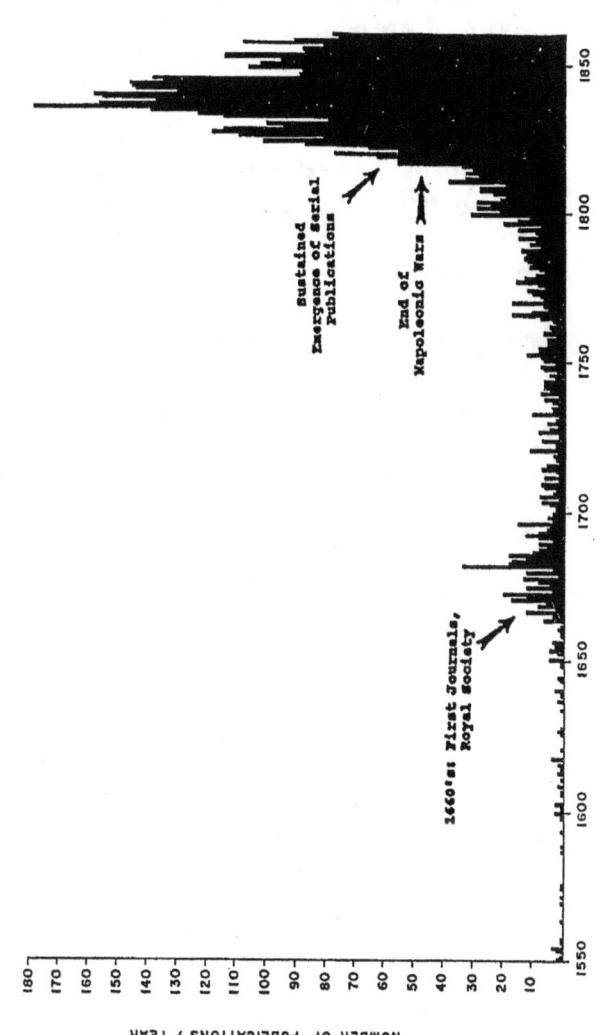

of research: for instance, whether to attribute a publication to the country where the work was done, to the country where it was published, or to the home country of the scientists; or how to differentiate between many small papers of little consequence and one manuscript of great importance. They addressed these and many other problems and challenges of bibliometric research, most of which have been discovered, rediscovered, and re-rediscovered since the paper of Cole and Eales in 1917.

Perhaps the next major step toward understanding the patterns of globalization was the work of Derek de Solla Price, who first demonstrated broad-scale exponential growth, that is, relatively constant doubling times, in bibliometric and other global developments.[3] For example, GNP and important discoveries were doubling every twenty years; scientific journals and abstracts were doubling every fifteen years; literature in specific hot areas, the number of telephones, and the speed of transportation were doubling every ten years; while labor forces and populations, and numbers of universities, tended to be doubling much more slowly, every fifty years or so.

In 1969 Price published the first observation that national scientific size was closely correlated with national economic size; specifically, that the number of first authors of scientific papers lay on a narrow band, when plotted against economic size of their country as measured by GNP.[4] With the advent of Science Indicators this observation was further elaborated on by Frame,[5] and most recently by CHI Research in a study of European science done for the Commission of the European Communities (CEC).[6] Figure 2, taken from that CEC work, shows that the economic activity of a country, as measured by Gross Domestic Product (GDP), is highly correlated with number of scientific papers published in that country. Twenty-eight different research areas were considered—areas related to various current and future CEC programs and representative of a major portion of European research.

Using the same methodology, a parallel set of data is shown as Figure 3, for the number of assigned U.S. patents versus GDP for eighteen major countries.

Assigned patents are patents that are assigned to a company not owned by the individual inventor. Most of the patents in the U.S.

FIGURE 2

GDP VS. NUMBER OF PAPERS IN 28 EC FIELDS

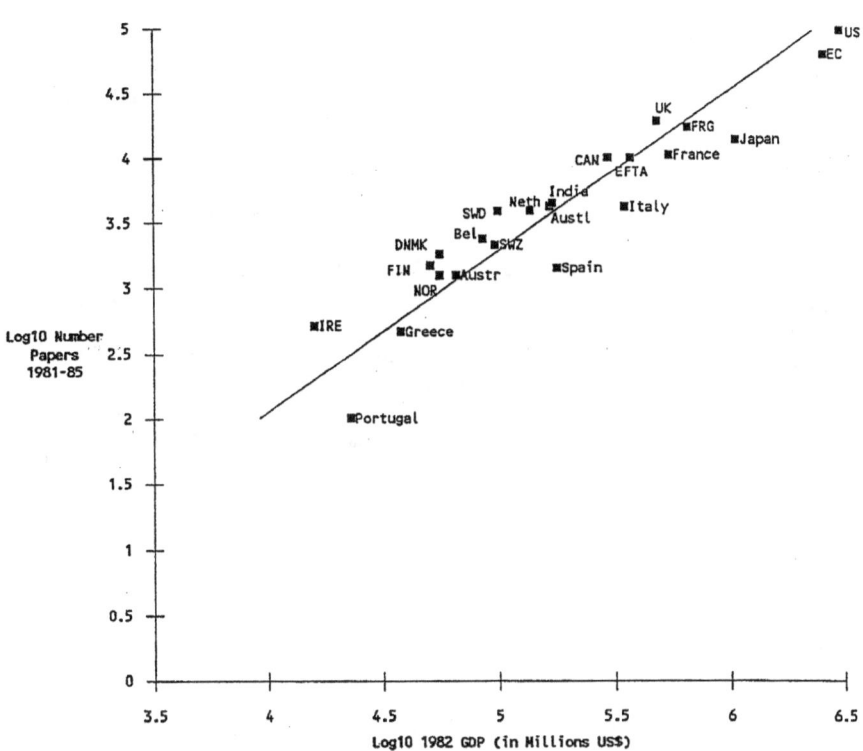

patent system are assigned to companies. Approximately half of all U.S. patents are U.S.-invented. Of these, about twenty percent are owned by individual inventors — typically consumer product inventions and relatively unimportant. For U.S. patents granted to foreign inventors, ninety to ninety-five percent or more are assigned to companies. Limiting this data to company-assigned patents tends to eliminate relatively trivial patents.

Given this general relationship between numbers of scientific pa-

FIGURE 3

GDP VS. NUMBER OF ASSIGNED U.S. PATENTS

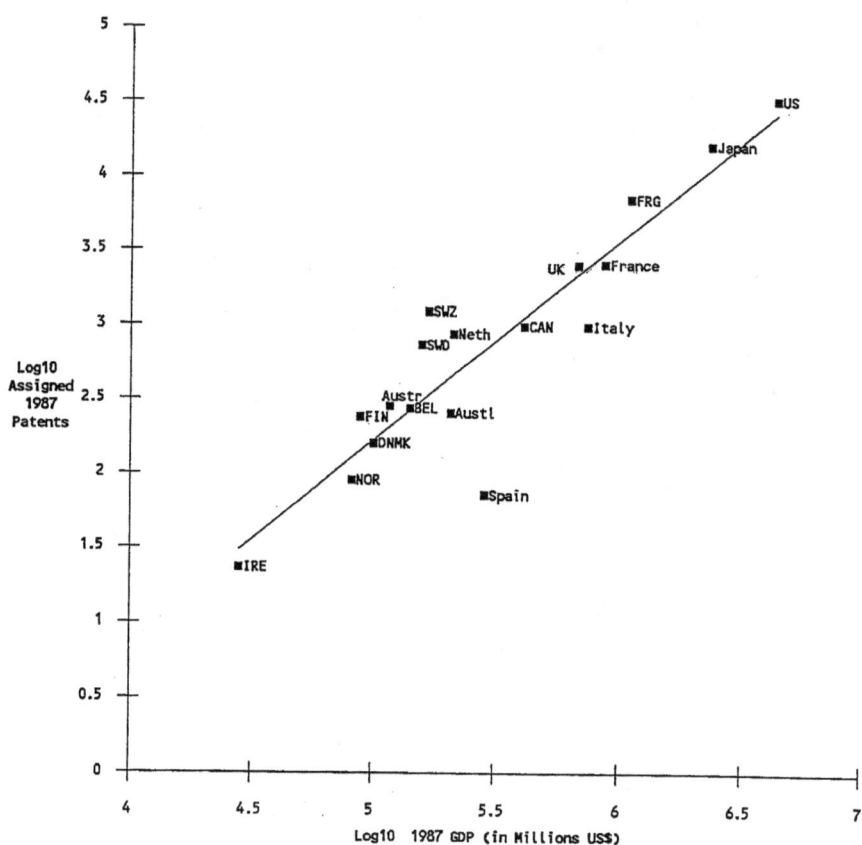

pers, numbers of patents, and GDP, the interesting phenomena are the deviations from it, which represent the leads and lags in national developmental cycles. For example, Japan tends to be above the regression line in technology and below it in science, while the UK is just the opposite — high in science, low in technology.

The evidence seems to indicate that the national development cycle goes economics first, technology second, and science third.

That is, a country must first function at certain basic economic level in order to begin to develop technology, and then it must reach a certain level of technological development and wealth in order to have a significant role in science. The Japanese economy following World War II is perhaps typical. First the economy began to recover as a low-wage producer of low-technology products, next it accumulated enough wealth to develop a technological base, and finally evolved into the high-technology powerhouse it is today. Japan is just now emerging as scientifically significant, especially in research areas linked to its technological base. More specifically, Table 1 shows the percent of papers in the *Science Citation Index* which are Japanese-authored and the percent of patents in the U.S. patent system which are Japanese-invented, two basic indicators of long-term trends. There is a steady increase in both cases: Japanese papers have been increasing at about 0.2 percent a year, Japanese patents at about 0.75 percent a year, so that the gap between the two is still getting wider, while the Japanese economic position continues to strengthen.

The Japan/UK and the Japan/Europe comparisons are also interesting over time, with Europe perhaps displaying the down side of

TABLE 1

JAPANESE SHARE OF PAPERS AND PATENTS

Japan Share of World Papers in SCI (1981 Journal Set)

	1981	1982	1983	1984	1985	1986	1981-86
Percent	6.8	7.0	7.1	7.3	7.6	7.8	7.2

Japan Share of All Patents in the U.S. Patent System

	1985	1986	1987	1988	1989	1990	1985-90
Percent	17.8	18.7	20	20.7	21.1	21.6	20.1

the cycle, with its relative technological position weakening more rapidly than its science.

As a final observation, the growth of Japan first technologically, then scientifically, follows the pattern shown by the United States in the earlier part of this century. The great technological growth of the United States following World War II was based on European research: on science developed earlier in the century by the Europeans; on large numbers of talented expatriate scientists, from Einstein to Szilard and many others, who brought with them to the United States their learning and knowledge from Europe; and, on many of the U.S. scientists who trained in the great laboratories of Europe in the first half of this century.

The remarkable growth in the U.S. economy and U.S. technology following World War II was followed quickly by an ascendance of the U.S. to its current preeminent position in science—a preeminence funded by the enormous economic growth in the United States and aided by the close ties of the science and scientists in the U.S. with their colleagues and mentors in Europe. If one went back to the beginning of this century, science in the United States was a barely perceptible blip across the ocean. No one dreamed in the early 1990s that the scientific world's center would shift so totally to North America. Whether the scientific center will shift again, in the next century, to an equivalent or even to a central locus in Southeast Asia is an important question. Clearly, the wealth exists in Japan to make that possible. Whether the tendency toward group rather than individual discovery and development in Japan will allow science to flourish there, as it has in the United States, is one of the questions that remain to be answered.

COOPERATION AND LINKAGE

In the earlier parts of this paper the data were presented on science, technology, and economic growth, as if they were occurring in parallel to one another, with only inferential remarks on linkage—both linkage between the various scientific centers, and direct linkage between science and technology. This is clearly not the case; one of the major characteristics of modern science is the increasing amount of scientific cooperation, and the parallel increase in the amount of that cooperation which is international.

Coauthorship data provide the indicators to measure this cooperation. Coauthorship can be gauged from the number of individual authors per paper, which has been increasing steadily, or from the number of institutional coauthorships, papers with two or more addresses for their authors, which has also been increasing steadily. For example, under the heading "clinical medicine" the average number of individual authors per paper listed in *Science Citation Index* has increased from about 2.6 to 3.5 between 1973 and 1985. Under "chemistry," "engineering," and "earth & space sciences," where there are fewer authors per paper, there has also been an increase, from about 1.8 per paper to 2.1 per paper between 1973 and 1985. Even in "mathematics," the least coauthored field, there has been an increase from 1.3 to 1.4 individual authors per paper.

This trend is also apparent in institutional coauthorship, which is shown for EC in Figure 4. Note that figure is for corporate authorship, that is, institutional addresses. Overall, forty percent of the EC papers are now multi-institutional. Of this forty percent, slightly more than half have authors from two institutions in the same country, the other half have international coauthorships: between authors in different EC countries; between authors in EC and non-EC countries; and, of course, between EC countries and the United States. Parallel to the spread of scientific publication and patenting throughout the world, there has also been an increase in the portion that is internationally linked.

There has also been a marked increase in linkage between technology and science, which is illustrated by Figure 5, the patent to science linkage.[7] The average number of "other references cited" on the front pages of U.S. patents are plotted by country of inventor of the patent. These "other references cited" refer to a wide variety of sources: scientific papers, scientific meeting notes, newspapers, technical reports, disclosure bulletins, and so forth, but, over the span of time indicated, approximately half are references to scientific papers in refereed scientific journals. The number of these references has increased dramatically, at least three-fold between 1975 and 1989, with the most rapid increase for the United States, and the least rapid increase for Japan. Some of that difference is due to

FIGURE 4

COAUTHORSHIP TRENDS IN 28 EC FIELDS

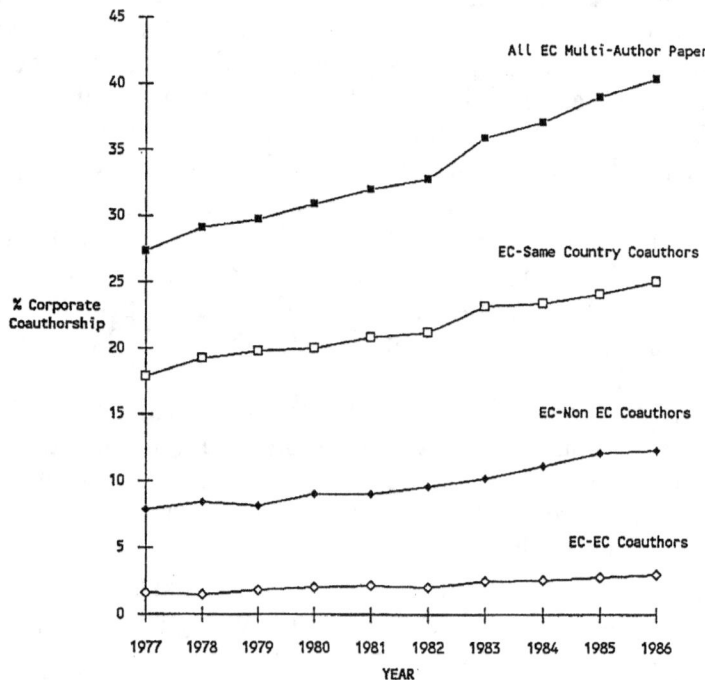

the relative emphasis of the two countries in the U.S. patent system. U.S. inventors are patenting heavily in the pharmaceutical and biotechnology areas, the most science-linked areas of technology, while the Japanese are patenting most heavily in electronics. Although electronics is more science-linked than the older mechanical areas of technology, it is not as science-linked as pharmaceuticals and biotechnology.

In measuring the science-linkage of patents, the European coun-

FIGURE 5

NATIONAL PATTERNS OF SCIENCE LINKAGE

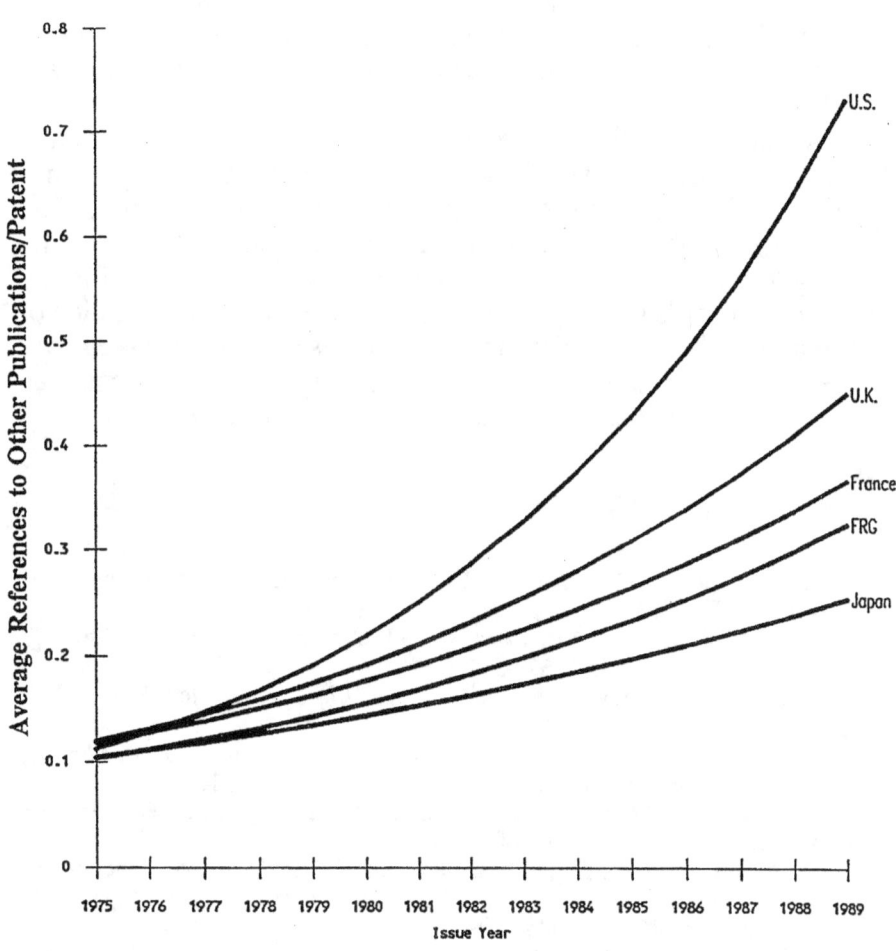

tries tend to be midway between the highly scientific United States and the more technological Japanese. Much of the science-linkage from German patents is due to their emphasis on chemistry, whereas the UK and France tend to emphasize pharmaceuticals and biotechnology.

A very important point should be made about the age of these science references in patents. Many of these references are to very recent science, and the scientific papers cited in biotechnology and electronics patents are, in particular, only three or four years old, about the same age as the scientific papers cited in other scientific papers.[8] There is little or no lag today between technology and science. The scientific and technological communities are quantitatively linked by the dependence of modern technology upon modern science.

A final observation: the bibliometric data does not indicate any slackening in the rate of increase for linkage and cooperation. Whether this is due to ease of travel, ease of communication, or just to the geographical spread of science and technology today is something to be debated by sociologists. But I see no evidence for any slow down in these trends, and would guess that the globalization of research, scholarly information, and patents that we have seen over the last decade, and, in fact, over the last century, will continue unabated, to the benefit of the entire industrialized world.

NOTES

1. William J. Broad, "In the Realm of Technology, Japan Looms Ever Larger," in *The New York Times,* 28 May 1991, p. C-1.

2. F.J. Cole and Nellie B. Eales, "The History of Comparative Anatomy," *Science Progress* 11 (1917): 578-596.

3. Derek J. de Solla Price. *Little Science, Big Science,* New Haven: Yale University Press, 1963.

4. Derek J. de Solla Price, "Measuring the Size of Science," *Proceedings of the Israel Academy of Science and Humanities* 6(1969): 10-11.

5. J. Davidson Frame, "Measuring Scientific Activity in Lesser Developed Countries," *Scientometric* 2 (1980): 133-145.

6. Francis Narin and Edith S. Whitlow, "Bibliometric Study for the Evaluation Unit, DGXII: Evaluation of Scientific Cooperation and Coauthorship in CEC-Related Areas of Science," May 1990.

7. Francis Narin "TECH-LINEsm Source Book: A Guide to TECH-LINE's Indicators of Corporate Technological Strength," CHI Research, Inc., 1991.

8. Francis Narin and Elliot Noma, "Is Technology Becoming Science?" *Scientometric* 7, no. 3 (1985): 369-381.

Europe 1992—
Implications for Scholarly Publishing and Distribution

John F. Riddick

On January 1, 1993 the European Community (EC) will begin operating as a single, integrated internal market. Since 1985, EC members have laid plans that would remove the barriers to free movement of goods, services, capital, and people among the twelve member nations. Economists predict that an integrated market containing a population of 324 million people will offer a market economy competitive with the United States and Japan. Because of the formation of a single European market, employment is expected to grow by 5 million new jobs, the gross domestic product will increase by seven percent, and prices for goods will be reduced by six percent.[1]

The Internal Market, known also as EC-92, has generated among Europeans heightened expectations for wealth and power after a decade spent in the economic doldrums. The initial thrust for an integrated market emerged from the consequences of the Second World War and resulted in the formation of the European Economic Community, provided for by the 1957 Treaty of Rome. In the years that followed, economic growth resulted, but the forces of integration diminished. By the 1970s, the Economic Community (also called the Common Market) was in the grip of a lethargic "eurosclerosis." Two men were responsible for breaking out of this lethargy: Lord Cockfield of England and Jacques Delors, President of the European Commission. As Vice President of the EC Commis-

---

John F. Riddick is Professor and Head, Acquisition Services, Central Michigan University, Mt. Pleasant, MI 48859.

© 1991 by The Haworth Press, Inc. All rights reserved.

sion, Cockfield drafted a 1985 White Paper introducing 300 proposals which collectively would steer the European Community toward an integrated internal market. The presentation of the White Paper paralleled the election of Delors as President of the EC Commission. His vision and force of personality have provided the drive behind the development of an internal market without barriers.[2]

The removal of barriers hindering the movement of goods, services, and people was essential for the formation of the EC Internal Market; prerequisites included the elimination of border controls, acceptance of differing national product standards, opening banking and fiscal services, standardizing tax rates, and allowing of the free movement of people within the European Community. Let's first examine current EC policies and goals, and then consider the implications of EC-92 for the serials information chain.

BORDER CONTROLS

One vital aspect of the Internal Market Agreement was the removal of internal border controls. In the past, crossing the traditional borders of the European Community's member states has imposed direct and indirect costs, which restrained the movement of manufactured goods. For example, widely ranging duties must be paid at each border, adding dramatically to product cost. The amount of time required to move a truck of goods across two or three national borders added further to the overall expense. Indirectly, each nation's need to collect statistical data about its exports and imports resulted in a vast amount of supporting documentation. In 1988 the EC nations agreed to and implemented the Single Administrative Document, which replaced at least seventy documents previously used to collect excise taxes and to record the passage of imports or exports. Although the document itself is complex, its implementation has reduced the time to transport a shipment 750 miles from 58 to 36 hours.[3] Further cost savings are expected with the removal of all internal border controls.

Paralleling the lifting of border controls on transport of goods is the removal of restrictions on movement of services and workers throughout the EC. Nineteen ninety-two will mark EC-wide competition in the European service sector. Dropping national restrictions on banking, telecommunications, and transport services will lead to significant savings of time and money. Also, EC's citizens will have the opportunity to compete for jobs throughout the member nations. This movement of workers could gradually lead to the mutual recognition of professional credentials and training requirements.

Some resistance lingers, however, to the total lifting of border controls. Of foremost concern is the import of illegal drugs and arms. Because of the unevenness of external border controls, movement of terrorists into the European Community is also a concern. But cooperation by EC members, and the increased sharing of police intelligence, promises more uniform regulation.[4]

As internal barriers to the flow of goods within the European Community disappear, EC's trading partners, particularly the Americans, fear that heightened external barriers to their goods by "Fortress Europe." Pragmatically, the integration of U.S./EC business through mergers, acquisitions and shared markets means a shutting out of U.S. imports is unlikely. On the other hand, EC officials have blatantly stated that regulations are specifically aimed at Japanese imports. This attitude reflects a tinge of bitterness toward Japan's closed-door policy to EC exports. Although the Japanese have set up some factories, particularly in the United Kingdom, these factories are generally dismissed as "screwdriver" plants; their products possess insufficient local content to be considered EC goods.[5]

At present the movement of goods across EC borders is subject to varying value added tax rates, which range from zero to twenty percent. For some EC nations, the collection of these taxes is of great importance to their national budgets, while for others, VAT is of little consequence. Because of these disparities, neither the elimination of VAT, nor its collection at "desirably high rates," is acceptable to Internal Market planners. Emerging compromises establish two bands of tax rates. The first band, a rate of four to nine percent, will apply to essential goods including food, domestic energy, public transport, and books and periodicals. The second band, a VAT rate of fourteen to twenty percent will apply to all other goods.[6]

HARMONIZATION OF STANDARDS

The acceptance of a product throughout the European Community will be based on mutual acceptance and adoption of technical standards and specifications. For example, twelve different sets of rules currently govern the making of a refrigerator. Marketing the refrigerator, or any other manufactured good, in all parts of the EC seemed to require a single product standard. However, after spending incredible amounts of time in often fruitless negotiation, planners decided instead on the "mutual recognition of products." That is, even if the technical standards for a Spanish produced refrigerator vary widely from one manufactured in Germany, if the Spanish version meets with Spain's technical standards, it can be sold throughout the Internal Market. If the EC meets the level of research and development it contemplates, the pace of technological change may be faster than the ability to write standards.[7]

This principle of mutual recognition of standards will attempt to paper over some serious weaknesses in the European Community's approach to its differences, at least for the immediate future. The principle was derived from a 1979 European Court case, which judged that a French alcoholic beverage could be marketed in West Germany despite its failure to meet German standards.[8] Only in the areas of health, safety, the environment, and telecommunications will products have to meet a single specific standard.

EUROPEAN MONETARY SYSTEM

Closely associated with the development of the Internal Market is the emergence of the European Monetary System (EMS). The EMS has set up guidelines for the issue of the European Currency Unit (ECU), and Exchange Rate Mechanism (ERM), credit facilities, and the transfer of capital.[9] To date, the EMS has succeeded in bringing stability to the exchange rate values of the European Community currencies.[10] Ultimately the development of a single currency, the ECU, occupies the dreams of many planners and the nightmares of politicians. Emerging from the experiences of the EMS is recognition of the need to form the European Monetary

Union (EMU). This body would establish monetary policy addressing price stability, full employment, sustaining of economic growth, exchange rate stability, and a financial system. Essential for the success of any financial system is the development of a Federal Monetary Authority and a series of national central banks.[11]

BANKING AND CURRENCY

The development of the Internal Market has elicited the consolidation of the EC's banking system to support the expected growth of business. With the removal of barriers, capital will begin to flow beyond traditional national limits. Already, in anticipation of 1992, numerous banks have merged, traded shares, or otherwise made acquisitions. In support of these developments, several regulations have emerged governing banking, insurance, brokerage, and securities.[12]

THREATS TO THE 1992 INTERNAL MARKET

The developing processes, culminating in the implementation of the Internal Market Agreement by January 1, 1993, are fraught with many perils. As the old German aphorism says, "the devil is in the detail." Besides the internal threats, many external forces require resolution.

Since 1947, the General Agreement on Trades and Tariffs (GATT) has governed and regulated most aspects of world trade. Periodic reexamination and reform of these measures occur through negotiations or rounds of talks. The current Uruguay Round, begun in 1986, has failed to resolve serious differences between the European community and the United States over issues regarding agriculture, a subject of great importance to the success of the Internal Market. The threat of trade restraints and tariff wars looms between the United States and the European Community. At issue are agricultural subsidies, especially those of the French.[13] Some economists dismiss GATT as outdated and call instead for a new framework for world trade, but under the current system, success of the

GATT talks could influence the success of the European Internal Market.

In response to the organization of the initial European Economic Community in 1957, the United Kingdom organized the European Free Trade Association (EFTA). Although the UK subsequently left EFTA for the EC in 1973, the remaining EFTA members possess mature industrial and service economies. Over the past decade trade between the two economic blocs has added significantly to the economic welfare of both. The future of EFTA appears questionable; Austria and Norway have openly expressed their desires to join the EC. It would appear that the EC will find it necessary to admit at least some EFTA members to insure the benefits of their mutual trade. One concept which has gained some creditability involves the development of a European Economic Zone which could include certain EFTA members in the economic benefits while exempting them from the political encumbrance of full EC membership.[14]

The reunification of the German nation also may have an impact on the successful completion of the Internal Market. For centuries *Ost-Politik,* or "look to the East," has been integral to German economic and foreign policy. Germany's catastrophic eastern adventures in the twentieth century led to the partitioning of the country. The subsequent growth of West Germany economically and politically, and its alliance with other western countries, seemed to signal the demise of *Ost-Politik.* The prosperous West German economy has been at the core of all EC planning. To what degree the reunification of the two Germanies will affect German economic conditions and fiscal contributions to the EC causes concern. Also, the extent to which German vision will refocus on the newly opened markets of Eastern Europe remains an open question of great importance to the completion and success of the Internal Market. Without the strength and focus of the dominant German economy the development of an EC-92 is of little economic significance.[15]

In broader terms the development of EC-92 requires a stable political world. Serious political or economic turmoil either in Eastern Europe, the Soviet Union, or elsewhere would slow or threaten successful completion of the Internal Market. The distraction caused by the recent Persian Gulf War provides a clear example.

SERIALS AND EC-92 – THE EUROPEAN SCENE

EC-92's Internal Market Agreement will offer the serials publishers, subscription agents, and serials librarians a mixture of opportunity and uncertainty. Serials publishers and subscription agents already possess a Euro-view if not a world view, and exhibit developed business practices not yet apparent in other business sectors. With twelve months remaining before the implementation of EC-92, let's consider the possible developments for each member of the serials information chain.

The Publisher

The major European serials publishers presently manifest an international perspective and are doing business much as though the national barriers to trade had already been removed.[16] Perhaps the most serious question remaining is: What level of value added tax will apply to journals? Here the British could throw a spanner into the works due to their dearly held VAT exemption on books, periodicals, and newspapers. Elsewhere in the European Community the VAT ranges from zero to twenty percent. In the end, a range from four to nine percent seems likely. A more level playing field may result in a broader market available to all EC publishers and slightly higher prices for British publications.

In other areas, publishers may indirectly feel the impact of EC-92. A key premise of the Internal Market is the open movement of goods, services, capital, and people. In this more competitive environment, the cost of paper, printing and binding services, and transportation for a periodical issue should be less. Likewise, the publisher could reduce labor charges by taking work to less expensive areas. The publisher's use of financial services in a highly competitive banking environment may also offer savings. As the Internal Market develops, the trend toward merger or acquisition of serial publishers is predictable as control of wider markets translates into profits for some and not for others. The recent acquisition of Pergamon by Elsevier is one such example. The opportunities offered by the EC-92 environment will likely create other mergers and acquisitions.

Although the Internal Market will offer savings in some areas, additional expenses also seem inevitable. Small- and medium-sized publishers who currently do little business internationally may need to train staff in how best to take advantage of this new environment.[17] Travel expenses may also increase as publishers' representatives seek entry into new markets. Success in new markets may demand the establishment of branch offices, the recruitment of staff with special skills, and additional communication expenses to tie the satellite operations to the home office. Firms entering into new markets and doing business under the new terms of the Internal Market may require expensive legal aid to support the firm's operations.[18]

The Subscription Agent

The European subscription agent faces many of the same issues, potential profits, and additional expenses as the publisher, plus a series of additional challenges. The basic premise of the Internal Market is to increase potential market size through the removal of barriers to doing business. Accepting this premise and its potential, will not the German agent contemplate entry into the British market, or the Frenchman into the typically Dutch sphere? As in the publishing world, additional competition may engender a series of mergers or acquisitions among the subscription agents.

The subscription agent and the publisher should be vitally interested in improvements in telecommunication proposed by EC-92 planners. Of particular interest is the development of EC-wide telecommunication capabilities in facsimile, telex, videotext, voice-mail, and electronic banking.[19] These improvements will decrease the amount of time required to conduct business. In the future, broadly available and highly sophisticated telecommunications systems might offer new ways of moving publications, i.e., information, from writer to reader through the assistance of publisher and agent.

The Serials Librarian

EC-92 will also open opportunities for the European serials librarian. With steps underway to harmonize the professional standards and credentials of librarians throughout the EC, the Northern European librarian may be able to consider moving to Athens, Rome or Madrid for reasons other than a sunny vacation.[20] Perhaps in the short-term this will not be common, but as library schools standardize curricula (including courses in European languages and comparative librarianship) and foster an international sense of information distribution and service, librarians will probably enjoy greater mobility.[21]

SERIALS AND EC-92 —
THE AMERICAN SCENE

On this side of the Atlantic what do American librarians, publishers, and subscription agents face? The serials librarian may perceive a whiff of distraction exhibited by their international subscription agents. The European agent's attention may not be focused on protecting the market-in-hand, but on competing for new and nontraditional clients in the European Community. American firms with an international scope may be preoccupied with establishing or maintaining a presence in the EC market. Expect here also a series of acquisitions and mergers. But for many years publishers and agents in North America and Europe have worked cooperatively. For the serials trade, "Fortress Europe" is less a concern than an opportunity to take advantage of more competitive costs for financial services, transportation, and perhaps telecommunications. The publisher appears as the least exposed member of the serials world due to a previously established broad international posture. Where the rub may come is with special marketing agreements and pricing deals among publishers and agents; many of these beneficial arrangements will not be allowed under EC-92 trade directives.

The movement toward an integrated market and the place of the serials world within it will, however, be complicated by the present unsettled state of the serials industry. Increased costs and subsequently increased subscription prices for journal publications have led to increased cancellations by subscribers. The profits of the subscription agency, significant research and development automation costs, the fight to retain traditional markets, expensive competition for new markets, cash flow problems, and wildly swinging exchange rules will cut further into profits, complicate fiscal planning, and even threaten the existence of some firms.

SUMMARY

The development of the fully integrated Internal Market by January 1, 1993, is doubtful. But if we view EC-92 as a process rather than as a fixed date, we see that considerable progress has been made. Completion of the Internal Market appears threatened by unresolved issues in the GATT negotiations. German intentions and development within the European Community are becoming increasingly unpredictable because of the economic weakness and drag effect of the former East Germany. Germany's view to expansion in Eastern Europe conflicts sharply with EC needs both politically and economically.

Other concerns include the increasing disfavor expressed toward EC President Jacques Delors. Many EC leaders have accused him of moving too fast and of seeking too great a level of political and social integration. The power of Delors' personality has stimulated and carried forward to success much of the EC-92 program. A sense of resistance is growing, however, and without some display of flexibility and compromise by Delors, the thrust for completion of the Internal Market may be seriously weakened.

Another concern is the European Community's lack of credible planning for relationships with third world nations. Current planning reveals a narcissistic tendency. We need only to look to the Middle East's oil to sense the external bridges which will be necessary for an effectively operating European economy.

A great deal has been said in the literature about the interaction of the American economy with that of the European Community. The fears of "Fortress Europe" shutting out American products is nonsense. The two economies are too intermixed and mutually beneficial. But one question has not been asked: How deeply involved in European integration does the United States want to become over the next fifty years? The United States is looking increasingly to the Pacific Rim for new markets, as exemplified by President Bush's granting of most favored nation trading status to China. The current wave of immigration is Asian rather than European. The American vision is slowly pivoting from East to West as California's populations now outnumbers New York's, and the Los Angeles/San Francisco banking complex begins to rival that of Wall Street.

If the integrated Internal Market successfully translates into the growth of the gross domestic profit for the European Community, that bodes well for the serials world. One of EC's key goals is increasing its research and development functions. Accordingly, greater monies should flow to the universities, research institutes and special libraries, which will necessarily acquire published research or automated access to research results. These forces should proceed hand-in-hand with the development of an integrated telecommunications system and the electronic transmission of research results.

Significant concern has mounted in recent months about the incursion of the Japanese into the control of key portions of the Internal Market. Journalists envision a divide-and-rule scenario as the Japanese pick off weak firms in automobile and computer industries, particularly in Britain. On the Continent the Japanese have provided enormous investment funds for electronic firms and are buying chunks of companies. Up till now, we've seen no Japanese invasion of the EC's publishing industry, but if bad times were to strike and capital support were needed, the Japanese certainly possess the funds to make inroads.

The formulation of the White Paper in 1985 and the subsequent Single Market Agreement of 1987 coincided with a period of relatively good economic times for most of the European Community. In prosperous times it is easier to be magnanimous, cooperative, and far-visioned than when facing recession, unemployment and soup kitchens. EC planning, forecasts, and general attitudes have struck a consistent note of euphoria until recent months. Concern about giving up traditionally held elements of national sovereignty, the stalemate in GATT negotiations, fear of the Japanese, questions raised by German reunification, and a weakened economy cast shadows of doubt over the progress of integration. To a large extent, the members of the serials information chain can stand aside in their previously gained international posture to take advantage of the best opportunities which emerge.

NOTES

1. Michael Calingaert, *The 1992 Challenge from Europe* (Washington, D.C.: National Planning Association, 1992).
2. Stanley Hoffman, "The European Community and 1992," *Foreign Affairs* 68, no. 4 (Fall 1989): 27-47.
3. James W. Dudley, 1992, *Strategies for the Single Market* (London: Kogan, 1989).
4. "Where Nationalism Dies Hard," *The Economist* 312, no. 7610 (July 8, 1989): 18-20.
5. Stephen Cooney, "The Impact of Europe 1992 on the United States," *Proceedings of the Academy of Political Science* 38, no. 1(1991): 100-112.
6. "Europe's Internal Market," *The Economist* 308, no. 7558 (July 9, 1988): 5-44.
7. A.D. Van de Gevel and David G. Mayes, "1992: Removing the Barriers," *National Institute Economic Review* no. 129 (August 1989): 43-51.
8. Paolo Cecchini, *The European Challenge 1992* (Aldershot: Wildwood House, 1988).
9. Gary C. Hufbauer, *Europe 1992* (Washington, D.C.: 1990).
10. Jeffery Harrop, *The Political Economy of Integration in the European Community* (Aldershot: Edward Elgar, 1989).
11. Jacob A. Frenkel and Morris Goldstein, "Europe's Emerging Economic and Monetary Union," *Finance & Development* 28, no. 1 (March 1991): 2-5.
12. Serge Bellanger, "Toward an Integrated European Banking System: 1992 and Beyond," *Banker's Magazine* 171, no. 4 (July/August 1988): 54-59.
13. Jagdish Bhagwati, "Jumpstarting GATT," *Foreign Policy* no. 83 (Summer 1991): 105-118.
14. Thomas Dyllick, "Switzerland and 1992," *Atlantic Economic Journal* 18, no. 3 (September 1990): 26-37.
15. "Make Way for the Germans," *The Economist* 313, no. 7624 (October 24, 1989): 13-14.
16. W. Gordon Graham, "The Shadow of 1992," *Publishers Weekly* 234, no. 26 (December 23, 1988): 24-26.
17. David Mitchell, "1992: Implications for Management," *Long Range Planning* 22, no. 1 (1989): 32-40.

18. Neil B. Krupp, "Overseas Staffing for the New Europe," *Personnel* 67, no. 7 (July 1990): 20-25.
19. Ralph Miller, "Europe 1992: The Impact on the Information Industry," *Online* 14, no. 2 (March 1990): 51-55.
20. Jo Haythornthwaite, "1992 and the Information Specialist," *Journal of Information Science* 15 (1989): 365-368.
21. M.A. Lowe and C.M. Baggs, "Are You Ready for EC-wide Employment?" *Library Association Record* 92, no. 11 (November 1990): 803.

Zastroika, Perestroika, Rasstroika, Dostroika, and Us

Edward Kasinec

In Russian, the noun *stroika* means "building." With the prefix *pere-*, it means "rebuilding" or "reconstruction." Change the prefix to *ras-*, and it can mean "deconstruction," or even "destruction." Adding yet another prefix *do-* to *stroika* results in a term meaning "enhancement" or "completion." Using the meaning "behind" of the prefix *za-*, one can create a noun *zastroika*, that is, the time before Gorbachev, which is usually referred to as the time of *zastoi* or "stagnation." Except for *perestroika*, these terms are neologisms of my own coinage. But even if the words do not exist, a reality did and does exist, and it is to these realities of the Russian/Soviet and East European book world that my remarks today are addressed.

ZASTROIKA

In the period of *zastroika* or *zastoi*, the book world in the Soviet Union and its satellite states was dominated by the government and its political arm, the Communist Party. There was a monochromatic quality to this book world, and a predictability as to which authors were published and the themes that were expressed in their writings. Dissident viewpoints (expressed in *samizdat* and *tamizdat*) were ruthlessly extirpated, and books and writings representing these viewpoints were secreted in the *spetskhrany* or special divisions of libraries and other curatorial institutions. Card catalogs in

---

Edward Kasinec is Chief, Slavic and Baltic Division, and Aitken Fellow, New York Public Library, 42nd Street and Fifth Avenue, New York, NY 10018.

© 1991 by The Haworth Press, Inc. All rights reserved.

libraries could better be termed guides to "recommendatory reading," rather than reflections of what the library actually held. Bibliographical work was sadly tendentious and failed to reflect not only dissident viewpoints, but also the writings of Western and émigré scholarship.

My colleagues in other area studies fields would often tell me how they envied my lot. Selection and collection development were based on a limited number of national and trade bibliographies, and a set number of intermediaries or vendors (the now-defunct Les Livres Étrangers, Victor Kamkin, Kubon & Sagner, etc.) provided what we wanted, with the assistance of centralized book distribution agencies in the Soviet Union and Eastern Europe. The names of these agencies are familiar to all who have dealt with Slavic and East European books: Mezhdunarodnaia Kniga, Ars Polona, Hemus, Artia, and so on. Because of the absence of a freely-convertible currency, other titles which fell out of the structure of official trade and academic publications were supplied through a system of barter and exchange. Our lives were easy, predictable, but also constricted and, at the base of it, maybe a bit dull.

RASSTROIKA

From this *zastoi* came Gorbachev, Raisa Maksimovna, and *perestroika;* and from that *perestroika* has now come *rasstroika:* confusion, deconstruction, excitement, opportunity, frustration, and a future that seems somewhat unpredictable. First let me deal with some of the features of *rasstroika*.

Just as Soviet military and political power dominated Eastern Europe, so too did its system of publishing, bibliographical work, and librarianship dominate and cast a pall over the satellite countries of Eastern Europe. The methodological work of the Lenin Library was deemed authoritative for the librarianship of Eastern Europe, and the officers of this institution often dominated delegations of the Eastern Bloc to international conferences such as IFLA. Even within the Union republics of the Soviet Union, the role of the Lenin Library was dominant and often stifling, monopolizing as it did large portions of the budget of the Ministry of Culture, as well as carefully harboring unto itself international exchange relations.

One result of this is the accumulation of large stocks of duplicate books in various provincial libraries. In the period of *zastoi,* the number of foreign trips accorded to librarians was limited, and most travel was confined to other countries of the Soviet Bloc or *sotsstrany.* Such trips as were made to the capitalist countries often fell to representatives of the Lenin Library.

Now, in the period of *rasstroika,* the role of the Lenin Library has inevitably changed. Its longtime director, N.S. Kartashov, was forced to retire under pressure in 1990, and a younger and more politically sensitive director, A.P. Volik, was named in the spring of 1991. The library is now drawing in its resources in an attempt to cope with massive problems of automation, physical preservation of collections, and rebuilding of its stack areas. This has, in turn, widened the opportunity for foreign contacts to libraries in the various Union republics (especially in the Baltic, Ukraine, and Byelorussia), some of which have declared their political autonomy. It has now become commonplace for librarians from the Union republics, and even the autonomous republics, to visit colleagues in the West. Within the last several years, numerous colleagues have visited me not only from the Ukraine and Baltic, but also from the Tatar and Chechen-Ingush Autonomous Republics. Within the Russian Republic, the president of which is Boris Yeltsin, other libraries, such as Leningrad's Saltykov-Shchedrin (formerly the Imperial Public Library), have begun to assert their legitimate interests and needs vis-à-vis the government. In recent months, officials at the Saltykov-Shchedrin Library even have begun to organize a group of "Western friends," somewhat along the lines of the Friends of the British Museum Library.

Other collections too—the Library of the Academy of Sciences among them—have been the recipients of Western support and benefactions, this in part to repair the egregious losses suffered in the fire of 1989. Thus, much has changed on this front. During my student days, officers of the Lenin Library were self-satisfied to the point of complacency. They felt secure in their exercise of political, methodological, and financial dominance over other libraries, not only in the Soviet Union but in the socialist camp as well. In the last several years they have become the objects of considerable political criticism and have been relegated to the role of less than *primus inter pares*. And this leads me to a second characteristic of *rasstroika* in the book world: professional ferment.

Before Gorbachev, bibliographers and librarians were, to use the title of Dostoevsky's novel, "the oppressed and humiliated," but barely sensed it, for so was the rest of society. They did not feel the full weight of their economic deprivations, some earning 120-150 rubles a month, because the standard of living of most of their compatriots was modest, and there was still a modicum of respect for individuals who worked with things of the mind. Now, from the societies in Eastern Europe and the Soviet Union have sprung millionaires. Cooperatives and free enterprise are encouraged, and privatization is on the lips of many economists. Thus, along with the political demands articulated by people involved in book culture have come economic and social demands. This has given rise to the development of professional organizations and publications such as the newspapers of the Moscow and Leningrad Library Societies. Further, representatives of these organizations have come to the West, seeking to study Western professional organizations such as the American Library Association, Special Libraries Association, and so on. They are striving to raise their prestige, social standing, and income. They have had some moderate successes: at one major Moscow research library, for example, they were successful in displacing a director and in gaining increased time for personal research. In another library in the now independent Ukraine, the salaries of some of the senior staff members were increased by a third. And this leads me to yet a third feature of *rasstroika*, the commercialization of library and book culture.

Many of the economies of Eastern Europe and the Soviet Republics are in a shambles. The central governments are less capable than David Dinkins of providing support to cultural, educational, and research institutions. Both publishers and library directors are seeking ways to supplement their incomes and to replace the monies formerly supplied by the central governments. This has led to a frenetic attempt to publish works which are sensational and revenue producing, and to engage in joint ventures with Western firms in order to bring equipment and foreign capital into libraries and publishing enterprises. Many library directors have begun to institute what we in the West call fee-based services, or to institute admission charges to exhibits, in a desperate attempt to draw to themselves nascent entrepreneurs from their societies. Some libraries have lost their government-supported mailing privileges, and traditional publishers now face severe competition from newly-created private and cooperative publishers. That which was formerly proscribed is now freely published and distributed. There is no longer effective censorship in any of the countries of Eastern Europe. Even the contents of the *spetskhrany* I alluded to above have been disgorged and thrown open to public view. One of my most memorable recollections of recent years was seeing such a display in the Historical Library in Moscow — a collection in which I had worked many years before in the period of *zastroika* and *zastoi*.

And now, to a fourth point. All of these factors — travel to the West, reacquaintance with publications long proscribed, increasing criticism of the professional practices of the period of *zastroika* — have led to a great deal of *Angst,* or to use another good foreign term, *anomie:* a sense of disorientation and lack of direction. In some of the countries of Eastern Europe, library buildings and repositories are being reclaimed by the religious orders and communities which were their former occupants. In the space of two months last year, I saw a significant portion of the building of the Strakhov Monastery Library in Prague (i.e., the Institute of Czech Literature) revert from the state institution which had occupied it for the last thirty years back to the hands of the *opat* (abbot) and his confreres of the Premonstratensian Order. And in still other library institutions, elaborate microfilming equipment has been set up, only to find that the ancient pipes cannot accommodate sufficient water pressure for the processing of the film. FAX and telecommunications equipment has been set up, only to discover that the overload of international telephone lines prevents using it. Publishers and journal editors sign contracts to print manuscripts with Western authors, and then realize that paper shortages preclude them from fulfilling their commitments.

DOSTROIKA

But if these are some of the characteristics of *rasstroika,* I also want to deal with some of the building blocks of *dostroika,* or those factors which are integrating, positive, and which are tending to draw our Soviet and Eastern European colleagues more closely to patterns of work and behavior on the Western model.

One of the strongest evidences of *dostroika* on the part of East European and Soviet bookmen and women has been their attempt to recapture the culture and literature of their respective emigrations. For decades, the literatures, archives, libraries, and museums created by Czechs, Russians, Ukrainians, and Bulgarians living abroad was forbidden fruit to their compatriots in the homelands. Now, publishers in the homelands have begun to publish the works of the Masaryks, Solzhenitsyns, Havels, Slavovs, and scores of others who were formerly tarred with the brush of "bourgeois nationalists" or "enemies of the people." In addition to publishing imaginative literature and memoirs of former émigrés, publishers in the homelands even have attempted to sign joint venture agreements with numerous publishers in New York, Paris, Stockholm, London, and other centers of the Slavic and East European émigré communities.

Scholars from the homelands are now traveling to the West to study archival and library collections belonging to their compatriots. Teams of bibliographers, textologists, and specialists in the auxiliary historical disciplines are now coming to the West in an attempt to recapture manuscripts, books, and archival collections held not only in established research libraries, but also those in private hands. (I might note parenthetically, that in some cases their zeal to recapture borders on the macabre, as in the case of the Soviet government's successful attempt to disinter Feodor Shaliapin from his Paris resting place, and reinter him in Moscow.) There are many projects in the wind which will attempt to publish Slavic and East European materials held in the West in journals and annuals published "over there" in the homelands. Soviet and East European bibliographers, too, are extremely anxious now to record what was published about their cultures in Western and émigré sources. In all of these ways, our colleagues in the Soviet Union and Eastern Europe are manifesting their desire to reintegrate elements of their culture that had been separated by the political vagaries of the 20th century.

In addition to the scholarly *dostroika,* our colleagues are also attempting to bring themselves closer to us in all sorts of organizational and technological ways. The Lenin Library has attempted to adopt the Virginia Technical Library System as a model for its technical processing services. The All-Union Bookchamber in Moscow has successfully reconciled the tapes of its database to those of Library of Congress's MARC system. The Institute of Scholarly Information in the Social Sciences (INION, or Institut Nauchnoi Informatsii po Obshchestvennym Naukam) in Moscow has now offered American library collections ten nodes through which to access its rich database in the social sciences and humanities. A number of institutions in the Soviet Union—for example, the Archeographical Commission in Kiev—are now subscribers to the Moscow-San Francisco Teleport. Publishers, bibliographers, and librarians from the homelands now appear with great frequency at international symposia and conferences. They attend meetings of the American Association for the Advancement of Slavic Studies, the International Congress for Slavic and East European Studies, the American Booksellers' Association, the American Library Association, and even more recondite conferences, such as the recent Online Conference in New York.

Now I must interject one cautionary note to this otherwise optimistic description. This is definitely a period of transition, and of parallel structures in the book world of the Soviet Union and Eastern Europe. There are still many members of the "old guard" who are entrenched in libraries, publishing houses, archives, and research institutes. While their power may be considerably diminished, they are often in a position to impede or decrease the speed of change. This having been said, what are some of the implications of both *ras-* and *dostroika* for our community in the West and, more specifically, here in North America?

1. *Escalating Costs.* First and foremost, it means a greater amount of work, and a greater degree of complexity and subtlety in this work. Anticipate an increasing amount of correspondence, visitors, difficulties, and delays in obtaining materials to stock our great research collections. In addition to the increasing labor costs of acquiring and processing research materials, also anticipate considerable inflation in the unit costs of books, serials, and other library materials. Before 1986, the cost of Slavic and East European materials was artificially low because of government subsidies not only

to publishers, but also to libraries. With the removal of these subsidies and the creation of an internationally-convertible currency in a number of the countries of Eastern Europe, the cost of research materials will continue to increase and the very structure of exchange relations will change. The situation in Yugoslavia is a case in point. In the last several months, the costs of many monographic and serial titles have trebled, thus provoking a strong organized protest among bibliographers in the United States.

2. *Völkerwanderung.* The relaxation of travel and emigration laws in the Soviet Union and Eastern Europe will increase not only the number of our professional colleagues coming to the United States, but also will precipitate the increase of many nationals coming to our major cities, requiring specialized library and bibliographical services. Their coming coincides with a period of contracting monetary resources not only for academic Russian/Soviet and East European studies in the United States, but also contracting resources for the support of public libraries and their social programs. (While the Warsaw Pact was perceived as a military threat, these funds were plentiful.) The burden of receiving scholars from the Soviet Union and Eastern Europe is now often borne by private individuals or small, newly created foundations, such as that established in New York by philanthropist George Soros.

3. *Changing Constituencies for Soviet and East European Studies.* The cost of processing Russian/Soviet and East European materials, as well as their unit prices, are escalating; the number of consumers for these materials is increasing; and the resources to service them are contracting—these are some of the leitmotivs of our reality. There is another: the constituency for Slavic and East European collections is changing. The commercialization and privatization of the Soviet Union and Eastern Europe have *seemingly* opened new frontiers for Western businesses, banks, law firms, and speculators. These interests require information which is specially packaged and not always easily retrievable from our traditionally humanistic and social science collections. Taxation law in Uzbekistan, the law codes defining joint ventures in the Ukraine, and reports on the natural resources of the Carpathian area, are all requests which have recently been posed to our Division in the NYPL. In the West, many enterprising spirits have begun to publish newsletters and bul-

letins describing business and legal developments in Eastern Europe, the Soviet Union, or even, in the case of the Ukrainian and Byelorussian business digests, for specific regions of the USSR. All are expensive, and require an ongoing commitment from our institutions. Staff will have to be sensitized to the needs of these law and business constituencies and made aware that their ways (and metabolisms!) are not those of our traditional humanists. Collections may have to be reconfigured in order to serve these constituencies, whose needs can become only more voracious.

Let me try now to sum up. Foreign language collections have always been a heavy cross to bear for the administrators of major research libraries in North America. They have been tolerated because funds for international studies were abundant in times past, and there always were the endowments left by the eccentrics to support these collections. Within the overall configuration of Judaica, Orientalia, and East Asian materials, Slavic and East European materials have been sustained by significant governmental funding through Title VI, as well as through entitlements such as the Public Law 480 for Polish and South Slavic materials. The trough is now becoming drier, and the complexity of servicing these collections ever greater, especially as the post-war émigrés who served as bibliographers and catalogers retire from the scene. Just as these cultures in the homeland become intellectually more interesting and vivacious, *our* abilities to channel and use these opportunities are becoming more limited and problematical. The next several years will tell whether the first manifestations of *dostroika* will devolve into a greater *rasstroika*.

Scholarly Information and Serials in Latin America: Shifting Political Sands

Margarita Almada de Ascencio
Sylvia Pérez de Almada

THE NATIONAL AUTONOMOUS UNIVERSITY OF MEXICO AND ITS AUTOMATED SERIALS ACQUISITIONS SYSTEM

The National University of Mexico, known as UNAM (Universidad Nacional Autónoma de México), was founded in 1551. It is one of the oldest universities on the North American continent. During its 439 years it has undergone political, social, and economic crises. However, it is still the largest university in Mexico and produces about 38 percent of the country's research. It has certain characteristics that make it interesting from the point of view of serials acquisitions and the flow of scholarly information.

UNAM has a Central Library that coordinates the UNAM Library System of 165 department libraries dispersed throughout the different schools, institutes, centers, departments and units. These department libraries support all the University's activities in research, education, cultural extension, educational support and the university administration offices. UNAM has two main computer

---

Margarita Almada de Ascencio is Director and Sylvia Pérez de Almada is Head, Subscriptions Department at the Centro de Información Científica y Humanística, Universidad Nacional Autónoma de México, Apartado Postal 70-392, Cd. Universitaria, 04510 México, D.F.

The authors wish to extend their appreciation to T. García Zúñiga, A. Herrera, R.M. Serrato, and G. Silva for help in preparing materials.

© 1991 by The Haworth Press, Inc. All rights reserved.

centers, which provide technical support for academic and administrative departments, oversee implementation and maintenance of the computer network, and coordinate the computer departments spread out in the schools, institutes, centers, etc. Also closely linked to the Library System are the Science and Humanities Information Center (CICH), the University Press, the printing shop, and other publishing and editorial offices.

The 1991 budget for serials acquisition (Figure 1) is U.S. $5,563,842. The distribution of the budget is as follows: 52 percent for the libraries of research departments, institutes and centers (45 percent for science research, 7 percent for humanities and social sciences). The schools, both undergraduate and postgraduate, have 42 percent of the budget. Four percent of the budget goes for the smaller holdings of cultural extension, educational support, and administration offices, and 2 percent is for subscriptions for the pre-university system of the University (which has the 15 schools directly associated with the National University of Mexico).

The University maintains 14,135 serials subscriptions, not including titles received by gift or exchange. Unique journal titles for UNAM are shown in Figure 2. Distribution of the titles, which corresponds closely to the distribution of the budget is shown in Figure 3. The countries and regions of origin of the journals are: 46 percent from U.S. and Canada; 27 percent from Europe, Asia, Africa and Oceania; 14 percent from Mexico journals; 12 percent from Latin America, and 1 percent from Japan (Figure 4). This means that we have to import more than 85 percent of the serials for our libraries; most third world countries are in the same situation.

The serials acquisitions procedure is difficult in Latin American countries, with local regulations varying from country to country. Acquisition is complicated by excessive customs regulations, import permits, reduced budgets, lack of availability of foreign currency, slow or unreliable postal services, costly transportation, and varying pricing schemes. Some of these problems have been overcome in the past few years. In Mexico, import permits have been deregulated, customs procedures have been simplified, inflation has been reduced and foreign currency is more broadly available. However, budgets are still tight; this affects all acquisitions, both domestic and foreign. The annual increase in prices of Mexican serials

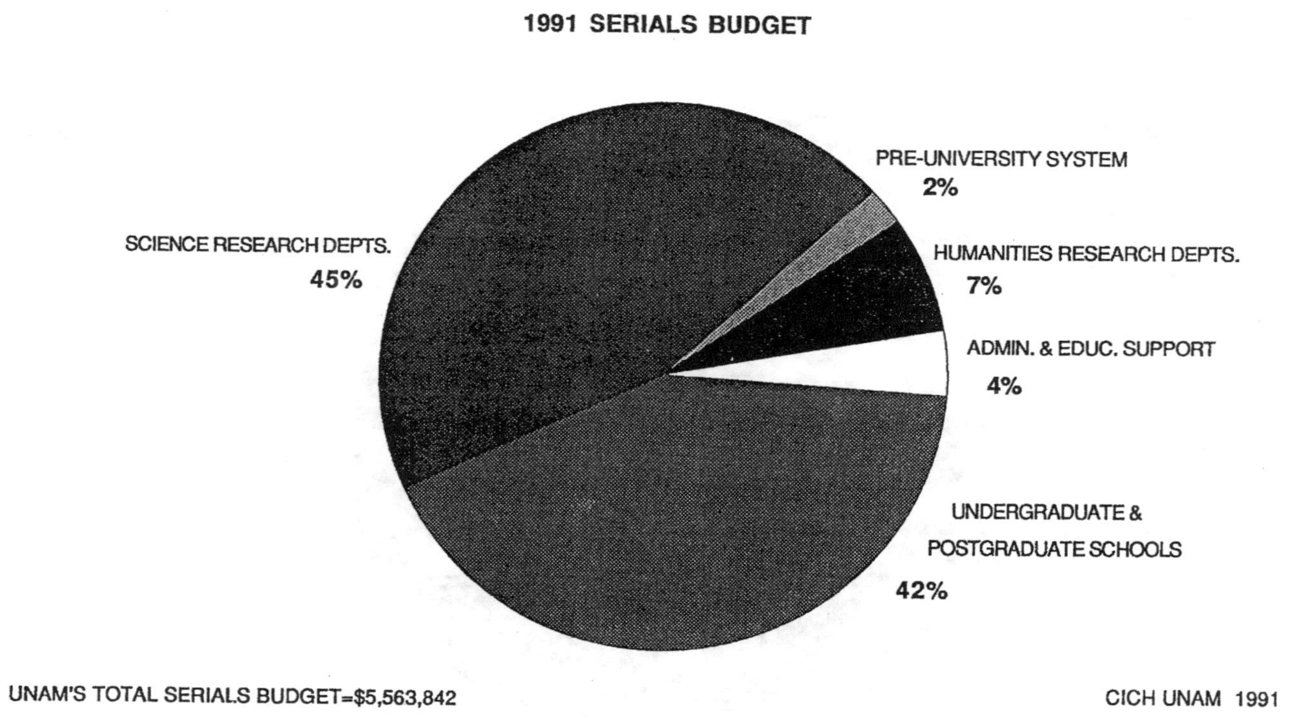

1991 SERIALS BUDGET

PRE-UNIVERSITY SYSTEM
2%

HUMANITIES RESEARCH DEPTS.
7%

ADMIN. & EDUC. SUPPORT
4%

UNDERGRADUATE &
POSTGRADUATE SCHOOLS
42%

SCIENCE RESEARCH DEPTS.
45%

UNAM'S TOTAL SERIALS BUDGET=$5,563,842

CICH UNAM 1991

FIGURE 1

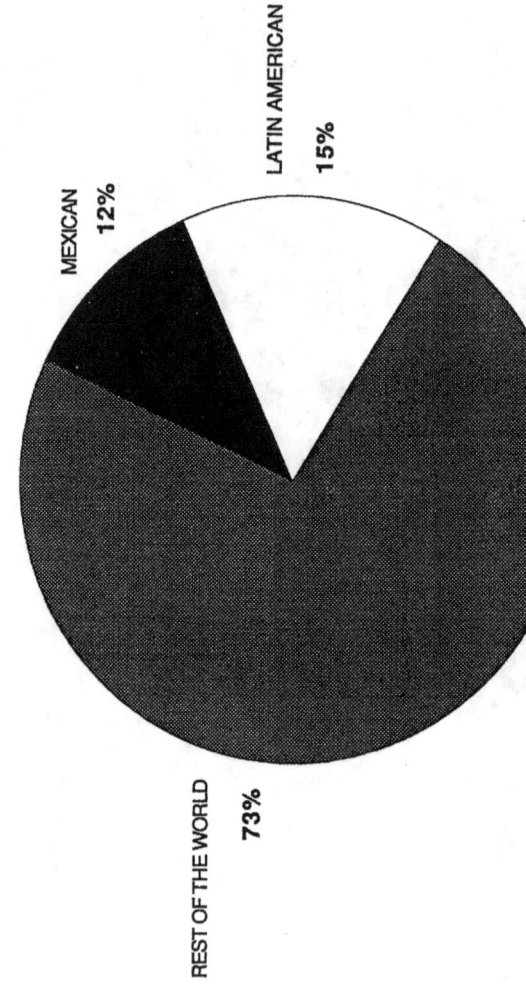

FIGURE 2

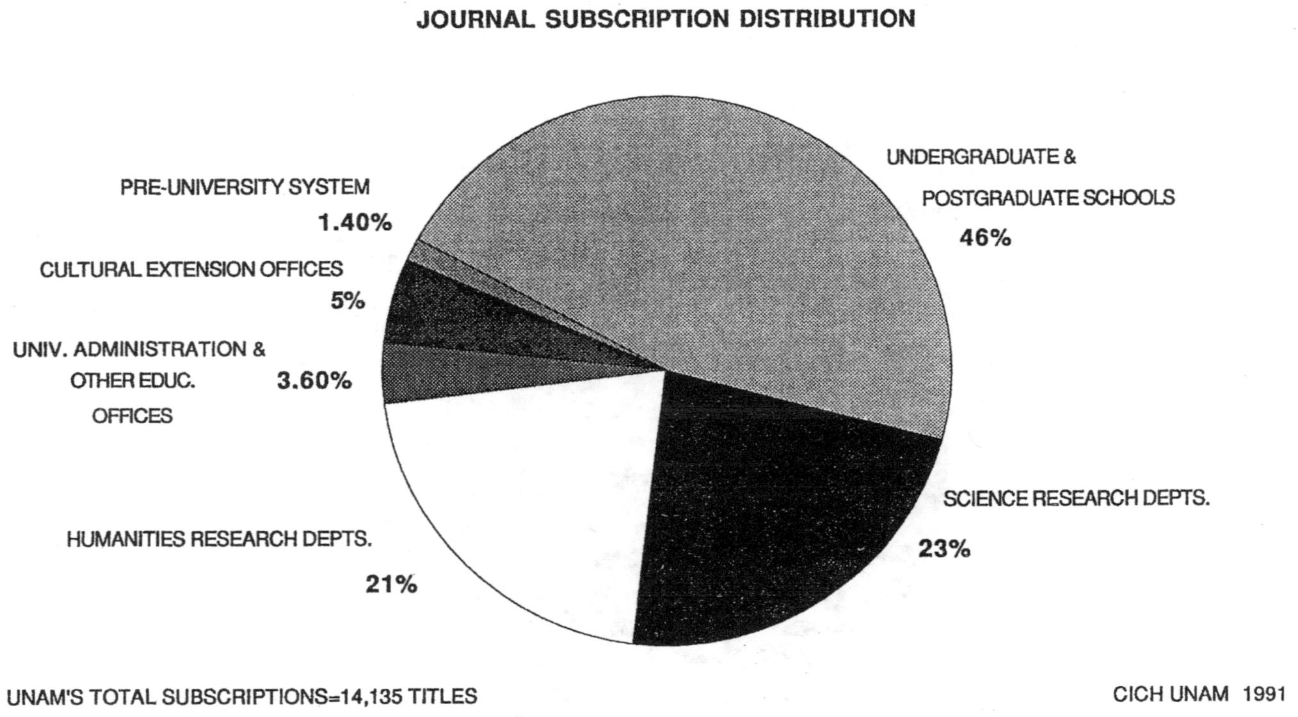

JOURNAL SUBSCRIPTION DISTRIBUTION

- UNDERGRADUATE & POSTGRADUATE SCHOOLS: 46%
- SCIENCE RESEARCH DEPTS.: 23%
- HUMANITIES RESEARCH DEPTS.: 21%
- CULTURAL EXTENSION OFFICES: 5%
- UNIV. ADMINISTRATION & OTHER EDUC. OFFICES: 3.60%
- PRE-UNIVERSITY SYSTEM: 1.40%

UNAM'S TOTAL SUBSCRIPTIONS=14,135 TITLES

CICH UNAM 1991

FIGURE 3

GEOGRAPHIC DISTRIBUTION OF JOURNALS

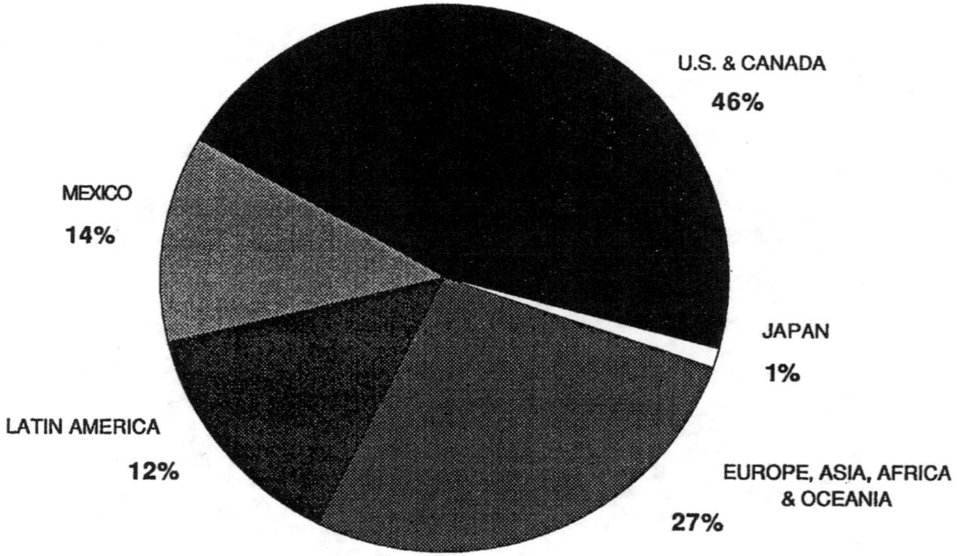

- U.S. & CANADA **46%**
- JAPAN **1%**
- EUROPE, ASIA, AFRICA & OCEANIA **27%**
- LATIN AMERICA **12%**
- MEXICO **14%**

SERIALS ACQUIRED BY SUBSCRIPTION=14,135 TITLES

CICH UNAM 1991

FIGURE 4

reflects high inflation rates of local currency; however, as inflation decreases the prices tend to stabilize. In general, Latin American serials prices are increasing (Figure 5).

One of the main problems of importing serials is the high cost of transportation and, in many Third World countries, an unreliable postal service, which means that journals arrive late or can be lost, thus making successful claiming almost impossible. At UNAM we receive almost all subscriptions by air service: either by air mail, air freight or messenger service. Even though the air transportation cost is high, timely receipt of information is required to support current research; that is why UNAM in 1985 decided to receive all journals by air. Surface transportation is used only for countries in South America and some Central American countries.

Another difficulty is that some publishers set up variable pricing schemes, determined by origin of order. Countries with fewer economic resources may have to pay higher prices, which deflates their purchasing power, and mean fewer titles for their collections. The majority of serials, especially those imported from regions other than Latin America, are ordered through subscription vendors. At UNAM we use e-mail communication for claiming, as well as all other technical and financial exchanges with vendors.

Serials acquisitions at the National University was centralized in 1972. The administration hoped to gain a better understanding of financial, clerical, administrative, and technical activities involved in the process. They hoped to make these activities more efficient and to achieve a better cost/benefit ratio. Centralization may not prove to be the best permanent arrangement, but it has helped to organize the system, to find out all the problems and drawbacks, and to be able to offer better alternatives to the University administration.

Centralization compensated for insufficient technical and professional staff in the department libraries, who had tried unsuccessfully to cope with all the subscription activities. Individually the libraries had been unable to negotiate their budgets with the Central Administration of UNAM. In the 1970s many of the department libraries did not have professional librarians, and the people in charge of serials acquisitions usually did not speak English or any other foreign language. Few department libraries had the necessary

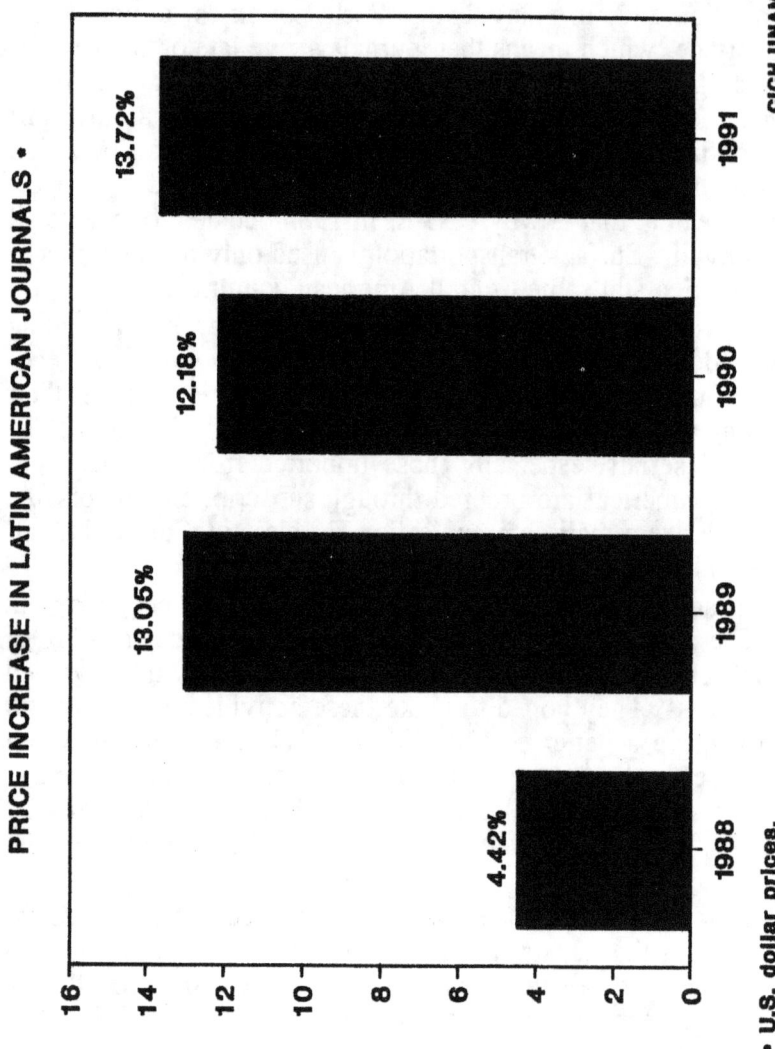

Figure 5

reference sources for ordering. Not everyone had sufficient awareness of publishers and vendors. There was little knowledge of computerized systems and, in general, the libraries were overburdened with hundreds and thousands of readers per day. The centralization scheme helped to overcome some of these problems.

Serials activities were consolidated under the Science and Humanities Information Center (CICH), which was given responsibility for the serials acquisitions in all department libraries. This centralized system is still in place today. CICH is in charge of negotiating with vendors and publishers, according to the requests from the library committee of each department library. The power of decision for selection of titles, and even vendors, was never centralized. Once the libraries determine their renewal list (new titles are added throughout the year according to the remaining balance), it is sent to CICH for ordering. The libraries can choose an entirely centralized system including ordering, receiving, claiming, etc.; or they can undertake some of the tasks themselves. CICH anticipates probable domestic and foreign inflation rates that could affect the price of serials titles and then proposes a budget for each library, based on each library's original request. The CICH proposals are reviewed by the Central Administration of the University as a top priority. Most of the journals are shipped to the Information Center, but invoiced separately per department library. Other journals are sent directly to department libraries who inform CICH of their receipt. Budgeting, payment, check-in, claiming, and distribution are primarily the responsibility of the centralized system at CICH.

Centralization has helped the libraries improve their infrastructure. Decision makers, because of CICH participation, have realized the priority and importance of timely serial receipt and the complexities of the financial, accounting, and administrative tasks. CICH usually negotiates budgets higher than the libraries original requests. The University's budget comes primarily from federal funds. Thus, the economic crisis of the 1980s was a major problem. Funds to pay the subscriptions often were not received until April. Payments in advance were not possible. As a result, receiving all the issues for a complete year was becoming more difficult and more expensive, because we could not take advantage of prepayment discounts. Finally in 1986, some of these constraints were eased and by 1987 all subscriptions could be paid in advance. Gaps in holdings for the years 1983-1985 have been filled in, and new subscriptions are added every year.

Severe domestic inflation during the 1980s forced the University authorities to negotiate continuously for budget increases and to lobby for a share of the available foreign currency. If each small department librarian had tried to negotiate separately, their voices would not have been heard, but CICH representatives speaking for the needs of the entire University collection were successful. During the years 1982 to 1985 very few new titles were added, but overall, the number has always increased.

There was also an effort to reduce the number of duplicate subscriptions, but some duplicates were indispensable, because of the widespread campuses. The National University has one main campus with over 170,000 students and five other campuses with undergraduate and postgraduate programs, located in or near Mexico City. The fifteen pre-university schools are spread out through the Mexico City and surrounding state of Mexico.

In 1975 CICH began automating the serials acquisitions and financial control, and still functions on a local system not linked to the University telecommunications network. CICH is now considering the decentralization of materials receipt and check-in. In 1990 we started training technical and professional staff from different groups of libraries—the research department libraries, the postgraduate, the undergraduate libraries, and then the high school libraries, so that they could start using software packages for automated control of serials within their own libraries. CICH is now implementing an integrated network for distributed subscription receipts, which should lead to greater speed and efficiency. CICH will provide technical support for the system and maintain financial control.

The restructuring program for UNAM's serials acquisitions during 1991 to 1993 includes the following objectives: (1) to make serials holdings and acquisitions information more accessible to department libraries and patrons; (2) to keep up-to-date on developments in automated serials acquisitions and check-in; and (3) to increase training and staff development opportunities for professional and technical staff. Strategies to accomplish these objectives include: (1) developing joint projects with the UNAM Library System and UNAM Computer and Telecommunications Network; (2) diagnosing more effectively current and potential needs, as well as examining the infrastructure available to meet those needs in terms of human, technological, information, and financial resources; and (3) to improve access and dissemination of information in serials acquisitions and handling.

CICH will act as a permanent service to help and to update library and information staff on information access and the use of information technologies. CICH's role is supplementary to the libraries' activities and is done in conjunction with the other departments that participate in information transfer. CICH's services are neither imposed, nor generic; they tend to be "ad hoc" designs for the specific needs of the intermediary and the end users.

Several other university libraries and special libraries in Mexico, and elsewhere in Latin America, have automated their serials acquisitions. Some use electronic communication, especially with the vendors; however this is not widespread. Serials vendors have become increasingly interested in the Latin American market. This interest is an advantage for libraries in the region. Vendors are now offering better services as they gain a more understanding of the problems that Latin American libraries face. Most of the larger serials vendors have tried to include Spanish-speaking personnel, which aids the communication with libraries throughout the Spanish-speaking countries.

The selection of serials also poses a problem for libraries in Latin America. Not all library committees include qualified academic and library staff; and not all the libraries are aware of the appropriate sources for serials selection. However, as a direct result of the economic crisis within the region, there has been an effort to select journals that best suit the academic goals of the universities. Inflation, lack of local funds, and difficulty in acquiring the foreign currency are common in most, if not all, of the Latin American countries. The awareness of the importance of timely serials acquisitions is increasing, but in places where inflation and economic crisis is most severe, the lack of continuity in budgets, and thus in collections, is quite apparent.

We hope in the future that there will be a more equitable pricing scheme among countries around the world. It does not aid developing countries to inflate the prices they must pay. It is true that some publishers have, for limited periods, aided developing countries by offering discount prices, but this has not been continuous, nor has the money always been available in time to take advantage of these prices. In some of the Latin American countries there has been a concerted effort to maintain or increase holdings and to use online or CD-ROM databases for current awareness services. Several countries have developed shared acquisitions programs.

In summary, it is difficult for countries that must import all of their materials. They must deal with local restrictions and lengthy paperwork in order to transfer funds, receive journals, and claim. Transportation poses a problem. If journals are to be received in a timely manner they must be shipped by air. The journals take so long to arrive by surface transportation, that it becomes almost impossible to report valid claims for missing issues. Several vendors have traveled extensively throughout Latin America in order to better understand local problems and share in overcoming them, which has resulted in an increase of orders from Latin America.

As the region continues to develop the awareness of the importance of timely information for development will increase (especially among decision makers). Telecommunications and computer networks continue to reduce costs and increase efficiency in communication. Vendors and publishers are improving their computerized services and communications. They are also giving more attention to the needs of their clients. All of these developments promise to make serials acquisitions a less taxing job, and give us reason to hope that our goal of more timely information flow for the advancement of knowledge and well-being will be achieved.

LATIN AMERICAN JOURNALS AND SCHOLARLY INFORMATION FLOW

CICH has published Latin American bibliographic indexes, through its computerized databases, since 1978. These indexes, entitled *CLASE, PERIODICA,* and *BIBLAT,* are available on paper, through online access to our CICH host, or on CD-ROM. The indexes include articles published in Latin American journals and abroad and cover most subject areas—humanities, arts, social sciences, economics, natural sciences, hard sciences, and technology. The articles are either written by Latin American authors or focus on Latin America. The CICH library currently receives over 1500 Latin American journals—most, but not all, of these titles are included in the indexes. A breakdown of the 1932 titles currently indexed is shown in Figure 6.

Many difficulties arise in Latin American journal publication: lack of continuity because of reduced budgets, lack of sufficient editorial infrastructure for scientific journals, and lack of a proper publishing scheme to maintain a sufficient number of quality papers. Inadequate refereeing and limited experience in marketing and promotional techniques further complicate the situation. These factors result in irregular publication schedules and a disproportionally high number of failed titles.

Few Latin American titles are included in *Science Citation Index* or the major online indexes, but Latin American peer review boards rely heavily on citations from these indexes. As a result, there is a pressure for authors to publish in internationally known journals, rather than local ones, so that peers can be confident of the papers' excellence.

Changing socio-economic and political situations in Latin American countries make it difficult for journal publications to maintain continuity. Sometimes a journal ceases in one country and reappears in another. It's also difficult to keep track of changes in title and publisher's address. The limited funds of some small publishers mean they cannot maintain adequate communication with subscribers to inform them of address changes, price changes, status of claims, or even renewal deadlines.

Many universities want to publish their own research, but decision makers don't always understand the necessary infrastructure, standards, and investment required to produce a good journal that will be accepted and cited internationally.

CICH's decision to start the Latin American journal collection and databases was prompted by these difficulties. All references that appear in the CLASE or PERIODICA database indexes are supported by an immediate document procurement service.

CICH has published bibliometric studies since 1976 and over the past few years has increased the application of bibliometrics for

TITLES INCLUDED IN CICH DATABASES

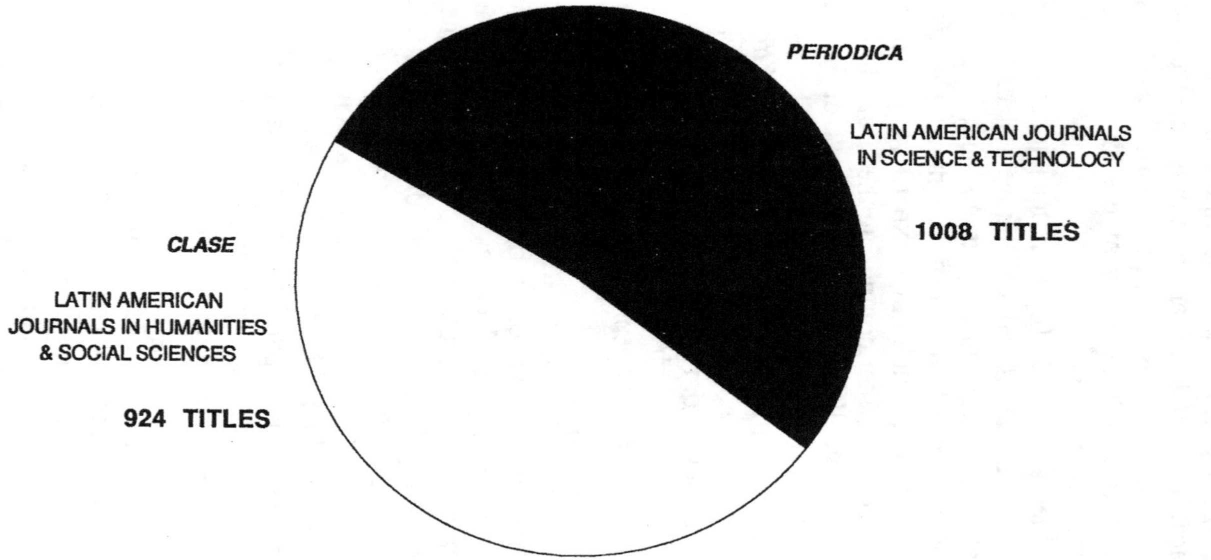

PERIODICA
LATIN AMERICAN JOURNALS
IN SCIENCE & TECHNOLOGY

1008 TITLES

CLASE
LATIN AMERICAN
JOURNALS IN HUMANITIES
& SOCIAL SCIENCES

924 TITLES

CICH UNAM 1991

FIGURE 6

science indicators within its new R & E program. Two recent studies looked at the journals where UNAM scholars publish their papers. We originally thought that we would find, especially in the science and technology field, a few "most used" journals for publication; we expected the excellent papers to appear in core journals and the others in a rather small number of well known journals. However, our initial findings are quite different. Our samples from the National University, both in "biomedicine" and "science and technology," conclude that a very widespread range of journals are included. In our samples taken from studies by Delgado and Russell, 2192 science papers, published between 1979 and 1987, appear in 692 different journals. During the same period, 628 biomedical papers by authors from the National University of Mexico UNAM appear in 208 different journals. This makes it difficult to understand the various paths of publication, and in turn affects serials acquisition. Authors will pressure the library to purchase journals in which they are publishing, not all of which are needed.

Is there a future for publishing Latin American journals? I believe there is, if standards for content, presentation, international refereeing, adequate marketing, and financial strategies are clearly understood and followed by the smaller publishers, editors, and learned societies.

One factor that might aid journal production in Latin America is better information technology, telecommunications and computer networks; electronic journals and other electronic communication are as important to developing countries as they are to the rest of the world. The current electronic communications possibilities in Latin America, although still less than in other developed regions, are already helping to bring about regional publication projects. I believe that, in the future, we shall see a blend and balance between electronic and non-electronic publications; between online access, optical disc, CD-ROM, and future technologies; and between local computer systems and wide area networks. The growth of cellular technology in communications, linked to electronic handling of information, will surely enhance information exchange. The Americas seem to be heading toward better economic integration and prosperity. The information flow and exchange will increase as methods improve.

In conclusion, I would say that current changes in economic and political policies in Latin America might positively affect information flow in the future. However, even though the people of Latin America seem to be striving for a more balanced development, the economic crisis is still far from solved and the problems are many. The democratic changes in Latin America seem to enhance collaboration, not only within countries, but also among countries. There have been several meetings of Latin American information professionals, with very open discussions, seeking cooperation for the future development of information markets. Much of this cooperation is achieved through closer communication by electronic mail. It actually has increased the collaboration within the region. We hope for a better global communication and more promising future for all the Americas. I am sure that advances in the use of information technology along with improved "info-structures" and awareness of the importance of information for development, will produce local efforts that will trigger information industry in more countries. A better balance in this industry might improve unbalanced economies. A more balanced economy throughout the continent might be one way of improving the well-being of societies. Political sands usually shift like a pendulum shifts (from good to bad; from bad to good). The nineties seem to be directing Latin America toward a better future for information services, including publications.

BIBLIOGRAPHY

1971-1991: XX Aniversiario Centro de Información Científica y Humanística. Edited by Ruiz Mariscal. Mexico City: Universidad Nacional Autónoma de México, 1991. All dates and statistics were taken from this title.

Almada de Ascencio, M. "Las actividades del Centro de Información Científica y Humanística en apoyo a la transferencia de la información en las Escuelas Nacionales de Estudios Profesionales y Facultad de Estudios Superiores Cuautitlán de la UNAM." In *I Seminario de Integración de Sistemas Bibliotecarios ENEPS-FES Cuautitlán.* Mexico City: Universidad Nacional Autónoma de México, 1991.

Delgado, H. and J. M. Russell. "Impact of Studies Published in the International Literature by Scientists at the National University of Mexico." In *Proceedings of the International Conference on Science Indicators for Developing Countries, Paris, France, 15-19 October 1990.* In press.

Pérez de Almada, S. "La desconcentración de servicios de suscripciones."In *I Seminario de Integración de Sistemas Bibliotecarios ENEPS-FES Cuautitlán.* Mexico City: Universidad Nacional Autónoma de México, 1991.

Russell, J. M., H. Delgado, A. M. Rosas and G. Blancas. "Estudio bibliométrico de la producción biomédica internacional de los investigadores de la Universidad Nacional Autónoma de México." *Revista Española de Documentación Científica.* Forthcoming.

PLENARY SESSION 3 – STRATEGIES AND RESPONSES

Automated Library Systems: What Next?

Carol Pitts Hawks

In a recent letter, Jonathan Waring of Collets referred to this as the "Monday morning graveyard slot." So while I'm very pleased to have been invited to speak to you today, I'm extremely pleased to see the number of you who actually made it to this meeting after last night's festivities!

In a presentation in 1985, Richard De Gennaro began by saying:

> The standard keynote speech at library technology conferences begins by describing, in glowing terms, the wonders of the new information processing technology and then exhorts the assembled company to embrace that technology or be left behind on the ash heap of the technological revolution.[1]

The pace of technological change and innovation is phenomenal. Technology that was state-of-the-art five years ago is inadequate

---

Carol Pitts Hawks is Head, Acquisition Department, The Ohio State University Libraries, 1858 Neil Ave. Mall, Columbus, OH 43210-1286.

© 1991 by The Haworth Press, Inc. All rights reserved.

today, and what is considered leading edge today will seem primitive in five years. As technology improves and costs go down, we librarians demand additional functions and capabilities, and our requirements and expectations are always one step ahead of what is currently available. Thus, the features and ideas proposed in this paper are functional requirements which are within reach, but not yet commonly available. I hope that when we look back on this paper in five years, these features will have become commonplace items in most systems.

Automated serials control systems have made significant strides in the last five to six years, but many still lack key features which are fundamental to our success. On the acquiring side, our management report capabilities still fail us when any new wrinkle is introduced. On the cataloging side, we must grapple with rapidly multiplying formats and the need for bibliographic control and representation of items for which we provide access, but not ownership.

As background, let me begin by telling you what has been happening with library automation in the state of Ohio. I currently manage a combined acquisitions/serials department, which includes all traditional serials activities except serials cataloging and binding. My library is one member of the Ohio Library and Information Network, known as OhioLINK. OhioLINK will link the seventeen state-supported university libraries in Ohio so that they will appear to the user as a single resource of approximately 19 million volumes. Each institution will have the same state-of-the-art integrated library system which feeds into a centralized database. Over the past two years, the OhioLINK network of committees completed a Request for Information, a Request for Proposal (with 3,000+ specifications), eight days of vendor demonstrations, and four site visits to the users of the four systems selected as finalists in the bid process. As a result, Innovative Interfaces was selected as the vendor for this project. These activities have provided a wealth of information on the current state of automated library systems.

My remarks today will synthesize my experiences as the chair of the Acquisitions/Serials Control Committee and as a member of the Site Visit Team to form an analysis of what is next for automated serials control.

Specifically, I will discuss five areas in which we should see major improvement in the 1990s: enhanced management reports, including serial cost projections; improved mechanisms for migration from one system to another; introduction of expert systems and artificial intelligence; external interfaces to vendor/publisher databases; and finally enhanced serials check-in including SISAC barcodes, a shared publication pattern database, control of new formats such as electronic journals, and issue-level records of vendor performance.

ENHANCED MANAGEMENT REPORTS

First let's examine management reports. Recent events in serials publishing, pricing, automation, and the economic climate have made librarians' decision-making processes far more difficult and also more critical to our continued ability to fulfill our mission. Published cost studies of serials prices, for example, are useful for general trends in publishing, but are of limited use in actual budget projection, since they reflect data on costs in a selected geographic area or a selected group of titles monitored from year to year. Each library's mix of titles is unique enough to make the variations from published data significant. In order to predict accurately the cost of serial title renewals in a given library, automated systems must provide accurate data and analysis.

Economic pressures are also increasing the demand for a diversity of local management reports. Data collection based on factors such as publisher, subject, and country of publication coupled with serial expenditure is routinely being requested. Reports that combine classification with costs require linkages between cataloging and acquisition files.[2] While the audit/security trails in most systems ensure the provision of accurate data, the sophisticated analysis needed is not uniformly available.

Carol Chamberlain has discussed the need for management reports that calculate average prices of books and serials by subject categories and project expenditure based on average prices, actual expenditures, and average inflation rates.[3] And Jean Houghton has highlighted one of the fundamental difficulties with using data from automated systems for cost projection.

> For projection purposes, what is important is consistency. Not whether an invoice is paid in July or November, but whether it is paid on the same basis every year. Successful projection also depends on a large enough statistical pool to blur inconsistencies, or a small enough pool to do an item by item check.[4]

However, these difficulties can be surmounted by a system which can prepare serial renewal cost projections by individual title. For each title, the program calculates projected costs using previous payment data and percentage increases. Individual variations based on data such as country of publication and payment history can be accommodated. The most sophisticated program has been available on the original Geac system; plans indicate that the program will be carried over to the Geac Advance System. The program recently released by Innovative Interfaces provides comparative data by fund, but not by individual title.

To clarify further, I will explain the Geac version in more detail and suggest some minor improvements. The report predicts an estimated cost for renewal of a title based on past invoices/expenditures, plus an inflation factor. In a more sophisticated system, the inflation factor could be adjusted based on variables such as country of publication, fund, or subject classification. The method used would weigh the most recent invoice patterns more heavily than older trends. By dividing the invoice history into periods and determining the increase/decrease between periods, a prediction would be made with the most recent change given twice the weight of changes in older periods. The simpler Innovative Interfaces program analyzes the payment history by fund for two designated time periods in the aggregate. Individual title information is not given. Instead, librarians can use this report to evaluate the renewal cost increases (after invoicing) for all chemistry titles as a group. Both of these reports are major steps forward in budget prediction and analysis. We can, and should, expect the number of management report programs to increase in number and in sophistication. Thus, the crystal ball we've been using up to this point might get just a bit clearer.

MIGRATION FROM ONE SYSTEM TO ANOTHER

Let's turn now to improved mechanisms for migration from one system to another. Much of the acquisitions literature in the 1980s was devoted to selecting and implementing an automated system. Libraries in the 1990s and beyond will be faced with migration to a second generation system. The library profession's emphasis and insistence on adherence to bibliographic standards will stand us in good stead for such transitions. However, acquisitions/serials control systems are based on fewer standards; the USMARC Format for Holdings has not been adopted by systems vendors as uniformly as the MARC Format for Bibliographic Data. Libraries with fully implemented serials control systems will have concerns in a number of areas: transferring fixed field data that has no equivalent in the new system, migrating variable length field data such as free text notes, and, most significantly, loading serial check-in parameters, frequency data, and publication patterns in non-standard format.

Once a library has completed the tedious and costly process of converting bibliographic, holdings, and check-in parameter data into an automated system, it would be difficult to justify the labor costs involved in a second conversion. In the OhioLINK environment, we included specifications to provide for the automated conversion of these records to the new system. Beyond this essential conversion, Jean Houghton has coined the phrase "payment system migration" for the process of electronically moving payment histories from one system to another.[5] The ability to transfer these histories would allow continued information analysis for collection management without having to wait the requisite number of years to rebuild payment data into the new system. Currently this type of conversion would require custom programming.

INTRODUCTION OF EXPERT SYSTEMS AND ARTIFICIAL INTELLIGENCE

In some of the country's larger libraries, expert systems are beginning to move out of the prototype phase toward marketable products. Vendors in the acquisitions/serials control arena have been slow to investigate opportunities for this new technology. However, as more user-friendly tools for building expert systems become available, we can expect more applications. At least one application of artificial intelligence technology is currently being used for acquisitions. Pam Zager at Iowa State University has developed an expert system to assign vendors to monograph orders. The system is designed to enable a student assistant to assign vendors by identifying order characteristics, such as country of publication, which would affect vendor choice.

Expert system technology can also be used as a mechanism to control, assess, and analyze the mass of data available from the automated serials control system. For example, Carol Chamberlain has proposed an allocation formula that incorporates an academic profile including number of faculty, student enrollment, and degrees granted. The acquisitions/accounting system would generate an acquisitions profile based on payments, the rate of fund expenditure during the year, average prices, and comparison figures from the publishing industry. A selection profile would include requests for expensive purchases, requests for purchase based on circulation and interlibrary loan analyses, and collection policies.[6] Each of these profiles would interact in various ways depending on the question posed to the system.

Norman Desmarais extends Chamberlain's proposal by predicting the application of artificial intelligence techniques to large databases. Such applications "could facilitate collection development by suggesting titles for purchase, to develop profiles of buying patterns, or to produce selection lists."[7] Aveney suggests the possibility of programming a system to print titles for consideration only when they have received a predetermined number of reviews.[8]

In another article, Brian Alley proposes one of the most interesting and viable expert systems. His model includes a main menu that lists eight vendor databases, each of which is linked to the library's acquisitions/serials control system. The vendors are in priority order and the system automatically seeks out the top priority for the initial search. If the vendor cannot supply the title, the system automatically queries the next ranking vendor until the title is located and ordered. In this model the vendors also have the advantage of quick, effortless access to their databases, which in turn allows them to keep more items in stock.[9] I can only imagine how useful such a system would be for locating elusive serial back issues.

EXTERNAL INTERFACES TO VENDOR/PUBLISHER DATABASES

Alley's model fits well with my next area, external interfaces. The possibilities for interfacing are growing at a remarkable rate and the adoption of the X12 standard will only accelerate that growth. The databases of book vendors, subscription agents, back-issue dealers, and publishers are assaulting acquisitions/serials librarians on a daily basis. Optical disc and online products such as *Ulrichs' Plus* for title availability, *BT LINK* from Baker & Taylor for inventory availability, and *SerialsQuest* from Faxon for serial back issues are appearing in libraries as stand-alone tools, often in CD-ROM format. Greater integration of these tools with the library's automated system is an essential ingredient for future development.

We often think in terms of downloading between systems, but our sights should be set higher toward true integration. Such seamless integration results in simple, straightforward movement from one database to another. For example, Carol Chamberlain[10] and Fred Lynden[11] have envisioned collection management workstations as a tool for selection in college and university research libraries. Such workstations would link administrative academic records, providing data on enrollment and subject emphasis to databases such as *Ulrichs' Plus* to determine existing literature in a field and its cost. We could extend this model to include online review of titles and sources, as well as online ordering. Desmarais predicts that separate discs for categories such as in-print material and serial issues will become obsolete. Instead we will be able to search multiple databases, making greater use of "hot keys" or macros to toggle out to other sources without disrupting work in progress.[12]

For example, Baker & Taylor's *BT LINK* provides inventory data updated weekly. Development of linkages with the library's automated system would allow the acquisitions clerk to locate a title in the database, toggle to the acquisitions system, load the data located in the vendor's record, generate the purchase order number, toggle back to the vendor's system, and enter an online order, effectively placing a hold on the book until it can be located and shipped.

Others have predicted the replacement of union lists with online links between article citations, journal holdings, and full text displays. "Ed Brownrigg has suggested that eventually the cataloging that publishers do to advertise titles in online searching and electronic buying systems will replace the cataloging done by libraries."[13] Additional possibilities include direct loading of standing order status reports into the local system and the online downloading of a checklist of issues that have been mailed.[14]

In summary, the next generation of systems could allow libraries to issue cancellations, claims, and orders to vendors without leaving their automated workstations. In response, vendors could acknowledge online the receipt of orders, claims, and cancellations. Status reports and responses to claims could be transmitted and recorded in the library's database without manual rekeying. The interfacing possibilities and the benefits to be realized from them are endless.

ENHANCED SERIALS CHECK-IN

The final area I would like to cover today is enhanced serials check-in. We have all waited for years for the development and acceptance of the SISAC barcode. This standard marks the beginning of a future which focuses on processing the contents of serials, rather than the container. Individual issue barcodes will allow cost-effective check-in by scanning and the elimination of input errors. Faxon representative Fritz Schwartz announced last July that Kluwer, Pergamon, and Elsevier had already begun printing the barcode on issues or had committed to provision of the barcode in the near future. In a recent *Newsletter on Serials Pricing Issues,* it was announced that Taylor & Francis, Wiley and the Royal Chemical Society had been added to this list. Although few automated system vendors have yet to incorporate the use of the barcode into their systems, it is safe to assume that the market will soon demand that vendors include this capability.

The era of electronic publishing is also upon us; the number of peer-reviewed electronic journals is growing steadily. Ohio State "mainstreams" these publications through the INNOVACQ system, creating traditional order and check-in records. The actual journal issues will be transmitted via the Internet and received in a generic mailbox for the Acquisition Department. The new skills required of staff will be knowledge of Internet protocols, e-mail procedures, and file transfer protocols. Once received, the issues will be transferred electronically to University Systems for access via the university's campuswide information system. Information such as enumeration will be recorded in the INNOVACQ system. I'm sure our next speaker will provide more detailed information on these new methods of acquisition.

In other areas, new developments in serials control will make it possible to compile vendor performance statistics based on the check-in record. Acquisitions librarians have grown accustomed to vendor performance information for one-time orders generated from automated systems, but only issue level performance assessment will provide an accurate, on-going measure of service provided by the serials vendor.

Subscription maintenance will be enhanced by mechanisms which can detect when subscriptions are due to expire. Analysis of serials check-in parameters will alert clerks when titles need evaluation—these alerts will be activated based on receipt patterns. Finally, the serials publication pattern database proposed by Bonnie Postlethwaite would include "information used to describe the frequency of publication and the method of identifying each issue of a serial publication."[15] Such a database would have uses in claiming, binding, preservation, copyright, and resource sharing, to name just a few areas.

CONCLUSION

The future of automated library systems is increasingly bright. We can expect to see significant changes in management reports, improved mechanisms for migration between systems, the introduction of expert systems and artificial intelligence, external interfaces to other databases, and enhanced serials control and check-in. Existing library systems will serve as a firm foundation from which libraries can build for the future. Many of the very early growing pains are behind us, but the next steps will have their own dilemmas, turning points, and obstacles to be overcome. As Richard De Gennaro has said:

> The point is that our field thrives on visions. Some of those visions turn out to be pipe dreams; others . . . eventually become realities — one way or another. The fun and frustration of it all is that it is so hard to distinguish the pipe dreams from the prophetic visions. . . . Our task is to pool our knowledge so that we can do a better job of telling one from another.[16]

NOTES

1. De Gennaro, Richard, "Integrated Online Library Systems: Perspectives, Perceptions, and Practicalities," in *Libraries, Technology, and the Information Marketplace: Selected Papers,* ed. Richard De Gennaro (Boston: G.K. Hall & Co., 1987), 229.

2. Aveney, Brian and Luba Heinemann, "Acquisitions and Collection Development Automation: Future Direction," *Library Hi Tech* 1, no. 1 (Summer 1983: 45-53, 50-51.

3. Chamberlain, Carol E., "Fiscal Planning in Academic Libraries: The Role of the Automated Acquisitions System," in *Advances in Library Administration and Organization* 6 (1986): 143-144.

4. Houghton, Jean, "Automating Serials Payment: The Right Tool for the Job," *Serial Librarian* 13, nos. 2/3 (October/November 1987): 108.

5. Houghton, p. 112.

6. Chamberlain, p. 148.

7. Desmarais, Norman, "Microcomputer-Based Acquisitions Systems: Where Have We Come From: Where Are We Going?" *The Acquisitions Librarian* 1(1989): 283.

8. Aveney, Brian, "Electronic Transmission in Acquisitions Systems," *Technical Services Quarterly* 2, nos. 3/4 (Spring/Summer 1985): 22.

9. Alley, Brian, "WYSIWYG Acquisitions: We're Nearly There . . . Well, Almost," *Technicalities* 10, no. 6 (June 1990): 1.

10. Chamberlain, pp. 147-8

11. Lynden, Frederick Charles, "Collection Management by Automation," *Library Acquisitions: Practice & Theory* 13, no. 3(1989): 182-3.

12. Desmarais, p. 284

13. Aveney, p. 21.

14. Vanderporten, Mary Beth, "The Development of Standards for Electronic Subscription Renewal," *Technicalities* 8, no. 9 (September 1988): 13

15. Postlethwaite, Bonnie, "Publication Patterns, the USMARC Holdings Format, and the Opportunity for Sharing," *Information Technology and Libraries* 9 (March 1990): 80.

16. De Gennaro, p. 234.

Embracing the Electronic Journal: One Library's Plan

Gail McMillan

The work of serialists is rarely static and now another exciting new challenge awaits us: the electronic journal. In this paper "electronic journals," also called e-journals, will mean any serials produced, published, and distributed nationally and internationally via electronic networks such as Bitnet and the Internet.[1] Electronic journals offer many potential benefits, including timely document delivery, direct links from online catalogs, less expensive subscription prices, and easy gathering of statistics on their use. They also pose new problems, such as: How does a library provide access? Does the library's computer have room for complete electronic journals without making sacrifices such as response time or implementation of new software? Who will archive these e-journals and how will this be accomplished?

From the point of view of the medium-sized, academic research library at Virginia Tech, the electronic journal is seen as another technological advancement to be incorporated into the collection of information sources already available from the library. Considering its mission, resources, and users, University Libraries has decided on a "near-term" approach to electronic journal access for the community we serve.

Two years ago the Scholarly Communications Project began at Virginia Tech "to explore, through management of actual journals, new ways of scholarly communication to reduce the expense of distributing print journals through commercial publishers."[2] Last

---

Gail McMillan is Serials/Maintenance Team Leader, University Libraries, P. O. Box 90001, Virginia Polytechnic Institute and State University, Blacksburg, VA 24062-9001.

© 1991 by The Haworth Press, Inc. All rights reserved.

summer when University Libraries learned that the Project was going to issue an electronic journal, many of us at the Libraries already knew that we had the resources and expertise to handle this and other electronic publications. We did not question *whether* we should welcome this new format into our library; rather, our questions were *how, when,* and *where?*

To address these questions and others, the University Librarian established the Task Force on the Electronic Journal. In a memo to the task force chair, he charged the group "to investigate and recommend how electronic journals can be integrated into library processes and procedures."[3] He urged us to be creative and act quickly.

The task force consisted of faculty and classified staff from each of the principal areas that would process and handle electronic publications. It was chaired by the Principal Bibliographer and had representatives from the following departments: Reference, Systems Operations, Automation Services, Database Administration, Acquisitions, and Serials Team/Cataloging, which I represented.[4] From the first task force meeting last October, it was evident that everyone was enthusiastic about the potential of online publications. Within six months the task force had delivered its report[5] and was invited to begin testing after the Libraries' management committee discussed our recommendations at a public forum. Present at that meeting were all the Libraries' department heads, assistant directors, members of the Task Force on the Electronic Journal and the University's Vice-President for Information Systems. After clarification of some issues, the University Librarian accepted our recommendations and reassigned the task force to oversee implementation. What follows are most of our recommendations, decisions, and accomplishments as of June 13, 1991.

From our initial, free-flowing discussion we quickly agreed on several points. First, an electronic journal should remain online at every step of the way, from internal processing through the point of use by the Libraries' patrons. Therefore, any consideration of the Libraries' printing to paper, binding, or where or how to shelve these publications, was moot. In fact, the task force report referred to printing to paper as "retrograde" and not a business our library should engage in. Second, an electronic journal is a serial and in most respects does not need to be treated any differently from serials in hard copy, microform, or CD-ROM formats. A third point was the identification of the appropriate medium for storing the electronic contents of the journals. The task force's discussions for the next several months focused on storage of and access to electronic journals.

In our final report we wrote:

> The Task Force on the Electronic Journal believes that, as agents standing between information producers and information consumers, libraries should support electronic journals. The fundamental reason for this is simply that libraries exist as conveyors of academically relevant information. We have not previously discriminated against information because of its format, and this is not the time to start. Furthermore, as customers of information, we want to encourage a means of dissemination which has the potential for considerable cost savings. Finally, we are sensitive to the complexities of bibliographic control and the perishability of unarchived information and we fear that information in electronic form will be at risk of disuse or destruction without the intervention and support of information professionals.[5]

The task force recognized that electronic journals have their limitations. For example, they require hardware and software. Furthermore, electronic transmission of graphics is a problem. Graphics can be mixed with text and transmitted as a Postscript file, but when Postscript has been used for electronic journals, file transfer problems between computer systems have resulted. The electronic journals we initially want to receive do not yet have graphics and are all available in ASCII format. ASCII file transfer between systems has not been a problem. When graphics file transfer protocols become standardized, we will be in a better position to make illustrated electronic journals available to our patrons. In the meantime, transmission of graphics files poses a problem, but graphics per se are not a limitation of the storage options we considered. Ultimately, the information industry will establish patterns and protocols to which libraries will adapt.

Keeping in mind these and other limitations of electronic journals, we identified several storage and access options and selected four as the most likely to meet our needs.

1. *PC-based local area network.* Storage and public access could be provided by expanding the existing PC-based Local Area Network (LAN), designed for our CD-ROM network. For over a year our Electronic Reference Area has used the LAN, which provides access to several (currently more than sixteen) CD-ROMs. As many as eight users may simultaneously search these databases from workstations in the main and branch libraries. Soon users outside the library-wide system will also have access to the CD-ROM network. Electronic journals could be copied onto the hard drive of this network server and made available as a selection added to the existing menu; but some development work would be necessary to determine the best method for data management, retrieval on the network, and off-campus access to the network.

The task force considered lags in system response time as the principal disadvantage to this PC-based LAN. As the number of electronic journals increased, additional disk space would be required to store the journals. If demand for access increased, a shared system for both electronic journals and CD-ROMs might become impractical. Response time could gradually increase until users would no longer be able to effectively search either database. A similar but separate network would then be necessary, thus increasing equipment and support costs.

2. *PC-based local bulletin board system.* Another storage and access option the Task Force on the Electronic Journal considered was a local bulletin board system. We liked this model because it was the least restrictive system, providing university-wide access via the campus network (the CBX), as well as in-house access at a public use workstation. Our systems representatives were confident they could design the bulletin board, without restricting the file format of e-journals (i.e., ASCII, Postscript, etc.). Disadvantages to the bulletin board system, however, include the difficulty of maintaining yet another network within the library, the cost of software, and the possible cost of hardware if no existing microcomputer workstation was available for this project.

3. *The Libraries' mainframe computer.* The task force consid-

ered using the Libraries' Hewlett-Packard 300, series 960 mainframe with VTLS, the Libraries' online catalog (an obvious choice for storage as well as access to electronic journals). It would be the optimal situation for both University Libraries and our patrons. With the online catalog as a gateway to the full text of electronic journals, we visualized achieving total integration of bibliographic information and document delivery. It would be ideal for VTLS users, who for years have been able to access our system both locally and remotely through the University's mainframe computer, to access the contents of electronic journals from the online catalog. From the Libraries' perspective, such integration would emphasize our responsibility and role in document delivery, establishing our ability to deliver traditional services in a nontraditional environment. The Libraries' retention of full responsibility would also guarantee that bibliographic and preservation issues receive proper attention.

Storing electronic journals on the Libraries' computer is not now currently a viable option, because most patrons cannot switch easily between the online catalog and source files. New programs would need to be written in order to give VTLS users direct access to the contents of electronic journals, and the task force recommended that the administration pursue this.

An alternate VTLS option would be to copy electronic journals into a separate database, providing VTLS users with an initial menu of options including the online catalog and electronic journals. VTLS users who select the electronic journal option would then see a menu of journal titles. Selecting a title would lead to the table of contents from which to select an article.

However, University Libraries currently has the largest database in the world running on the Hewlett-Packard 3000, series 960. Both of these options employing VTLS as the storage and access medium would require considerable additional resources, such as the purchase of more disk drives at a time when money is very limited and other system priorities such as keyword searching outrank electronic journal access.

4. *The University mainframe computer.* The task force considered a fourth option for access and storage, the University's IBM 3090-300E mainframe computer with a RoLM CBX, referred to

here as VM for Virtual Machine. This option has several advantages: (1) Virginia Tech is "heavily wired" and VM is readily available from offices both on and off campus. For example, whether in southwest Virginia at the Blacksburg campus or at the northern Virginia campus, every library staff member has a user ID and is expected to check regularly for electronic mail. Many faculty also use VM for on-campus e-mail as well as national and international communications with their colleagues through Bitnet and the Internet. (2) The means already exist for storing and transmitting large files, whether data, text, or graphics, and many of us regularly transfer, download, and print files. These procedures are routine and already well understood. (3) The electronic journals would be received and posted online with relatively low maintenance (i.e., no uploading or downloading of files from one computer or format to another). (4) Data storage costs would be relatively low since VM computing resources are not presently part of the Libraries' operating budgets. The task force, therefore, concluded that with VM we could readily make electronic journals available.

VM at Virginia Tech also has disadvantages: (1) It is outside the control of the Libraries,[6] and (2) its editing, word searching and printing capabilities have distinct limitations. (3) At this time access to VM is limited to those faculty, staff, and students who have user IDs. However, anonymous access will soon be available so that the university community can more readily access INFO, the online information system. INFO includes the menu option LIBRARY, which accesses another menu of news and information relating to University Libraries. Electronic journals could also be posted here.

Based on the advantages and disadvantages of the four options considered, the task force recommended that the text of electronic journals be made available on VM, accessible from the University Libraries' information display system, INFO LIBRARY.

The availability of electronic journals through VM would automatically facilitate access by a large component of the university community. But we realized that, in spite of the extensive automation within University Libraries and on our campus, a large component of faculty, not to mention students, are without terminals, mainframe accounts, or both.

Therefore, the task force agreed it was imperative that the Libraries also provide access to patrons lacking user IDs or access to terminals. We recommended that the library provide terminals with anonymous access to VM and INFO LIBRARY; access would still be limited, however, because these patrons would be required to come to the library and use the terminals provided. We recommended that the Libraries initially provide two terminals, one in the Electronic Reference Area and one in the Science Reference Area. The necessary wiring and lines are already in place. From these or any other terminals with a VM connection, users could choose the "E-JOURNL" selection from the INFO LIBRARY directory and get a list of the electronic journals available. Selecting a journal title would lead to a list of article titles that could be read at the terminal, downloaded to diskettes, or printed.

Although we acknowledged that the Reference Department would want to weigh this service in the context of other services they provide in the electronic environment, the task force anticipated that direct costs to download onto diskette or to print to paper would be the patron's responsibility. Rather than putting printers at these terminals, printing could be centralized; perhaps the Photocopy Services Unit should be expanded to include printing electronic articles on a cost-recovery basis.

Having addressed the storage issue and determined how access could work in one scenario, the task force then considered internal processing of electronic journals. We decided to handle them much like serials in other formats. Electronic journals would receive full treatment following CONSER guidelines, including Library of Congress call numbers and subject headings, linking entries, name authority work, etc. The bibliographic record would also describe the means of access in a general note (MARC tag 500) and in a local note (MARC tag 590).

> 500bb Mode of access: Electronic mail on BITNET ([userid] @ [node]) and Internet ([userid] @ [node]).
>
> 590bb This electronic journal is available for viewing on the University's INFO system on VTVM1 or VTVM2 under the entry INFO LIBRARY E-JOURNL.

Additional VTLS HELP screens would clearly explain what electronic journals are and how to access them. The VTLS MARC holdings record, besides listing the full extent of electronic journal holdings available online, would explicitly direct patrons to the electronic journal source text and identify the sites of dedicated access terminals. This information could go into a textual holdings field (MARC tag 866) and would display a public note:

> This electronic journal is available for viewing on the University's INFO system on VTVM1 or VTVM2 under the entry INFO LIBRARY E-JOURNL
>
> Terminals are available for free public access in the REFERENCE ROOM and at the SCIENCE REFERENCE DESK

In cooperation with Acquisitions Department personnel, the task force addressed other internal processes such as ordering, receiving, and claiming electronic journals. Here we anticipate making some adjustments for handling serials in this new electronic format.

Orders for new titles would be initiated by subject bibliographers, with the Principal Bibliographer's approval required even for new subscriptions to free journals. When a subscription is placed for a new electronic journal, the ordering clerk would ask the publisher to invoice Business Services (if indeed there is a subscription fee) and to send the text to the VM account maintained by the Acquisitions Department and dedicated to ordering and receiving electronic journals. Serials Receiving staff should open this account weekly to receive the issues—weekly because after one week, unopened files are automatically deleted by the system. These procedures assume a typical case in which publishers distribute journal issues to subscriber mailing lists, with receipt a passive activity for the library once its account has been established.

Somewhat more proactive procedures are required for electronic journals that notify subscribers via e-mail that issues are available, rather than sending issues to each subscriber's user ID. Sometimes an electronic journal issue may be so large that it must be sent in multiple files. In these cases, Serials Receiving will establish procedures for directly accessing the online host accounts and receiving text according to the schedules announced by journal publishers.

In both situations, Serials Receiving staff would give each file of the online issue a cursory check to ensure that basic conventions of text storage had been maintained and that the text is actually eye-readable. Serials Receiving staff would record the receipt of a new issue following the procedures now used for serials in all other formats (though electronic journals should be included in our current testing of online check-in). Claiming procedures should be straightforward, calculated by the same means now used for journals in other formats. These checks and procedures will certainly be refined with experience.

New titles would be forwarded to the Serials Cataloging VM account for cataloging and creating the MARC holdings records. Additional issues could be checked-in online and the MARC holdings record updated in Serials Receiving. As usual, Serials Receiving would forward to and notify Serials Cataloging of changes in title, frequency, or numbering. An explanatory e-mail note would 'accompany' the electronic journal when it is forwarded to Serials Cataloging.

The task force has recommended, as an interim measure, that the Database Administration Department be responsible for maintaining the E-JOURNL portion of INFO LIBRARY. At each stage where files are forwarded, the sending unit would purge the text from its own account after receiving e-mail notification from the subsequent unit that text transferred successfully.

In addition to clarifying technical processing, we addressed reference concerns. To handle the new technology the Reference Department has created a separate location, the Electronic Reference Area, with individual workstations that have both dedicated and multiple CD-ROM access. Reference Librarians have also had to become familiar with the new electronic tools, learning a variety of search strategies and commands as well as becoming acquainted with a variety of databases. All of these services require equipment, supplies, and a trained staff, able to train patrons in the use of these information technologies. The task force recommended that the Libraries' administration provide additional resources as the Libraries expand to include newer technologies, so that the introduction of this new service—access to e-journals—does not erode the level of service currently being provided. We included an appendix to our report that lists "resource considerations," because we wanted it to be recognized that monetary as well as organizational resources are necessary to insure the success of this endeavor.

We briefly touched on training issues in our report. While many within the Libraries are familiar with VM for receiving and sending e-mail, we wanted to insure that each step in receiving and forwarding files of electronic journals was uniformly understood. We also wanted the staff to feel comfortable with each phase of the processing and to know how all steps fit together to make electronic journals available to the Libraries' users. We recommended that initial training be carried out by our Automation Services Department after which each department would be responsible for training its own staff. Reference staff must also provide training for patrons. Ongoing review of new electronic publications would be necessary so that reference librarians could maintain their level of service and could incorporate new titles into training sessions for library patrons.

Having addressed these major issues surrounding electronic journals, the task force suggested testing our recommendations on five e-journals:

Newsletter of Serials Pricing Issues
   Bitnet: tuttle@UNC

Postmodern Culture
   Bitnet: pmc@ncsuvm
   Internet: pmc@ncsuvm.ncsu.edu

Journal of the International Academy of Hospitality Research
   Bitnet: jiahred@vtvm1
   Internet: jiahred@vtvm1.cc.vt.edu

Electronic Journal of Communication
   Bitnet: comserve@rpiecs
   Editor's Internet: winter@ucc.uwindsor.ca

New Horizons in Adult Education
   Bitnet: horizons@suvm
   Editor's Bitnet: ltnewell@suvm

These titles cover a variety of subject areas and include one international publication. The five we chose will also give us the opportunity to work with serials that do and don't have tables of contents, issues available in single and multiple files, and active as well as passive receipts. Since these electronic journals are available to us without subscription fees, we have postponed developing procedures for processing subscription costs and other considerations important to our Business Services Department.

I have described for you many of our deliberations and how we resolved procedural issues. Our report concludes:

> We feel strongly that local storage and access of full text electronic journals is a major step in the migration towards the concept of "access and ownership." The handling of electronic journals has important implications for future use of full text document delivery in fulfillment of the goals of the University Libraries.[5]

There are still many issues for libraries to address concerning electronic journals. Some of these are: (1) How will we handle interlibrary loan and copyright considerations? (2) How much, if any, reformatting of e-journals is necessary to make articles more easily accessible or readable for library users? (3) What is the role of serials vendors? I opened my paper by suggesting the benefits and problems of electronic journals and now I will leave you with these possible solutions as well as many more issues provoked by electronic publications.

NOTES

1. *Internet* is an electronic network providing high speed data transfer among all major educational institutions in the United States and worldwide. It also connects government, military, commercial and other types of organizations. Internet access is not limited by type or size of computer system. Its services include e-mail, text and binary file transfer, and remote login. The language of Internet is TCP/IP (Transmission/Control Protocol/Internet Protocol) which means that, in part, there is a common language between computer systems.

Bitnet (Because It's Time NETwork) is a subset of the Internet that allows data transfer between educational and research institutions. Its services include e-mail among Bitnet nodes, text file transfer, and interactive messaging.

2. Lon Savage, "New Electronic Journal Launched," *Spectrum*, 18 April 1991: 5.

3. Paul Gherman (University Librarian) to Paul Metz (Principal Bibliographer), 28 September 1990.

4. The task force members included: Bill Dougherty, Beth Hanson (implementation team chair), Buddy Litchfield, Paul Metz (first task force chair), and Kelly Queijo. The implementation team was later joined by Harry Kriz and Bill Kownacki, with input from Eleanor Garrison and Brenda Pratt.

5. "Report of the Task Force on the Electronic Journal," University Libraries, Virginia Polytechnic Institute and State University, 21 April 1991. The report was revised for distribution 17 May 1991.

6. Storage on the university mainframe computer could become a problem if electronic journals become extremely popular and proliferate to such an extent that "old" issues cannot be left online, but must be stored on off-line tapes. These would be loaded for users upon request, but would not be as immediately accessible as current issues.

Information Technologies and the Transformation of Libraries and Librarianship

Charles B. Lowry

IMFORMATION TECHNOLOGY AND THE LIMITS OF CHANGE

Until very recently libraries have been fundamentally nineteenth-century institutions that could be characterized as labor-intensive craft workshops. As such, their organization has centered around specialized skills and knowledge applied to complex manual filing systems. This organization is based on the storage and retrieval role which libraries undertook as part of the task of managing information represented in the print form codex, the bound volume as it has existed for centuries. Today, the library is being transformed into a capital-intensive, high technology light industry. The increased use of technology in libraries over the past ten or so years is unprecedented in scope and impact.[1]

If there were no "smart machines," then there would be no reason for this paper, because the basic model or paradigm of the library which was put into place around the turn of the century would remain dominant. Although it is tempting to do so, the purpose of this paper is not a recapitulation of the discussions of information technology. Instead, the purpose is to focus on the effects information technologies will have on libraries as systems and librarianship as a profession. Necessarily, this means touching also on "knowl-

---

Charles B. Lowry is Director of Libraries, University of Texas at Arlington Libraries, Arlington, TX 76019.

edge workers," to use Drucker's term, in other sectors including publishing and computers.

Predicting social change is always a "dicey" business. As that seer Samuel Goldwyn noted, it is "dangerous to make predictions, especially about the future." However, little guesswork is required about what information technologies will affect the future of libraries. At present the list would be as follows:

- microcomputers with improved processor cycle time, memory capacity, and access times;
- substantial improvements in the power of microcomputing systems and other software/hardware engineering advances, such as artificial intelligence, expert systems, and fuzzy technology, as well as the potential for a dramatic breakthrough presented by the photon chip, recently announced by Texas Instruments, the same firm that developed the silicon chip;
- removable optical mass-storage media with dramatic improvements in capacity and error rates, including the digitally-coded video disk, an offshoot of the analog video disk, and CD-ROM, the digital offshoot of the audio disk;
- the R & D currently underway on mainframe peripherals — optical mass storage and long awaited "bubble memory" — which portend vast improvement in storage cost and capacity over standard magnetic storage;
- several devices which may well have the most far reaching effects of all as a medium with the potential for "acting" like a book or magazine — the optical media card (OMC) developed by Drexler Technology Corporation, "The Smart Book" and the accompanying "Text Pack" composed of ROM chips developed by a joint venture company called Megaword, and finally, Sony's recent announcement of a mini-CD/ROM "Data Disc Man Electronic Book"; and lastly,
- the emergence of telecommunications networks as a vital backbone for sharing information, research knowledge, and library resources, and which include international high-speed networks, wide area networks, campus area networks, and local area networks.[2]

A steady stream of new applications are being added to the traditional print mission of the library at a fast pace. As the library profession begins to cope with it, we should be strongly reminded that we are not in the business of simply providing access to books, journals, or databases. Librarians knowledge workers, whose particular mission is to provide access to the body of knowledge and the tangible products of this exchange, are the means to fulfill an intangible information need. Today, the product may be a faxed article and tomorrow it may be an optical media card or a ROM chip, but the mission will be fundamentally the same, access to and delivery of what has been called "second-hand knowledge" or "public knowledge" — that is the public record of the work of the other knowledge professions.[3] The knowledge occupations or professions — both inside and outside of the academy — have a charter to produce and evaluate knowledge in specific areas of study. However, that body of knowledge is under constant modification, not only in the social sciences and humanities, but in the hard sciences as well. Within each discipline there is always the question of validity, and estimates of what is not worth publishing run as high as seventy-five percent, even in the sciences.[4] The place of librarianship within this "knowledge industry" is to constantly organize and provide access to the changing body of knowledge so that public ignorance of it can be converted into private knowledge.[5]

Thus far, this discussion has intentionally avoided use of the all-purpose weasel word "information," using "knowledge" instead for a very good reason. Information is not knowledge.[6] It is vital to the understanding of the information technology-driven change libraries are experiencing that we avoid the more trendy and overly enthusiastic paean to the information age — as Roszak puts it, the "megahype" of the "data merchants."[7] At a recent conference, Michael Schrage asserted that:

> The information age is a dangerous and misleading myth. The real value of the medium [of information technology] is not in the information it carries, but in the communities it creates. The use of information technology will be effective to the extent that they support relationships and collaboration which arises out of them.[8]

We should remember that information-seeking behaviors will always be motivated by individual needs which are attenuated by avoidance behavior. People will continue to seek information in the quickest way they can find it and not out of a fascination with information technologies—that is, except for those who have been unkindly called "technogeeks." In fact, to the extent that information technology is a nuisance, people will not use it.

The problem is that there has been a fundamental shift in the way we look at machines in the last four decades.

> The machines we have invented might be said to fall in two major categories: strong machines and smart machines. Strong machines (the steam engine, dynamo, airplane) have had their share of appreciation; but smart machines have elicited a very different response, a sense of self-effacing awe, that has more than a touch of the pathological about it.[9]

This public awe of the machine that "thinks" is part of the reason that computers are the cornerstone of the whole notion of the "information age." Moreover, it has numbed the public mind against the more rapacious salesmanship in the microcomputer industry. Two examples come to mind. In thousands of homes microcomputers sit on desk tops and bookshelves gathering dust or serving as very expensive toys, because they did not fulfill the inflated promises of enriching our private lives. The home computer industry collapsed when the cant confronted reality. Apple and other manufacturers moved quickly to greener pastures—first education, then business. Likewise, *Time* magazine recently characterized the applications of the microcomputer in education as "the revolution that fizzled."[10]

These examples are not offered out of some sort of neo-Luddite impulse, but as a reminder of the need for a balanced view of the true meaning of information technologies. Otherwise, we will veer between extremes driven by our own individual attitudes either hyping the "revolution" or resisting it. A strong case can be made that we may expect more evolution than revolution for a number of years as the face of libraries, like our society, are dramatically changed.

KNOWLEDGE FORMATS—
THE MESSAGE IN THE MEDIUM

Many in the library community believe that the salient feature of publishing in the future will be variety. The logic will be to select a type of publication medium which fits the use and economics of the information being published. To rephrase Marshall McLuhan, the message will decide the medium in which it is produced. A model (Figure I) describing how this might work is predicated on the current economies of various information technologies, including print. For instance, to consider publishing in CD-ROM format, which involves the cost of mastering and the delay which accompanies it, there has to be both market demand and added value, as well as low time sensitivity. By contrast, using the OMC format, which requires no mastering and can be copied more cheaply, may be attractive as a format to publish on-demand materials which are primarily alphanumeric and contain a few low-level graphics, such as a technical report or problems to accompany a sophomore accounting textbook to be used as homework on a spreadsheet. On the other hand, a scientific monograph, say one in biology, with more complex graphic requirements might demand the greater capacity of The Smartbook or Sony Data Disc Man Electronic Book. Online candidates will generally fall under that category of information which is highly time sensitive, probably proprietary and profit-oriented such as commodity prices or securities information. This model reflects the complexity of the problems and great opportunities facing commercial and not-for-profit publishers and libraries.

On the other hand, there are many imponderables in this model, since right now most of it is guesswork. Standards are lacking, specialized peripherals are not available, interfaces with other technologies have to be developed, and the model does not comprehend the effects of low-cost access to knowledge via publicly funded telecommunications networks.[11] It is possible that this latter form of delivery will help us rethink dependence on discreet ROM packages, be they books, CD's, or OMC's.

Allan Baratz of IBM recently titled a conference address, "A Living Textbook: National Network Perspectives."[12] This title is a thoughtful reflection of the potential impact of changes in telecom-

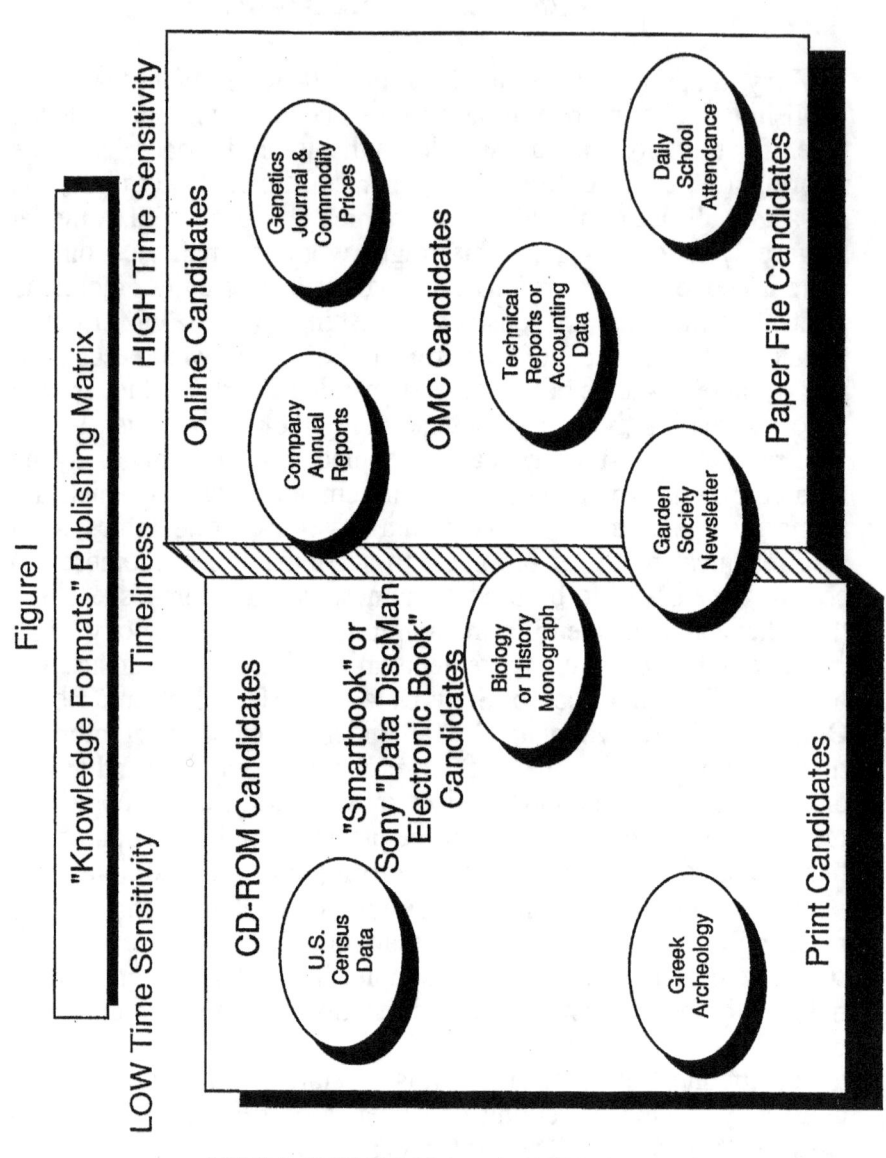

Figure I

munications. Somewhat fancifully, Figure II illustrates the essence of what is happening. If we think about the telecommunications network as water pipes draining a reservoir, then we may have a notion of the change that is occurring. In 1971 the T1 telecommunications network of NSFNET made available a resource of high value. The T3 networks of ten years later have a much higher capacity, and finally, the gigabit or even terabit network of the 1990s will have a vastly larger capacity. The basic problem with a T1 level network is simply that the computers of this world could overwhelm it, and perforce there were limitations in the quality, quantity, and character of data transmitted. The "data stream" easily filled up this electronic pipeline. As gigabit network of NREN becomes a reality, we will reach a point where all of the computers available cannot fill up the pipeline any longer. This has profound implications for higher education and libraries. Networked knowledge is vital to research, scholarship, and teaching. As the T3 network and then gigabit network are installed, there will be excess capacity available to support multi-media applications connecting local area networks on campuses to the Internet.

As the user interface is improved and a seamless network is developed, many applications will emerge for individuals who are not experts in computing or telecommunications. The uses of such high speed networks are many (Figure III) and include file transfer, electronic mail, multi-media transfer, video conferencing, super computer visualization, and distributed and parallel computing. The implications for higher education are illustrated in Figure IV. Remote lecturing by experts, joint authoring of publications, and the video conference classroom are fairly obvious, as are some of the dimensions of research applications. However, it is useful to speculate on the publication and library applications of the gigabit network.

First, let us assume that the pipeline is so big that the "data stream" cannot fill it up and as it becomes more available its uses proliferate. This assumes that the gigabit telecommunications do not stop at major nodes, but continue to selected points on campus, especially the library. Second, we may hope that the development of high definition television and other forms of multi-media display will overcome the problems of low quality graphic presentation in

Figure II

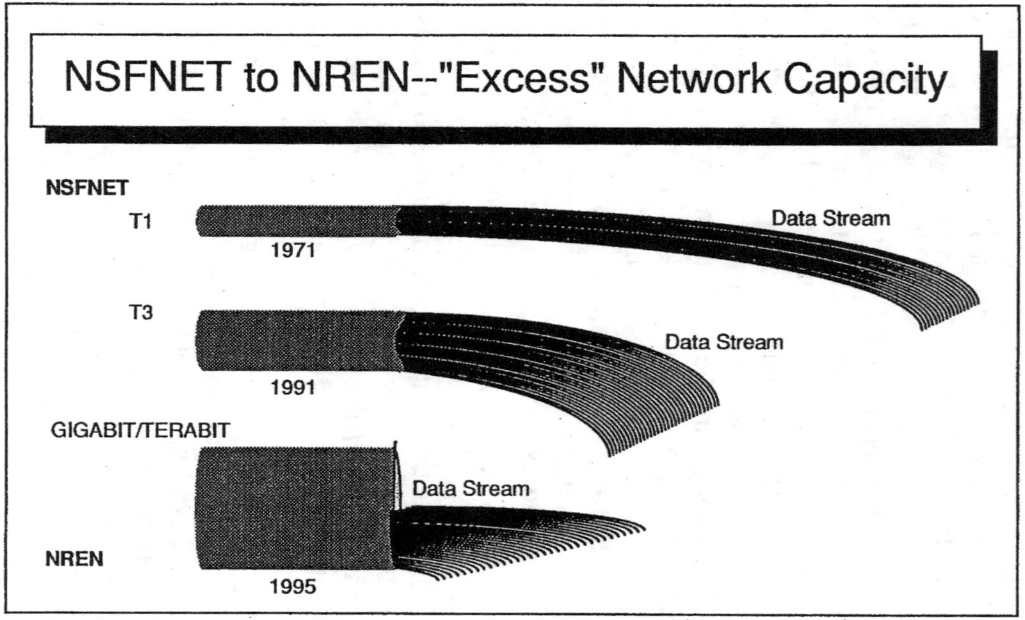
NSFNET to NREN--"Excess" Network Capacity
NSFNET
T1
1971
Data Stream
T3
1991
Data Stream
GIGABIT/TERABIT
NREN
1995
Data Stream

Figure III

Generic Uses of High Speed Networks

- File Transfer
- Electronic Mail
- Multimedia Transfer
- Video Conferencing
- Supercomputer Visualization
- Distributed and Parallel Computing

Figure IV

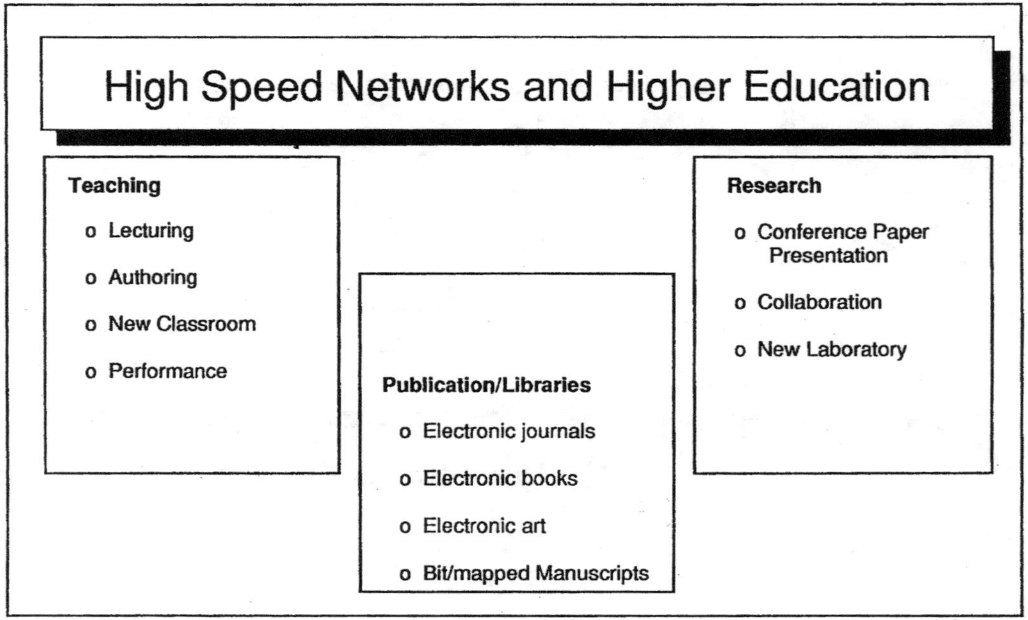

High Speed Networks and Higher Education

Teaching
- Lecturing
- Authoring
- New Classroom
- Performance

Research
- Conference Paper Presentation
- Collaboration
- New Laboratory

Publication/Libraries
- Electronic journals
- Electronic books
- Electronic art
- Bit/mapped Manuscripts

the next five to ten years. The combination of these two information technologies means that full motion video media will become a reality. It also means that the technical obstacles to publication of traditional scholarly material in electronic format at relatively low cost may be removed. Figure IV indicates a number of potential applications including electronic journals, books and art, as well as bitmapped redistribution of existing eye-readable knowledge, for instance, original manuscripts or out-of-print books. Eldred Smith may be correct to make the case that electronic information will solve the acquisitions dilemma — that is, the declining ability to provide access to published knowledge from the local collections.[13]

So far, the Internet has stimulated a flurry of development of electronic journals, and this is reflected in the publication of the *Directory of Electronic Journals, Newsletters, and Digests* by the Association of Research Libraries. At this time there are at least twelve e-journals that combine the application of computer and telecommunications technology with the traditional requirements of scholarship, including peer review and editorial oversight. Moreover, the Coalition for Networked Information, a sort of joint venture between ARL, CAUSE and EDUCOM, is a powerful signal of the importance of networking to the future of libraries.

What is happening in the library landscape is then surely the proliferation of what may be called, "knowledge formats." There are two central questions — how will users get access to new knowledge formats and how will the information they find be carried away for personal use? Let us momentarily put aside the question of access and turn to the second question — getting a copy. Users will have an array of new optical WORM devices to choose from for storing electronic knowledge formats, as well as much improved magnetic storage. It is also likely that circumstances will induce publishers, particularly university presses, to provide ROM versions of e-books, which are equivalent to the experience with "read only" print books and journals. Most of these electronic knowledge formats will be viewed through microcomputer technology except those which exceed the microcomputer's graphic capabilities.

PARADIGM SHIFT—
LIMITS OF THINKING

Having sketched the information technology which is driving the rapid transformation of knowledge formats, let us now turn to the question of user access and the role of libraries. Discussion in the professional literature of librarianship has emphasized the need to shift to a new paradigm for academic and research libraries.[14] The concept of paradigms developed by T. S. Kuhn is, after all, a powerful tool for thinking in both sciences and social sciences. "The paradigm is something which can function when the theory is not there . . . [and which] . . . has got to be a concrete picture used analogically; because it has got to be a way of seeing."[15] Recently Charles Martell summarized the extent of this discussion succinctly: "The warehouse, or collection-based paradigm still holds sway. The centerpiece of this paradigm is the provision of items shelved locally. A new access-based paradigm is emerging and gaining many adherents. Its centerpiece is the provision of items wherever they may be located. What happens between the user and the content of items is beyond the boundary of either paradigm."[16]

As far as they go, the current discussions of the new library paradigm have dealt with only one dimension of the change required of libraries, and have not done full justice to Kuhn's concept. Moreover, the discussion has been precipitated by a two-fold crisis — the dramatic expansion of publication and rapid rise in the cost, particularly of scholarly literature in the sciences and technology. By now, everyone understands the double-bind in which universities have placed themselves. "The irony, of course, is that our faculty do the research, write the articles, peer review them, frequently pay page charges to publish them, and cap the vicious circle by buying back the work from commercial publishers. We pay a dear price for our tradition of passing copyright from academic authors to commercial publishers.[17] The solution most often offered to this economic double-bind is the utilization of the power of computing and telecommunications, the general characteristics of which have already been sketched.[18]

No argument is being made here against this position; indeed, it is credible. However, it is past time to proceed further with the development of the paradigm and to give consideration to the effects of this change as the so-called "virtual" or "electronic library" becomes a reality. The central feature of this new library is a high degree of use of computers and related information technologies. How will this effect library organizations, human resources, and the need for professional education and training? Peter Drucker proposed the issues quite succinctly when he said that it is "right to ask if we are redefining libraries' mission. No, we are not redefining their mission, but we are redefining resources and as a result the role of librarians is changing."[19]

IMFORMATED LIBRARIES

To understand what is just beginning to happen in libraries, we need only look at what happened in other organizations when whole processes were automated. In the industrial setting, the introduction of a high degree of automation based on information technology has transformed the nature of work, but the products remain the same. Cars are still cars and televisions are still televisions even when CAD/CAM is used to design and build them. Banking services are highly automated and international, but they are still banking services. What has changed is the life of the workers in these new environments. That will happen for knowledge workers in libraries, as well. But there is an added dimension of complexity for libraries which is not present in the "knowledge based" private sector. As Drucker's comment implies, their product, the knowledge format, is also changing. One must assume that this level of abstraction and complexity, in which the tools of information technology also become the product distributed, will profoundly affect library organizations and librarianship as a profession.

Zuboff asserts that the introduction of automation in modern industry and business is causing a revolution as dramatic as that caused by the mechanization of workshops and factories in Britain between 1789 and 1848 at the dawn of the industrial age. In a ten-year study of applied automation, Zuboff analyzed these fundamental changes, and the insights are directly applicable in the library setting.

> On the one hand, technology can be applied to automating operations according to a logic that hardly differs from that of the 19th-Century machine system. . . . On the other, the same technology simultaneously generates information about the underlying productive and administrative processes through which an organization accomplishes its work. It provides a deeper level of transparency to activities that had been either partially or completely opaque. In this way, information technology supersedes the traditional logic of automation. The word that I have coined to describe this unique capacity is informate. Activities, events, and objects are translated into and made visible by information when a technology informates as well as automates.[20]

While automation of this type has long been associated with a general decline in the degree of know-how and a routinization of the role of the individual worker, there is plenty of evidence to indicate that automation also has extremely positive effects organizationally. In the first place, the broad application of information technologies can demand a dramatic "reskilling" so that the knowledge worker is "able to exploit the informating capacity of the technology, and to become a new source of critical judgment."[21] Whatever their purposes, in less than two centuries modern organizations have moved from oral to print, and finally to electronic authority. In the heavily computer-mediated environment, however, there are two important changes. A general requirement of higher intellectual skills and common access by all members within an organization to the information produced by the organization, that is, access to what Zuboff calls the "electronic text."

"The automating capacity of technology can free the human being for a more comprehensive, explicit, systematic, and abstract knowledge of his or her work made possible by the technology's ability to informate."[22] "The skills necessary for competent operation in an informated environment appear to be related to the kind of explicit, inferential, scientific reasoning traditionally associated with formal education."[23] At the same time, information technology presents several dilemmas in the informated organization. It can be used to make work more automatic and reduce skill levels, and as a means for managerial control and observation. At their best, however, information technologies corrode stratified hierarchical organization, make management supervision collaborative, and dramatically increase the responsibility for work of the individual.[24]

Zuboff's observations for the world of banking, paper manufacturing, and the telecommunications industry already could be made about many libraries. The "informating" technologies in libraries include integrated library systems and local area networks. After all, the integrated system provides the "electronic text" available to the whole library staff and increases the "intellective" skills and decision making that library work demands of all staff. Similarly, a local area network with a well developed management information system, electronic mail, and in-house conferencing capability is a powerful tool for reducing hierarchy, increasing staff participation and understanding of the organization, making management more approachable, and in general, opening up the organization. But this will require a conscious decision on the part of managers for these things to happen. We can choose another path, to use them for the purpose of increasing authority, hierarchy, and control.

COLLABORATION—
AN ORGANIZATIONAL IMPERATIVE

Historical parallels for the social change caused by technological innovation are many—the medieval castle, the printed book, and the automobile. These inventions stimulated change similar to the dramatic social transformation caused by the informating power of information technologies. But the most important change caused by the latter "is the increased intellectual content of work tasks across organizational levels that attenuates the conventional designations of manager and managed. This does not mean that there are no longer useful distinctions to be made among organizational members, but whatever these distinctions may be, they will no longer convey fundamentally different modes of involvement with the life of the organization. . . . Instead, the total organizational skill base becomes more homogenous."[25]

The task of rethinking library organizations brings to mind the old adage that "you have to know what you are going to do before you can do it," which contains the elements of both strategy and organization. Traditional hierarchical organizations have narrow spans of control and many reporting levels. Moreover, the quality of expertise increases as one moves up the hierarchy and is held closely by specialists and managers. In the informated organization, on the other hand, expertise and information often reside in software and anyone who has access to the system is an expert. In addition, as systems are networked expertise and information is distributed more evenly throughout the organization. By definition, networking overcomes the limitations of geography and hierarchy and allows communications across both. "Networks will not replace or supplement hierarchies; rather, the two will be encompassed within a broader conception that embraces both."[26]

Michael Schrage has hit upon the key difference that will characterize these new types of organizations—a high level of collaboration within the organization. He believes that one of the primary characteristics of information technology and the electronic text is as a tool for collaboration both in meetings and across the organization on a continuous basis.[27] When we invest in information technology as a solution, "we need to shift away from the notion of technology managing information and toward the idea of technology as a medium of relationships. Organizations need to get a better understanding of the complex ecologies of media that shape, deflect, and define one another."[28] However, collaboration is not a cure-all but has specific ingredients that define the organizational ways in which it may be useful:

- *Competence*—Individual collaborators must at least be competent to deal with the problem they face.
- *A shared, understood goal*—Collaboration is treated as a means to an end, not an end in itself.
- *Mutual respect, tolerance, and trust*—The collaboration exists precisely because the collaborators believe they need one another to get the job done.
- *Creation and manipulation of "shared spaces"*—Shared space is essential as a technique to achieve conversational clarity and includes old-fashioned blackboards, flip charts, and new col-

laborative technologies, such as e-mail, bulletin boards, conferencing systems, and electronic blackboards.
- *Multiple forms of representation* — Collaborations generally use a variety of forms of expression which may include mathematics, linguistics, structural representations, conversational and visual representation which allow the collaborators to grasp the key features of the task.
- *Playing with the representations* — Play here connotes playful and implies that participants do not have to commit to anything until they feel ready to do so.
- *Continuous but not continual communication* — Collaborators contact one another based on the need to resolve problems, not to meet organizational requirements.
- *Formal and informal environments* — Classic collaboration occurs in numerous formal and informal settings and is capable of surviving the change of scenery.
- *Clear lines of responsibility but no restricted boundaries* — Everyone remains responsible for their own duties, but each is encouraged to create a common understanding of the entire task.
- *Decisions do not have to be made by a consensus* — Collaboration is used as a tool to collectively generate the ideas which resolve the problem, but it does not imply consensus.
- *Physical presence is not necessary* — This has always been true to some extent but is increasingly so in the electronic environment.
- *Selected use of outsiders for complementary insights and information* — The collaborative group chooses when to go outside of itself to obtain vital information to stimulate the creative process.
- *Collaboration's end* — Long-term successful collaborations are rare. Because they are purposeful collaborations they of necessity come to an end.[29]

The obvious application of this notion of collaboration in the informated electronic library is to resolve internal organizational problems, and this will happen frequently. However, there is another not so obvious, but equally important, dimension of collaboration in the new library paradigm which Peter Drucker has referred to obliquely.

The greatest need is to look at a different role for the information provider, the librarian. Information resources are changing so fast that the librarian in the academic and research laboratory is at the beginning of a partnership with the faculty and researcher. Neither side has taken full responsibility for this partnership. . . . It is the librarian who knows the information resources and needs to be in on the planning of every research program.[30]

Amitai Etzioni has made a similar point.

For information to be turned into knowledge requires collaboration with other disciplines. . . . But if librarians would see themselves as knowledge managers and work together with other disciplines such as medicine, economics, sociology, physics—they would go a long way toward ensuring that the knowledge systems would be set up in such a way that they would make it easier to move from masses of unprocessed information to a specific number of conclusions.[31]

CHALLENGES IN THE NEW PARADIGM – CONCLUSIONS

In closing we should examine the challenges to the library profession presented by this new paradigm for the library as expressed both inside our informated organizations and in their relationships to what Patrick Wilson calls the "knowledge industry." What is provided here is only a sketch the four basic constellations of problems which the profession will be forced to address in the near future with fundamental change.

In the first place, if librarians are to truly enter into the necessary collaborations, then it is time to abandon the notion that role of librarians and libraries is to passively provide the basic information to patrons without a serious concern for judging the quality of what is provided. This is a tricky matter since it involves a core principle of the profession embodied in the American Library Association and Association of American Publishers joint statement, "The Freedom To Read." We must continue to build broad based collections that provide the full diversity of ideas and expressions of opinion, not some orthodoxy. However, concomitant with the responsibility of the profession to provide access to the whole of the record of knowledge is a new responsibility, one that Wilson calls "a true information service."

> Such a service would accept inquiries in the form of statements of a problem and respond with a description of what is presently known that bears on the solution of the problem. It would explicitly undertake to vouch for the accuracy of the information given as being part of the public knowledge, and would deliberately attempt to provide only such information as was of probable utility in the solution of the problem or the improvement of a decision situation.[32]

It could be stated in this way—that librarians must abandon a studied neutrality concerning the access to knowledge we provide since in many cases it is already an insupportable fiction. This means that we must explicitly begin to make judgements about the message in the medium, whenever we are asked to do so.

The second set of challenges surrounds the issues of educating new entrants into the profession and retraining active professionals. This is a large topic, and the subject of another paper. However, the voices of discussion and debate on the matter must become more active as the Committee on Accreditation of the American Library Association does its work of revising accreditation standards.[33] Likewise, library managers have a significant responsibility to ensure that retraining occurs, and the first criteria of their success is the extent to which they provide significant training and professional development resources for their staffs. Libraries must continue to make alliances with trainers on campus and in their city personnel offices. Similarly, they must work closely with library schools which will have an increasingly important role in the "re-skilling" of the library profession.[34]

The third set of problems will arise out of the collecting principles in the new library paradigm. So long as the focus was on collection centered provision of information, libraries might ignore one of the problems inherent in resource sharing, which merely took the form of a low level of ILL activity. With increasing emphasis on the access paradigm we will be forced to address again the question of how to fund expanded cooperation in modern library networks. The long running fee versus free debate arises out of the illogical conflation of the idea of free or open access to knowledge and the question of how that access will be funded. All information comes with a cost.[35]

Lastly, librarianship must come to grips once and for all with its fundamental inferiority complex. There is no profession which devotes more space in its literature to the question of its professionalism than librarianship. Certainly, the classic professions of law, medicine, and clergy don't even give it a second thought. In some measure, librarians' social esteem varies widely throughout the world. In the March 28 *Times* of London there was a story entitled "Persecuted Priest, to be Church Head in Czechoslovakia," in which it was stated that the primate of the Roman Catholic Church, Cardinal Frantisek, was stepping down and being replaced by Bishop Miloslav Vlk. The story states of Vlk that "during the 1970s, he was banned from parish work and had to take various jobs offered by the state, including sweeping the streets and working in the municipal library. But the bishop is on record as saying that the street-cleaning job was spiritually rewarding." The *Times* did not quote the primate-elect on his work in the library. Certainly librarianship in the United States has more respect, but we do tend to consider ourselves to be kind of knowledge street sweepers.

The truth is that in the general classifications of professional occupations librarianship maintains some of the highest requirements for independent responsibility and genuine autonomy. Moreover, the characteristics of librarianship overlap a large number of the other classifications for professions.[36] Recently, Etzioni characterized librarianship in this fashion:

> There can be little doubt that over the last twenty-five years librarianship has become more professionalized, as knowledge required to engage in librarianship by many measures, though not by all, has vastly increased. The development of computer sciences and all the attending technologies of retrieval systems have made the area and range of knowledge necessary consid-

erably deeper, wider and more challenging. So by that criterion, librarianship these days is more of a profession than it used to be. . . . In a sense, the librarian's discipline is moving closer to that of knowledge engineering, and that is where it will be for the foreseeable future.[37]

A friend and colleague is fond of saying that "the great libraries of the future will not be those with great collections, but those with great staffs." Why is this so? Simply because knowledge must be rediscovered in the library in order to be used and that process of rediscovery may be as important as the creation of knowledge itself. Patrons have always sought the assistance of librarians in this search to rediscover. In the "virtual" library of the future, a new more vital, and certainly a more challenging role, awaits the profession that emerges within the new paradigm as the mediator of knowledge. What profession should that be if not librarianship?

NOTES

1. Charles B. Lowry, "Converging Information Technologies: How Will Libraries Adapt?," *Cause/Effect* 13, no. 3 (Fall 1990): 35. This article discusses the author's views on how information technologies will be used by libraries and library patrons. The present article is, in effect, an extension of this earlier work, and discusses ways in which information technologies will effect library work, organization, and education, and librarianship as a profession.

2. Various applications and interactions of these technologies were explored by the author more fully in Ibid, p. 35-42. For another summary of the varied nature of "information technologies" see Shoshana Zuboff, *In the Age of the Smart Machine: The Future of Work and Power* (New York: Basic Books, Inc., Publishers, 1988), 415.

3. Patrick Wilson, *Second-Hand Knowledge: An Inquiry into Cognitive Authority,* Contributions in Librarianship and Information Science, no. 44 (Westport, Connecticut: Greenwood Press, 1983), 10,149-51; and Patrick Wilson, *Public Knowledge, Private Ignorance: Toward a Library and Information Policy,* Contributions in Librarianship and Information Science, no. 10 (Westport, Connecticut: Greenwood Press, 1977), 1-10.

4. Ibid., pp. 3-5, 16, 20; and Wilson, *Second-Hand Knowledge,* pp. 46-49, 39-40.

5. Wilson, *Public Knowledge,* pp. 91, 95, 101-09.

6. Fritz Machlup, "Semantic Quirks in Studies in Information," in *The Study of Information,* ed. Fritz Machlup and Una Mansfield (New York: Wiley, 1983), 653, 658.

7. There is probably still no better critique of the dangers of this kind of overselling than Theodore Roszak, *The Cult of information: The Folklore of Computers and the True Art of Thinking* (New York: Pantheon Books, 1986), see particularly pp. 14-46.

8. Michael Schrage, "Creating User Pathways to Electronic Information," (Reston, Virginia, April 28-30, 1991). This was the Keynote Address at the Faxon Institute 1991 Annual Conference; quotes are from the author's notes.

9. Roszak, p. 40.

10. Ibid., pp. 33-36, 47-71; and Philip Elmer-Dewitt, "The Revolution that Fizzled," *Time* 137, no. 20 (May 20, 1991): 48-49.

11. The original idea for this model was derived from figure 1 in "The Faxon Company: A Technicalities Profile," *Technicalities* 6 (May 1986):5. However, the current version differs significantly from the original, which was intended to distinguish how "published" knowledge would be presented in the future. The original model included four formats—print, paper file, CD/ROM, and online. It also had two determining dimensions timeliness and market value. The model used herein includes additional formats—optical media cards, "The Smartbook," and the Sony Mini-CD/ROM "Data Disc Man Electronic Book." It also adds the important determining dimension of "added value," as a significant factor which effects the decision to "publish" in electronic formats.

12. The discussion of telecommunications here draws in part on Alan E. Baratz, "A Living Textbook: National Network Perspectives," presented at Informa 1991, "The Academy at Work," (Long Beach, California, April 7-9, 1991).

13. Eldred Smith, "Resolving the Acquisitions Dilemma: Into the Electronic Information Environment," *College and Research Libraries*, 52, no. 3 (May 1991): 231-40.

14. See for instance, Duane Webster, "Organizational Futures: Staffing Research Libraries in the 1990's," in Minutes of the Association of Research Libraries, October 24-25, 1984 (Washington, D.C., Association of Research Libraries); Robert C. Heterick, Jr., "Networked Information: What Can We Expect and When?," *Cause/Effect* 13, no. 2 (Summer 1990): 9-14; and Robert C. Heterick, Jr., "Academic Sacred Cows and Exponential Growth," *Cause/Effect* 14, no. 1 (Spring 1991): 9-13.

15. Margaret Masterman, "The Nature of a Paradigm," In *Criticism and the Growth of Knowledge: Proceedings of the International Colloquium in the Philosophy of Science, London, 1965, volume 4,* ed. Imre Lakatos and Alan Musgrave (Cambridge: At the University Press, 1970), 59-89.

16. Charles Martell, "Mysteries, Wonders, and Beauties," editorial in *College and Research Libraries* 51, no. 3 (May 1990): 179.

17. Heterick, "Academic Sacred Cows. . . " p. 11; see also Richard M. Dougherty, "Turning the Serials Crisis to Our Advantage: An Opportunity for Leadership," *Library Administration and Management* 3, no. 2 (Spring 1989): 59-64; and Ray Metz, "The Impact of Electronic Formats and Campus Networks

on University Libraries in the United States," *Computers in Libraries* (May 1990): 30-31.

18. Heterick, "Academic Sacred Cows. . . " pp. 12-14.

19. Charles B. Lowry, "An Interview With Peter Drucker," *Library Administration and Management* 4, no. 1 (Winter 1989): 3-5.

20. Zuboff, pp. xiii, 9-10.

21. Ibid., pp. 23, 57, 62-63, 69-70.

22. Ibid., pp. 77-79, 114, 126, 179-181.

23. Ibid., p. 195.

24. Ibid., pp. 243, 285, 287, 290-91, 296-97, 303, 308-10.

25. Ibid., pp. 388-93.

26. Stanley M. Davis, *Future Perfect* (Reading, Massachusetts: Addison-Wesley Publishing Company, Inc., 1987), 24, 80-81, 86-90.

27. Michael Schrage, *Shared Minds: The New Technologies of Collaboration* (New York: Random House, 1990), 6, 7, 96-134.

28. Ibid., p. 142.

29. Ibid., pp. 135-63.

30. Lowry, "An Interview With Peter Drucker," p. 4.

31. Charles B. Lowry, "An Interview With Amitai Etzioni," *Library Administration and Management* 4, no. 1 (Winter 1989): 7; this theme of collaboration between librarians and researchers also appears in William D. Earvey, *Communications: The Essence of Science,* (Oxford: Pergamon Press Ltd., 1979): 10-12, 126.

32. Wilson, *Public Knowledge,* pp. 109-10,121-23; Wilson makes a similar case in *Shared Knowledge,* pp. 165-96.

33. For a good current perspective on the issues involved in curriculum revision for librarianship and information science see Bernie Schlessinger, June H. Schlessinger, and Rashelle Schlessinger Karp, "Information Science/Library Science Education Programs in the 1990's: A Not-So-Modest Proposal," *Library Administration and Management* 5, no. 1 (Winter 1991): 16-19; see also the American Library Association, Committee on Accreditation, Standards Revision Subcommittee, "Standards for Accreditation, 199X," which is the "preliminary final draft," subject to additional hearings and scheduled for adoption by ALA Council at the Summer Conference 1992 meeting in San Francisco.

34. A recent discussion of an expanded role for schools of library and information science in the education of new professionals and "reskilling" of practicing professionals is Raymond F. Vondran and Ruth J. Person, "Library Education and Professional Practice: Agendas for Partnership," *Library Administration and Management* 4, no. 3 (Summer 1990): 133-37.

35. See for instance Charles B. Lowry, "Resource Sharing or Cost Shifting? — The Unequal Burden of Cooperative Cataloging and ILL in Network[s]," *College and Research Libraries* 51, no. 6 (January 1990): 11-19.

36. Anne Roe and Patricia W. Lunneborg, "Personality Development and Career Choice," in *Career Choice and Development: Applying Contemporary Theories to Practice,* a joint publication in The Jossey-Bass Management Series

and The Jossey-Bass Social and Behavioral Science Series, ed. Duane Brown, Linda Brooks, and Associates (San Francisco: Jossey-Bass Publishers, 1990), 68-78.

37. Lowry, "An Interview with Amitai Etzioni," p. 5; this comment was by way of contrast to Etzioni's earlier analysis of librarianship and the changes in the level of professionalization which he believes have occurred, see *The Semi-Professions and Their Organization: Teachers, Nurses, Social Workers,* ed. Amitai Etzioni (New York: The Free Press, 1969), 201-03, 266-67, 276-77, 285-86.

Wrap-Up Session

Dan Tonkery

We've heard exciting plenary sessions and workshops that have indicated that the world is changing and changing rapidly. What I'd like to do is summarize some of the topics that were presented. Because I'm giving the wrap-up, I had the advantage of previewing the abstracts (I hadn't actually seen the papers) and have tried to put together a short presentation of what I thought we were going to hear from our speakers, based on those abstracts.

KEY FACTORS INFLUENCING CHANGE

One of the key factors, I think, in our changing world is information. We have a tremendous amount of information in a variety of formats, and it's available everywhere. The second thing I would like to stress is that the scholarly journal is still our most important information source. We heard in the presentations on Monday that "users still like print." At the Faxon Institute this year there was a presentation on usage patterns, and it was not surprising to hear that many researchers still keep private print files. Even though so much technology and gadgetry is available, at the end of the day researchers make print-outs for their files.

But information access is becoming more important than ownership. We've been the victims of our own success in terms of providing new tools. This is what I've heard here at this year's NASIG conference; I heard the same thing this year at SLA and MLA. It's becoming an established fact. One of the factors influencing this change is certainly the growth in user expectations. When I started

---

Dan Tonkery is President and CEO, Readmore, Inc., 22 Cortlandt Street, New York, NY 10007.

© 1991 by The Haworth Press, Inc. All rights reserved.

out in the Reference Department, I had to master about sixty different printed indexes. It was easy; things moved fairly slowly and I only had to think of one access point. Now we have CD-ROM databases and online systems—we can access information all over the world. Users are no longer satisfied with indexes to information, they expect to get the actual documents. Key technologies for telecommunications, software development, and the computer industry have all come together and we're sitting on a platform ready to be launched into a different world.

Technology is now affordable. The price of a PC, the price of a printer, and the price of telecommunications have dropped drastically. One of the major factors that's influencing the change, or at least pushing it, is an upset in the economic balance between the needs of libraries and the financial resources available to them. The publishers' pricing has outstripped our ability to pay. We've been pushed over the edge and we can no longer afford the collections that we want. Access is becoming more important than ownership, partly because the pricing problem is making ownership unaffordable.

Another thing, mentioned in an earlier talk, is the change in research methodology to include remote groups and the globalization of research. In Japan, a project may involve laboratories in five other countries. When General Motors builds a new car—and some of us wonder why they do that—they develop the technology in physically remote research labs. Remote groups are working on common problems and making heavy use of technology to transfer information.

STRUCTURES SUPPORTING CHANGE

I call the structures supporting change the "Five Ps": the platforms, the pipelines, the products, the patrons, and the publishers. The platforms are the computer hardware and software. When I think of the mainframe that cost millions of dollars only five or ten years ago and compare it to the super PC sitting on the corner of my desk, in terms of capacity and capability, I realize how quickly the technology has advanced. For less than $5000, a two or four megabyte machine does the equivalent of the work that NLM's machine did when Medline first started. That's been less than twenty years; I hate to think twenty years ahead, because even now the affordability of this equipment and the power of it actually outstrips our ability to use it. There are standards being developed for video display and multimedia that will provide systems with workstations that have graphics and color integrated with sound. We're going to have fully functioning workstations with document imaging, scanning, and retrieval. All of this is coming together, coalescing, to get us into the next world.

The pipeline is already laid. AT&T, Sprint, and MCI have tremendous capacity. If you travel down any railroad track, you'll see little signs warning you about optical fiber cable. I can buy a T1 line that runs from New York to Seattle for a couple of thousand dollars. Five years ago that would have cost me $10,000 a month. A move from T1 to a T3 line (that can handle a billion bytes per second) means a move to sound and video. Of course, someone's going to put a meter on that pipeline when you get into end RAM—it is not always going to be free. There are going to be commercial interests involved once it works. But the pipeline already supports e-mail and it's very effective. A graphics image file is coming within the next two or three years.

In terms of products out there that support change, even if you travel in Mexico or the Middle East you will find CD-ROMs. We sell them all over the world. You're starting to see multi-publisher database products, such as Adonis, where four, five, six or ten publishers get together and come out with one product. Probably the most interesting product around is the CARL system's Uncover database—one of the most innovative uses of technology that I've seen in a long time. A database indexing two million articles, with new articles captured the day a journal arrives in the library, really changes the way we do things. When you consider that Index Medicus takes two months to index, the speed in indexing Uncover is almost unbelievable. And when you add the article delivery capability of this system and of other systems like the Information Store, the result may revolutionize the way we think about collections and collection development.

IMPORTANT QUESTIONS ABOUT CHANGE

Everything is in place. We have the affordable platforms, the pipelines to move information around, the products that are being distributed worldwide and the patrons whose expectations for access are maintaining the momentum of change. But there are still some things that haven't been dealt with. One of them is the economics at the publisher's end. We haven't heard from the publishers in depth, but I think one of the important impacts the shift to article level document delivery will have is on publishing economics. Any journal has a certain subscriber base, and we know that journals may be profitable at say 500, 1000, 2000, or 3000 subscribers. What happens when a publisher starts to lose 10 percent, 15 percent, or 30 percent of that subscriber base? What is the threshold where the journal becomes unprofitable and therefore impossible to publish? That's something that needs to be addressed. If systems like CARL can deliver an article within 24 or 48 hours, many libraries are going to look at their budgets and say, "maybe we should reserve money for article delivery, and buy the hard copy only when necessary." Each year as budgets get tighter and the pressure to deliver information to patrons gets greater, librarians are going to review that decision.

The second question is: What changes are required in our infrastructure to support the new age? In case you haven't noticed, libraries traditionally have been built for print products. We've slipped in a few PC labs, but the stacks still constitute most of the usage. When I was at UCLA, the circulation in the main research library was over 4 million volumes. That's hard to replicate in terms of providing enough PCs and enough terminals and enough access to be able to support comparable volume in the electronic format. Vendors also have a responsibility; is the infrastructure of subscription services ready to support the new technology?

My third question is: Will the tools of technology be acceptable replacements for printed products? Assume for a minute that the printed product is in jeopardy, or it is too expensive. Will the current faculty be able to accept that the peer review information or the print journal they need is now available only in electronic form? The promotion and tenure system in our country still demands articles and books in print format. Some journals are available in electronic format, but often have a printed version that is still considered to be the archival copy.

I also have a question for the library profession. What changes in our professional education are required to support the next stage? The declining number of library schools says something. Our society and our universities do not value the educational system that produces professional librarians. What's wrong with library school education in our country? What changes have to be made to support the new age? When I went to library school there was not a single course in business or finance. Librarians were not expected to know how to manage for profitability, or how to read a balance sheet, or anything related to business operations. Yet one of the first things a librarian does in the library world is go through the budgeting process, and most of us don't have the skills to make a proper presentation. We're not intellectually stupid, we just haven't been exposed, and I think that's a failure in our educational system.

My final question is: How do we protect intellectual property rights? I believe that the current copyright legislation has not kept up with the electronic age. Litigation will occur between the publishing companies and the article delivery services. The publishers looked the other way when document delivery occurred. The volume of document delivery has not been large enough to cause a great deal of concern, except in a few cases such as the Williams and Wilkins suit against the National Library of Medicine for copyright violation. Fair use has been quietly accepted. This will change in the age of the FAX and rapid document delivery. The issue of copyright is going to become very meaningful and very timely. At SLA this week in San Antonio there were three sessions dealing with copyright and all three sessions were standing room only. I've never seen so much interest in copyright; and it's due primarily to document delivery. There are a lot of unknowns in this area, and it's one that I think is going to influence all of us.

That concludes my presentation. I tried to pull together the main themes for the changing world of libraries and journals. I think that all of us are going to have a job — I heard that there's an opening for a monk in . . . what country was that? Maybe I can't get a job as a monk, but there might be other possibilities. I think it is an exciting time to be in the library profession and to be dealing with serials. We're going to see change, and I think it's going to come faster than predicted. In some ways we're being forced into it by rising prices, but we're going to roll with it, and we're going to move on. And I think you are going to see some major changes in the distribution of information in this country. Thank you.

WORKSHOP SESSION REPORTS

Case Study: Starting a New Medical Journal

Gabriela Radulescu
Workshop Leader

Barbara A. Carlson
Recorder

Gabriela Radulescu, Executive Editor of the journals program of Springer Verlag, New York, spoke about the publisher's decision-making process when considering whether or not to start a new journal. The workshop summarized this complex subject, first with discussion of a generic blueprint for the entire process, second with data from an actual proposal that was ultimately rejected by Springer Verlag, New York.

Medical and scientific publishing is not an exact science. In spite of all the information available to and collected by publishers, publishing decisions still remain gambling decisions.

Radulescu gave an overview of Springer's New York journal program, suggesting that this year is typical. Six journal publica-

---

Barbara A. Carlson is Head, Serials Management, Medical University of South Carolina, 171 Ashley Ave., Charleston, SC 29425.

tions were discontinued, with four of the six to be continued by the journals' affiliated societies. One of the six was an outright cancellation, while one went through what is referred to as "modified death," that is, it was absorbed by an existing journal. However, as Springer discontinues these six titles, it will launch three new titles. Just three years ago Springer's New York program had fifty journals; now the count is fifty-eight. The question is: Why are there always more new titles?

According to Radulescu, the three major proponents of new titles are individual researchers, organized groups such as scientific/political societies, and commercial entities like publishers and advertisers. Researchers in emerging scientific fields argue that their papers are scattered throughout the literature, and, as a result, it is difficult and laborious to access literature in their specialities. Societies want to disseminate important new research in their fields, but they also have powerful political motivations to disseminate their members' work: to establish their society's scientific credentials; to establish new subdisciplines; to defend the economic position of the society in scientific turf battles; and to ensure the society's financial health by expanding membership that, in turn, profits from the journal.

If a journal is successful, several players benefit. For its editors, a journal provides financial benefits such as honoraria, paid travel expenses to meetings, support staff, and discounts on other Springer publications. To societies, a journal can offer income from royalties or profit-sharing arrangements, as well as from "subsidized" membership drives, where the publisher promotes the journal as a membership benefit. When profitable, the journal generates investment funds and covers overhead expenses for the publisher. Advertisers may gain from increased sales of products. Starting a new journal can enhance corporate image and visibility. Publishers are not alone in having motivations for starting new journals.

But before a new journal is started, publishers take certain steps to estimate its potential. A peer review is conducted among scientists in the given scientific field and among members of the intended readership. Opinions from editors of similar and competing journals are solicited as to the need for this new publication. Next, an internal review is done to predict the costs of publishing the journal. A market analysis is compiled comparing: the price of the new journal at the estimated break-even point with current prices of similar/competing publications; to postulate a competitive price for the first five years; and to find the true break-even point within the first five years. From this analysis the publisher can project a financial picture for the proposal.

This information is gathered into a checklist that summarizes the prospective journal. The editorial description offers the scope, content, source of manuscripts, and any associated society information. The publishing parameters set the initial size, frequency, and other particulars. The five-year forecast for circulation, projected price, estimated cost to the publisher, and calculated cost-recovery time measures the possible success of the venture. The results of the editors' survey are crucial, since they reflect whether or not there is a need for the publication. Finally, the recommendation—to publish or to reject—considers the possible effects of either decision and the steps that would follow.

A case study of an actual proposal for a publication on "neuroendocrinimmunology" was used to illustrate the process. Springer Verlag, New York considered a proposal to expand a newsletter of a pharmaceutical company into a quarterly journal that would provide a unique perspective on the union of three scientific disciplines. Showing that the peer review was indecisive while the five-year financial projection was quite favorable (since it could theoretically become profitable in its third year), Radulescu demonstrated how mixed messages create the gambling nature of the enterprise. Based on the newsletter's track record, the editorial conclusion was favorable for producing a quality publication. Likewise, the short-term profitability of the project was also positive. Yet the final recommendation was to reject. Because it appeared the journal would be useful, but not essential, to its intended audience, the decision was made not to publish it.

Radulescu's comment that publishers wish that they could publish their lists of rejected proposals, struck a chord with librarians and publishers in the audience. She reiterated that every publisher who rejects a proposal knows that there is someone else who will publish it and hopes that the rejected project does not become a lost, golden opportunity in an emerging scientific discipline.

Marketing a New Social Science/ Humanities Journal to Libraries, Then and Now

Patricia Scarry

Workshop Leader

Isabel Czech

Recorder

Patricia Scarry, Marketing Manager, Journals Division, University of Chicago Press, discussed the methods for marketing a social science journal in 1975 and how strategies for marketing a similar journal in 1990 had changed. The two journals involved were *Signs,* whose first issue came out in Autumn 1975, and *Journal of the History of Sexuality,* whose first issue was published in July of 1990.

Signs, dealing with women's studies, was a tough journal to launch, because there wasn't yet a clearly defined women's studies field in 1975. Proven mailing lists weren't available; they had to be created using a wide range of sources including directories to women attorneys, women deans, women's political groups, etc. Also, subscriber lists from other social science journals published by the University of Chicago were used. There were two pre-publication mailings, totaling 88,000 pieces. In the first year of publication, 110,000 pieces were drop-mailed. In total, eighty-four percent of the journal's initial marketing budget was spent on direct mail.

In addition to the mailings, ads were placed in a variety of publications, including the *New York Review of Books, Science, Ms.,*

Isabel Czech is Manager, Publications Selection, Institute for Scientific Information, 3501 Market St., Philadelphia, PA 19104.

© 1991 by The Haworth Press, Inc. All rights reserved.

and the *American Journal of Sociology*. Piggy-back mailings went out with EBSCO invoices, and exhibits were put up at the Modern Language Association conference, among others.

As a result of the mailings, ads, etc., pre-publication subscriptions numbered around 4,000. Over time, this number increased to 8,000, then leveled off at 5,500 in the mid 1980s. Subscriptions have stayed at this level for the past few years. It took ten years (from 1975 to 1985) to set up a mailing list of 30,000 appropriate potential readers. The renewal rate to *Signs* is seventy-five percent. It has a higher individual circulation rate (3500) than library (2000) circulation rate.

Journal of the History of Sexuality was launched in July 1990. This journal had a narrower potential market than *Signs*, though the subject was related. Marketing started eight months prior to the first issue, as it did with *Signs*. There was a key difference, however. The *Journal of the History of Sexuality* had an academic editor dedicated to the journal. He solicited manuscripts from contributors to *Signs*, and other similar journals, and was able to create a database of 10,000 names. This database was used not only for manuscript solicitation, but as a mailing list for the journal.

As with *Signs*, direct mail was the core of the launch. There were two pre-publication mailings, as with *Signs*, totaling 34,500 pieces (a significantly smaller number than used with *Signs*, as the potential market and journal focus were narrower). Again, more than eighty percent of the initial marketing budget was spent on direct mail.

Other similarities in marketing strategies included placing ads in relevant publications, setting up exhibits at the Modern Language Association conference, and sending out piggy-back mailings with EBSCO invoices.

For the first year of publication, the publishers anticipated that *Journal of the History of Sexuality* would acquire 1500 subscribers. So far, the journal has 1300; the ultimate goal is 3000. Because the journal is so new, the renewal rate cannot be calculated yet. Now that the journal has been launched, the publishers won't buy as many ads as they did for *Signs*, because money is tighter. Instead, they are exchanging ads with other publications. It is anticipated that it will take five years for the journal to make back the money invested.

In the next section of the workshop, Scarry analyzed the cost of marketing in 1975 for *Signs* and in 1990 for *Journal of the History of Sexuality*. In 1975, $20,000 was spent on pre-publication marketing; using inflationary estimates something close to $40,000 would have to be spent to accomplish the same things in 1990. Surprisingly, only $17,000 was spent in 1990! In the first year of publication, $28,000 was spent on marketing *Signs*, but in the first year of *Journal of the History of Sexuality*, only $18,000 was spent.

Next, Scarry discussed University of Chicago's approach to direct mail. They believe a direct mail piece sent to a librarian all too often goes in the trash, because librarians don't always decide which journals get purchased—the faculty decides. For this reason, they send direct mail to faculty members and field experts. If mail is sent to the library, they feel it is absolutely essential to address it to a specific person. Due to library staff cuts, mail could be tossed if it doesn't have a specific name on it. The same problem comes up if a sample issue is mailed to the library. If the person logging in the journal doesn't find the title of the sample issue in the serials records file, the title could be tossed onto a "problems" shelf and never be evaluated. One workshop participant, who is a librarian, commented that it's better to send direct mail to positions (Acquisitions Librarian, for example) rather than to names. This way, even if a particular person is no longer at the Library, their successor will receive the mail.

Scarry was asked if she thought it worthwhile to sell social science journals in bookstores. She said that *Signs* is sold in bookstores, because it has popular appeal, but on the whole, this doesn't happen. One person asked Scarry if advertising in *Signs* and *Journal of the History of Sexuality* brings in any sizable revenue. The answer to this was "no." Subscriptions account for ninety percent of the journals' revenue and ads for very little.

Towards the end of the workshop, the topic of when to start a promotion campaign and when to launch a publication was brought up. Scarry said that good times for mailing promotional pieces are late August-September and after Christmas. For a scholarly publication, mailings should never take place after May or during the height of the summer. Since libraries prefer to subscribe to journals on a calendar year basis, a new journal should start in January. Individuals don't like to be restricted to a calendar year cycle, so the University of Chicago will start or cancel a subscription with any issue.

SUPER-OPAC:
Records for Articles
and Chapters in Your Catalog

Bradley Dean Carrington

Workshop Leader

Birdie MacLennan

Recorder

Bradley Dean Carrington, Head of Cataloging at King Library, University of Kentucky, presented an overview of possible enhancements to the Online Public Access Catalog (OPAC), for providing access to journal articles and to chapter titles in monographs.

Carrington outlined two approaches: (1) the "separate file" approach, which uses the OPAC as a gateway to vendor-supplied indexes to journal contents; (2) the "integrated file" approach, which uses MARC-based records in the OPAC to provide: (a) keyword access to tables of contents in books via the addition of a contents note (505 field) in the bibliographic record, or (b) access to titles and authors of journal articles via the creation of brief separate records (as outlined in rule 13.5 — "In" Analytics — of AACR2, 1988).

After giving a brief overview of selected vendor software and services (CARL's UnCover database and NOTIS's MDAS — Multiple Database Access System — were cited as popular examples), Carrington described advantages and disadvantages of each approach based on his experience with implementation of the enhanced OPAC at the University of Kentucky.

Advantages identified with the "separate file" approach include

---

Birdie MacLennan is Serials Cataloger, Bailey/Hope Library, University of Vermont, Burlington, VT 05405.

the prevalence and availability of a great many commercial files (growing rapidly in size and scope), which provide convenient access to journal articles in a wide variety of subject areas. Disadvantages of this approach include the disparity of search protocols for different files, and the scarcity of records for book chapters. Licensing agreements with database providers can be limiting and article citation linkages to journal records in the OPAC—also known as the "hook to holdings"—can be inconsistent and difficult to maintain.

Advantages identified with the "integrated file" approach include no problems with linkages to separate files and ease in sharing MARC-based records for cataloging and lending purposes. Additionally, contents notes help the patron evaluate the item once it has been retrieved. Disadvantages cited were: few such records exist; authority control will demand labor-intensive inputting of records; also, if journals are cancelled or withdrawn, related "in" analytic records for article contents would need to be deleted.

As libraries begin to offer menu options through their OPAC terminals, the need for a standardized search language across all files becomes critical. A field linking the main and the analyzed record will also aid searching and bibliographic control. ISSNs were the favored common designator for this linking field; however, other industry standards, such as Serial Issue-Level Identifiers (SIIDs), CODEN identifiers, and OCLC numbers were noted as possibilities.

In his closing remarks, Carrington offered encouragement to librarians experimenting with the MARC format to provide enhanced access in the OPAC. He noted that MARBI (MAchine Readable Bibliographic Information), the interdivisional arm of ALA that sets the standard for MARC records, has made two Discussion Papers available: "Content-enriched and Enhanced Subject Access in USMARC Records," (Discussion Paper No. 42) and "Enhancing USMARC Records with Table of Contents" (Discussion Paper No. 46). Librarians interested in this topic can learn more about it by subscribing to MARBI publications (available from the Network Development and MARC Standards Office at the Library of Congress) and by attending MARBI meetings at the ALA Mid-Winter and Annual meetings.

Periodicals Receiving Units and Public Service Areas: A Productive Combination

Rosann Bazirjian
Lin Polson

Workshop Leaders

Phoebe Timberlake

Recorder

Rosann Bazirjian, Head of the Acquisition Department at Syracuse University Library, and Lin Polson, Head of the Serials Division at Simon Fraser University Library, began by describing the periodicals reading rooms at their institutions in terms of staffing, location, and reporting structures. They ended by providing guidelines for assessing the potential benefits available from the combination, to some degree, of a technical service receiving function and a public service reading room.

Bazirjian spoke from the perspective of a department head at an institution where check-in had previously been performed by reading room staff, but then in 1976 a decision was made to "free the public service staff from time consuming technical processing work." This decision was recently reviewed in light of the library's impending migration from SULIRS, a locally-developed online system, to NOTIS. The advantage of having serials holdings information available to the periodicals reading room patrons was acknowledged and it was decided that the existing periodicals reading

---

Phoebe Timberlake is Chair, Library Resource Coordination Department, Long Library, University of New Orleans, New Orleans, LA 70148.

© 1991 by The Haworth Press, Inc. All rights reserved.

room would remain part of the library re-configuration to accommodate the new system. But other points needed to be considered in weighing the proposal to transfer responsibility for check-in back to reading room staff. Would there be sufficient space for the additional staff and recordkeeping function? Would the public area be too distracting and therefore, affect the quality of work performed? Would the same staff members be required to fulfill technical and public service functions? Without cross-trained staff, would one of the advantages of such a unit be diminished? These and other staff-related questions were posed.

Reporting lines for the unit were another area of concern. Bazirjian suggested naming a single reading room supervisor, who would be responsible to both a technical service and a public service head. Since check-in and payment activities for non-periodical serials would still be performed in technical services area of the library, coordination of these activities would be critical.

A final consideration was the online system and its ability to respond to the information needs of the reading room patrons and staff. Bazirjian explained how the use of the NOTIS serials control module resulted in Syracuse's eventual decision to keep check-in within the technical service area and communicate information to other areas through the online system. In addition to check-in details and holdings statements, notes on issues claimed or pulled for bindery or replacement were added to the records. The availability of this information to anyone with access to a terminal eliminated the need to move the actual check-in procedure to the reading room.

Lin Polson discussed integration of a periodicals reading room with a receiving unit in a somewhat broader context. She described the six divisions of her library's organizational structure (Reference, Loans, Monographs, Serials, Collections Management, and Systems). The heads of those divisions all function as part of the library's management group. The Serials Division orders, receives, checks-in, pays for, claims, and catalogs all continuing titles, including newspapers, monographic series, and sets-in-progress. All units within the division except the bindery operate as part of the automated Geac system.

Polson described several events which had brought about total integration of serials functions approximately fifteen years earlier at Simon Fraser. At that time a task force had been appointed to review the problems of duplication of effort and materials, inconsistency of records, and the cost of labor involved problem resolution. As a result, a new definition of "serials" was drafted so that order staff could identify serials more easily at the point of ordering. The Cataloging Division agreed to send Serials any continuing title that arrived for cataloging without first passing through Serials. Also it was agreed that holdings would be posted to the serials holdings list instead of the shelflist.

These changes remedied some problems, but others became apparent. Records, staff, and processes for handling serials were still decentralized; for instance, each reference division maintained jurisdiction over its binding records. In 1976, the library created a serials unit with a periodicals reading room adjacent to the serials section. Administratively, this still left the serials section as part of acquisitions with an overworked Cataloging Division handling serial titles somewhat sporadically. Finally, in 1979, the staff of Acquisitions and Cataloging were reorganized into Monographs and Serials with a cataloger moving into the new Serials Division.

In discussing the pro's and con's of a fully integrated unit, Polson said strengths included: a knowledgeable staff, maintenance of important service goals, continuity, and backup personnel. The possibility of serials staff inadvertently assuming a reference role rather than an informational one and the broad functional knowledge required of the division head were cited as possible negatives.

In 1987, collection growth at Simon Fraser required a change in the physical location of the serials workroom—four floors away from the reading room. As at Syracuse, the presence of an integrated online system made it possible for the physical separation to occur without a serious loss of information to the reading room staff or patrons. At Syracuse, the decision resulted in the reading room staff remaining administratively under Public Services, while at Simon Fraser they remained administratively part of the Serials Division. Both libraries have continued to provide holdings information through computer terminals.

In the discussion that followed, the workshop leaders and participants agreed that the coding of holdings data and the displays of some online systems can result in holdings information that is difficult for infrequent library users, or even staff, to interpret. They stressed the need for help screens, uncoded statements on complicated records, and frequent communications between public service and technical service library staff.

The Continuations Saga: Converting Non-Periodical Serials

Joan Luke Stephens
Steven H. Murden

Workshop Leaders

Judith M. Shelton

Recorder

Joan Luke Stephens, Serials/Microforms Librarian and Assistant Head, Acquisitions Dept. at Georgia State University, and Steven H. Murden, Assistant Head, Acquisitions Services at Virginia Commonwealth University Library, collaborated on this workshop on the conversion to automated form of manual check-in records for non-periodical serials. Stephens focused on procedures, forms, and techniques, while Murden focused on the decision-making process and aspects of problem resolution.

Stephens began her presentation with an introductory sketch of Georgia State University and its Pullen Library. In 1985 when Pullen Library implemented the FAXON SC-10 system for periodicals check-in, Pullen had an online catalog and anticipated integrated circulation, acquisitions, and serials control modules. Non-periodical serials were not loaded into the online check-in system because it was expected that holdings information would show up on circulation records and on the serials control module.

Four years later the circulation module had been implemented and the acquisitions module was being installed, but the serials control module was found to be unsuitable. The implementation of on-

---

Judith M. Shelton is Serials Catalog Librarian and Assistant Head, Catalog Dept., Pullen Library, Georgia State University, Atlanta, GA 30303-3081

© 1991 by The Haworth Press, Inc. All rights reserved.

line periodicals check-in had been successful and the FAXON system had proved to be a good one. A recently completed cancellation project that cut the number of active titles by one quarter meant there were fewer titles to convert and consequently lower online costs. For these and other reasons the decision was made to load non-periodical serials into the FAXON system.

Stephens focused her presentation on the organization and implementation of this second-round conversion project. Planning for a second project was facilitated by the experience of the staff and their familiarity with the system.

- The resistance from public service staff, encountered in the initial implementation, was avoided by consulting with them early in the second-round conversion.
- Worksheets and procedures from the initial conversion could be used, with modifications, for the second-round conversion. An instruction packet was developed that included step-by-step instructions, examples of forms, definitions and explanations of fields, and illustrations of worksheets that had been processed properly.
- Training could be informal and quick since all the staff was experienced with the system and with serials.

Titles were loaded in three passes through the alphabetically-arranged kardex. First priority was given to titles with Reference call numbers. The second pass picked up general serials, and the final pass took in services and problem titles. The first step in each pass was data collection from the online catalog records and the kardex. Instead of copying cataloging information to a worksheet, coding was added directly to the catalog printout to reduce transcription errors and to speed processing. Kardex information was transcribed to a worksheet. The second step in each pass was data entry. This was done in two stages: all data except current check-in and payment information was entered first to limit disruption of actual check-in activity in the early stage and to speed input of this data in the later stage. The final step involved revisions and corrections. Stephens provided a handout with examples of conversion problems—titles with cumulations, services, memberships, monographic series, and items published out of sequence — and the ways they were handled. It took nine months to complete the project; a total of 3000 records were loaded into the system.

Murden described a similar conversion currently underway. He began with a comparison of Virginia Commonwealth to Georgia State and included a brief historical overview of automation at his institution. In 1987 all periodicals and a few non-periodical serials were being checked in on the OCLC serials subsystem, while most non-periodical serials were still being checked in manually. The library was about to discontinue the OCLC subsystem and was planning, but not yet ready, to migrate to a new integrated system. In 1988 the FAXON SC-10 system was selected to bridge the interim period and the records from the OCLC subsystem were converted to FAXON using a tape download and programming customized by FAXON. The decision was made to continue receiving non-periodical serials manually until a new integrated system was chosen and implemented.

Two years later the NOTIS system was purchased, and circulation, cataloging, acquisitions, and the OPAC have been implemented. Conversion of the kardex was delayed for various reasons (Murden viewed this delay as an opportunity for additional planning and for familiarizing himself with the system). Murden described the factors involved in deciding what information should be transferred from the kardex and what information from other sources should be included.

Murden also planned to accomplish the conversion in stages, divided by type of publication and vendor. FAXON records could wait till last, because SC-10 records had been automatically created for them. Records for another major vendor could easily be done first, because they had already been pulled out of the kardex in the process of resolving an unrelated problem. Conversion began in January 1991 and is not yet complete.

The disruption to normal operations due to dismantling the kardex led to the development of a check-in backlog, and new procedures had to be developed. In retrospect, Murden suggests that the alphabetical approach employed at Georgia State may be preferable to the breakdown by type of publication and vendor because it interferes less with ongoing operations.

In conclusion, both Stephens and Murden agreed that staff familiarity with the system being used and serials experience facilitate conversion. Familiarity with the system is essential to planning and anticipating problems, while serials experience is essential to timely problem resolution.

Interfacing Automated Environments: Linking the Integrated Library Systems

Lynne BrancheBrown
Katherine Hughes

Workshop Leaders

Christie T. Degener

Recorder

Lynne BrancheBrown, until recently the Acquisitions/Serials Librarian at Raytheon Equipment Division Technical Information Center, discussed the investigation of a possible direct link between two systems already in place. Katherine Hughes, Serials Librarian at Loyola University of Chicago Medical Center Library, defined a more abstract concept of "interface" — procedures shared by two or more automated systems (also referred to as disciplines) — and described how awareness of shared procedures affected automation efforts at her library.

BrancheBrown began by explaining why an interface between their integrated library system, BIBLIOTECH, and Ebsco's online service, EBSCONET, seemed desirable. BIBLIOTECH is used for all serials and acquisitions control, while EBSCONET is used for online ordering and claiming. BrancheBrown found herself manually moving information from one system to the other and inputting the same data into both systems. This inefficiency led her to consider the possibility of a BIBLIOTECH-EBSCONET interface; sub-

---

Christie T. Degener is Serials Librarian, Health Sciences Library, University of North Carolina at Chapel Hill, Chapel Hill, NC 27599-7585.

© 1991 by The Haworth Press, Inc. All rights reserved.

scription and claim information from BIBLIOTECH would be extracted as a file that could be read directly by the EBSCONET computer. Invoices or claim responses from EBSCONET would be sent on disk or via e-mail for uploading into BIBLIOTECH. Renewals could be handled by converting the floppy disk file received from Ebsco into new BIBLIOTECH records. This last process would avoid manually keying in the large numbers of records required for each annual renewal cycle (1200 records in 1989).

Planning began in August 1990 by examining the pro's and con's of the interface. The pro's included: eliminating the rekeying of information, improving accuracy (data entered correctly would be transmitted correctly), and reducing online connect time to EBSCONET (sending data as a file rather than keystroke-by-keystroke). The con's centered around automatic transmission of data entered incorrectly: incorrect subscription data; incorrectly entered check-in information generating unnecessary claims; incorrect entry generating inaccurate claims. This loss of quality control suggested that the benefits from rekeying data might outweigh the drawbacks.

The next planning phase identified the common data elements to be used for the interface, including subscriber, subscription information (down to copy level), and invoice information. BrancheBrown commended Ebsco for allowing the library to assign its own subscriber codes for generating electronic orders in BIBLIOTECH. Negotiating this innovation and acting as an intermediary between the two vendors involved was important since neither vendor knew exactly how a library was using its system. BrancheBrown also advised that a business-like approach will foster better understanding and increase the chances of successful planning.

BrancheBrown finished by mentioning procedural changes resulting from planning efforts. A proposal was written to pull new subscription data from BIBLIOTECH in the order they would be entered into EBSCONET. This streamlined the rekeying process for new subscriptions, which continued to be handled manually due to the small number of titles involved. Since the interface for handling renewals was not ready for use by November 1990, an alternative method was devised to convert Ebsco renewal invoice data into a form acceptable for batch loading into BIBLIOTECH. Ultimately, Raytheon dropped their pursuit of a BIBLIOTECH-EBSCONET interface since these other changes had brought about the main results desired: minimizing rekeying of information, but still keeping the serials librarian involved.

In the workshop's second half Hughes described the planning and implementation of an automated bindery system, the HERTZBERG CONNECTION. Planning began with an analysis of the manual binding operation. The data elements to be included in HERTZBERG CONNECTION records were title, buckram color, and spine information. These data elements for actively received titles constituted the online "preservation decision file." The form of title and the title filing arrangement (by significant words rather than word-by-word) came from the SILO (Serials of Illinois Online) union list; this filing arrangement was also used for shelving the volumes.

Hughes then reviewed the effect of NOTIS implementation on the automated bindery system. Bibliographic records for LUIS, the NOTIS online catalog, were downloaded from OCLC rather than from the union list. Records in LUIS file word-by-word rather than by significant title words. To match the form of title and title filing arrangement now available in LUIS, title information in the preservation decision file had to be verified against LUIS and modified where necessary. The physical volumes also had to be relabeled and rearranged.

Hughes continued with more detail about the implementation of both systems, including the serials and circulation data related to the binding process. Item records were created for individual bound volumes and for items being sent to the bindery, then barcodes were added to link item records to the appropriate bibliographic records. Circulation and serials staff devised five bindery "patron" IDs, each with a different date range to cover items sent out during a given period. Charging a volume to one these bindery "patrons" generated a message in the OPAC displaying the volume's bindery status and its due date. At the same time, bound holdings information was updated manually and the individual issue entries for that volume were deleted.

After using the NOTIS check-in function for one year, the library has now initiated the bindery alert system. When the first issue of a new volume has been received, the check-in staff person prints out the title's receipt history to use as a pull slip. This alert begins a sequence of activities in NOTIS and the HERTZBERG CONNECTION that together constitute a single process. Hughes concluded by briefly discussing the future of additional binding enhancements in NOTIS.

Questions at the workshop's end concerned future plans for both interfaces described, including the possibility of direct file transfer between the HERTZBERG CONNECTION and NOTIS, the timetable for NOTIS binding enhancements, and the intent of the BIBLIOTECH developers to produce the planned interface.

Conversion to Automated Serials Control Systems: From the Drawing Board to the Front Lines

Trisha L. Davis
James L. Huesmann

Workshop Leaders

Marla Edelman

Recorder

Trisha L. Davis, Head of the Continuations Acquisitions Division at the Ohio State University Libraries, acknowledged that members of the audience were at different stages of automating and were using different systems, but hoped that the workshop would provide general information and increase understanding of the process and results of automating serials control. This understanding may empower librarians to better negotiate with vendors regarding system capabilities.

After seeing other successful library systems, serials librarians may have unrealistic expectations for serials control. Unlike catalog records, serials records are "moving targets" due to variations in receipt dates, invoicing, fund accounting, and binding data. Another problem is the lack of national standards for serials control systems.

James L. Huesmann, Serials Librarian at the University of Wisconsin-La Crosse Library, continued the discussion by outlining

---

Marla Edelman is Head, Serials Department, Jackson Library, University of North Carolina at Greensboro, College Avenue, Greensboro, NC 27412.

© 1991 by The Haworth Press, Inc. All rights reserved.

system capabilities. He emphasized available functions and library needs. He stressed the need to realistically evaluate system performance (including response time, processing speed, capacity, and physical requirements) and to maintain flexibility and adaptability when specifying input and output requirements. He also emphasized the importance of enhancing and adapting a system to local needs; documenting and pursuing problems with the vendor; and participating in a user's group in order to encourage system development.

Few libraries have the option of creating their own system, but there are many vendor-supplied systems, stand-alone systems, and integrated systems to choose from. Here too, librarians must take an active role in determining what their libraries will purchase.

All of these systems are based on bibliographic records, which interact with serials data, acquisitions/fund accounting data, serials control, and binding data. Inadequate links between these four elements can make serials systems difficult to use. Some special considerations for serials control include: the interconnection of various functions and movement between functions without having to go through a menu; the types of menus and the information they displayed; security-protected functions; and public vs. proprietary data.

In her discussion of profiling, Davis compared it to buying a custom-made shirt as opposed to taking one "off the rack." Often the system purchased will not work exactly as originally demonstrated; the library has the responsibility to be assertive, to ask the right questions, and to create a database with records complex enough to test the system. Emphasis was placed on involvement of all levels of staff from all areas where the system will be used.

In profiling the bibliographic parameters, Huesmann advised librarians to determine what files to transfer to the OPAC, to eliminate the less useful and confusing fields, to include those subfields that are most helpful, and to decide what indexes are needed and what fields should be included in each index. He asked, "Can you create local fields and tags? Are there enough system-supplied fields and are they indexed? Do the fields display where they're needed? Are codes clear and can they be added or changed? Do you have the ability to add, change, and delete fields?" Davis cautioned staff to use local fields for local data; if you assign a currently unused MARC fields for local data, remember that these fields could later change or disappear.

As for hardware parameters, librarians should ask, "What is needed to get the system to run as fast and as well as required? Does the system demand color monitors or will it run without them? What type of processing takes place?" A central processing system runs on a mainframe computer. In distributed processing, more than one computer is involved (if part of the system slows or goes "down" the other components can still operate). The single workstation could be appropriate for some activities such as serials control.

Contracts with systems vendors should specify who does the installation of hardware and software. It is important to spell out who is responsible for environmental controls, communication links, and system administration, and who will bear any unanticipated expenses in these areas.

Systems testing and functional testing are the keys to success. Many people don't realize that they must negotiate not only for training and database loads, but also for testing. Systems (or benchmark) testing will reveal the overall speed and effectiveness of the system and how easy or difficult it is to use. Using students and other less sophisticated staff to test the system will give an accurate idea of how long it takes to learn the system. Functional testing will evaluate database integrity, specialized functions, and interactive processes. Is the full bibliographic record being downloaded? Are all the fields being properly indexed and retrieved? Do the menus and screen displays provide adequate information in an acceptable format? It is possible that posting, encumbering, and paying invoices could slow the system. In order to test for check-in and claims, "dummy" records with artificial claim periods should be created, so that tests can be completed within the time allotted. A great deal of planning is required beforehand.

Problem resolution falls into three categories: (1) simple problems that can be fixed easily, usually by the vendor (i.e., an inaccurate display or menu caused by miskeyed data); (2) major problems that will require large outlays of time and money (and the involvement of the developer) to fix, for instance reprogramming the indexes; (3) problems that fall somewhere in between, which can be solved by compromise between the vendor and the library.

Huesmann outlined a number of ways for adapting a system to the library's needs or vice versa. It's important to be able to redirect output into other programs if possible. ASCII output can be formatted as required using a word processing application or transferred into a database program to produce other statistics. A DOS-based system can easily create special menus to speed up special functions like check-in. Systems staff can devise special menus and customize screen displays, even in an integrated system.

Changes in workflow because of conversion to automated serials control can create special problems. It is important to bear in mind that data will be shared by all departments. It is especially important to keep information regarding frequency or title changes up-to-date. Non-catalogers know more than they realize about the nature of serials cataloging; they are familiar with the MARC fields and know how changes in these fields affect the database. Training staff to use the new system may be the most difficult part of the conversion. Staff members will have to learn many new skills and procedures and must learn to make the system work for them in a number of creative ways. However, training can also pave the way to job upgrades as sophistication and the level of responsibility increase.

Conversion to an online system will demand new attitudes and approaches to serials control. Davis stated, "Work files are not your own. They are shared in acquisitions, serials, cataloging, public service, and perhaps with the general public, so you have to think of your records in terms of all the others using them, as well as how [the records] will work for you." The success or failure of the system will depend on attitudes toward sharing that information.

Replacement Issues: Where Do You Find Them and at What Cost?

Beth Holley
Susan Malawski
John T. Zubal

Workshop Leaders

Lawrence R. Keating II

Recorder

Beth Holley, Head of the Acquisitions Department at the University of Alabama Library, began by defining a replacement issue as a substitute for an item once purchased and received, which now requires reordering/repurchasing to complete a binding unit. Libraries need replacement issues for a variety of reasons. Issues may be lost, stolen, damaged, or mutilated. Some issues are never received, but cannot be claimed due to the expiration of the claim period. Still others may be needed to fill in gaps caused when a subscription did not begin with the first issue of a title.

Several alternatives to binding were suggested, along with their drawbacks. Volumes can be bound incomplete or held pending a search for missing issues. In-house binding is a possibility, but some in-house methods lack permanence. Princeton file boxes may be used, or the volumes can be bundled with string or rubber bands, although neither method really protects the volumes from damage or loss. Finally, microfilm replacement is good for long runs, but a

---

Lawrence R. Keating II is Head, Serials Department, University of Houston Libraries, Houston, TX 77204-2091.

© 1991 by The Haworth Press, Inc. All rights reserved.

single volume on microfilm doesn't fit well on shelves with bound volumes and requires explanatory notes in the bibliographic record.

There are a variety of sources for replacement issues. The first choice is the publisher—not always the most economical source. "Duplicate Exchange" lists are labor intensive and frequently have a low success rate. Back issue dealers are an obvious source, but it is not easy to identify who's out there and what they're offering; once the dealer is located, it is necessary to find out their policies and procedures: whether they deal in single issues or complete volumes, what their subject coverage is, and so on. Interlibrary loan can be useful under certain conditions, but it has its pitfalls. UMIs photocopy service is costly.

Holley distributed a preliminary draft of her Directory of Back-Issue Dealers (which she intends to publish at a later date) as a hand-out. She indicated also that since June 1990, her department has requested 2,400 single issues, but has only been able to acquire 938 of these.

John T. Zubal, President of United States Book Exchange/Universal Serials & Book Exchange, presented a historic overview of back issue sources for libraries, starting with sources prior to 1945. Indexing services (H.W. Wilson, Chemical Abstracts) made back issues available to subscribers once indexing was complete. Of the commercial sources, American magazine services (e.g., Abrahams Magazine Service) were primarily back issue dealers, while their European counterparts such as William Dawson and Swets & Zeitlinger were subscription agents and news vendors first, and only secondly back issue dealers. Exchange operations such as the LC Exchange and Gift Division and similar departments in other libraries were also potential sources for issues, as were backfiles maintained by publishers.

Zubal characterized the period 1946 to ca.1973 as an era of rapid academic development spurred by the G.I. Bill of Rights. Larger student populations demanded well-stocked libraries; at the same time, scientific, and medical research underwritten by the Federal Government led to increasing numbers of periodicals to publish the research. Retrospective collection building became important and additional back issue firms (e.g., Kraus Periodicals, Walter J. Johnson) began operations. The United States Book Exchange was created as a clearing house for periodicals contributed by libraries and made issues available to other libraries for a small service charge. Additionally, reprint companies and manufacturers of non-print alternatives emerged to satisfy demand for backsets.

The mid-70s saw a switch from growth of library collections to maintenance of existing collections. This shift of policy was brought on by rising fuel prices, fiscal problems, and rising book and journal costs. For serials departments strained budgets had to be dedicated to maintaining ongoing subscriptions rather than acquiring backsets. As dealers reoriented themselves to new markets, they were confronted with additional problems such as warehouses overflowing with aging stock, the loss of key personnel, and a lack of customer orders.

The current back issue market is populated by many of the older firms along with smaller and newer suppliers. Generic back issue sources such as USBE and regional or defined exchange programs continue to supply issues, as do publishers and various vendor/bibliographic back issue services. A major consideration for back issue suppliers today is supplying serials in alternative formats such as CD-ROM, e-journals, and online databases.

Susan Malawski, Director of Subscription, Fulfillment and Distribution for John Wiley & Sons, Inc., focused on the publication process and inventory control. She stressed that publishers try to plan print runs carefully and systematically. In calculating the size of print runs, a publisher applies such considerations as circulation, volume year, supply of promotion copies, replacement copies, and back-volume sales. Periodical publishers were not affected by the Thor decision as were book publishers: back issues are warehoused rather than destroyed (storage space plays a more important role than tax considerations).

Publisher inventory policies for periodicals are based on such factors as expected demand over a period of years, anticipated sales, the cost of carrying inventory, the replacement cost of an out-of-stock item, and finally, the damage to customer relations by being out-of-stock. Malawski presented a hypothetical example of a sample print run which clearly illustrated the diverse factors that determine the final number of copies printed for a given issue. She also presented two hypothetical stock reduction plans for back issue management over a ten-year period, again emphasizing that stock reduction is space-driven and that reductions are sometimes unnecessary since attrition may have lowered the number of copies on the shelf.

Discussion after the presentations was lively and extended, and touched on such topics as how and when decisions are made to reprint issues, how back issue prices are determined, want lists vs. purchase orders, and rotation of want lists among suppliers.

How Vendors Assess Service Charges and a Publisher's View of Discounts to Vendors

John Breithaupt
Buzzy Basch
Tina Feick

Workshop Leaders

Kathleen Meneely

Workshop Recorder

John Breithaupt, Director-General, Marketing, Association of Management and Distribution Services at Allen Press, focused on a publisher's view of the discounts given to vendors and what impact the agent's discount has on the publisher's strategy. Next N. Bernard (Buzzy) Basch, Consultant from Basch Associates, addressed the issue of fees—bill backs, price increases, supplemental invoices, etc.—from a vendor's perspective. Tina Feick, Serials Specialist from Blackwell's Periodicals Division concluded the presentations by providing insights on service charges from the foreign vendor perspective.

Breithaupt's discussion focused on non-profit society-based publishers. These organizations are run by society officers who are professionals in their fields and who work on a volunteer basis. Breithaupt emphasized that the total circulation of these publishers is generally less than 10,000 (and in many cases less than 5,000) with society membership accounting for fifty percent of the total. Be-

---

Kathleen Meneely is Collection Development Librarian—Serials, Cleveland Health Sciences Library, 2119 Abington Rd., Cleveland, OH 44106.

© 1991 by The Haworth Press, Inc. All rights reserved.

tween 1987-1991, Breithaupt conducted two surveys of society publishers to determine if they provided discounts to the vendors they deal with and what kind of services these publishers were receiving (if any) from the subscription agencies.

According to the survey results, in 1987, 64 percent of the publishers were giving U.S. agencies discounts averaging 7.1 percent in 1991, 72 percent were giving U.S. agencies discounts averaging 6.7 percent. European agencies were receiving 7.3 percent discounts in 1987 and 6.4 percent discounts in 1991. Breithaupt noted that although the percentage had decreased, the dollar amount had increased 25 percent.

The second survey focused on the publisher's view of vendor discounts and the resulting vendor services. Publishers mentioned the following benefits from subscription agencies: the consolidation of subscription orders, answering inquiries, receiving claims, and saving publisher invoice and postage costs. Two other benefits, which have far less impact, were higher renewal rates and an increase in new subscriptions. The publisher did not perceive that subscription agents either promoted or recommended journals to the library or charged more for services based upon the amount of price discount that the publisher gave.

Publishers also remarked that the subscription agent provides more services to the library than to the publisher; that the agent price discount is expected in the scheme of operation from publisher to library, and since the publisher is receiving some benefits from the agent, the agent should receive the price discount; and finally, the agent receives sufficient payment from libraries for services provided to the library and the publisher. When asked what the publisher saved in dollars by having the agent consolidate library subscription orders, 76 percent of the publishers either did not know or left the question blank. Based upon this response, Breithaupt estimated that the agent discount has no impact on these non-profit, society publishers' strategies.

Breithaupt concluded that communication between the publisher, vendor, and the library should be reinforced. As members of a complex distribution chain, each participant needs to be aware of their individual and collective roles and the roles of others in the chain.

How much can a vendor charge and how does a vendor calculate library fee assessment? Basch stated that there are no rules governing what an agency can charge; they can charge whatever the market will allow. Calculation of fees is a complex decision-making process requiring the consolidation of many component parts.

Basch observed that all agencies provide the same basic services, but their methods for calculating fees are different. To calculate service charges, a vendor must look at many variables. Costs vary from organization to organization and include: labor costs, system charges, research and development, software/hardware, operating overhead, a variety of service packages, and profit objectives. Some agencies use formulas which incorporate: publisher discounts; maximum dollar charge per title; percent of subscription price; minimum transaction fee; maintenance of information lines on invoice; rounding up or down; service charge on shipping charges; non-vendor order titles; mark-ups on titles; etc. Other variables that influence fees are the volume of titles, the mix of foreign and domestic titles or whether there is a flat title charge.

Basch concluded that, although a vendor may be reluctant to discuss the service charge, librarians should not assume that these fees are not negotiable. Basch also advised that librarians should not assume that all of their invoices are charged the same rate and that their prior fixed agreements are still in effect. Finally, Basch emphasized that there is no direct relationship between the charge to the library and the vendor services that are used. The service charge is a single fee structure that covers invoicing, claiming, replacements, renewals listing, adjustments, and general housekeeping activities.

Tina Feick rounded out the discussion by focusing on foreign vendors. Feick emphasized that all foreign vendors do not deal with subscriptions and service charges in the same way. Some vendors market by geographic location, while others have one standard fixed price and service charge policy for all clients; policies can vary from country to country. The availability of prepayment plans and publisher or region-based plans also varies.

Feick discussed two concepts of service charges; bottom of invoice service charges and embedded service charges. With the embedded service charge, the total price of the journal includes the service charge. Many libraries prefer the embedded service charge, because it is easier to allocate costs to various funding accounts. The title prices charged to U.S. customers vary according to the prevailing economic environment. Feick advised librarians to check exchange rates in sources like the Wall Street Journal on a monthly basis—be aware of current economic trends; look at the previous year's prices; and inquire about the projected rates for the coming year.

Feick offered a few suggestions for selecting and negotiating with vendors. When asking for a quotation, send a sample of the list, including foreign and domestic titles (and titles that range in cost). Ask about method of delivery, membership rates, etc. Since exchange rates may vary among vendors, ask the exchange rate and when it was set. Ask for a sample invoice of prices actually quoted by the vendor.

In conclusion, Feick emphasized that librarians should know their collection; this will produce the best results for both the library and the vendor.

Case Study: Managing the Established Sci-Tech Journal

John Tagler
Workshop Leader

Brenda Dingley
Recorder

This workshop, one of four presented under the auspices of STM publishers, was a case study in which John Tagler, Director of Corporate Communications, Elsevier Science Publishing Company, described the management of a mature journal faced with the possibility of a severe competitive threat, and an unorthodox, but successful, solution to the problem.

Tagler described the *Journal of Photochemistry and Photobiology* (*JCP*) as a niche journal emphasizing theoretical research in a small, stable research field. The subscribers are virtually all libraries, mostly academic or government, so no reduced personal subscription rate is available. *JCP* is published in two sections, available separately, or together for a small price savings.

The journal was launched in 1972, under the title *Journal of Photochemistry*, and built ninety-five percent of its current subscriber base within ten years. In the next few years the journal expanded its subject scope slightly by merging with two struggling journals in related areas, and by affiliating with a related society. At that time, *JCP* changed title and sectionalized.

Brenda Dingley is Head of Acquisitions, University of Missouri, Kansas City, 5100 Rockhill Rd., Kansas City, MO 64110.

© 1991 by The Haworth Press, Inc. All rights reserved.

In 1988 Elsevier learned that the society was not happy publishing its journal as a section of an established title, and was considering publishing in concert with two other societies. If the society decided not to renew its contract with Elsevier, *JCP* would lose papers from the society membership. This was considered a serious threat to *JCP*, because without a good manuscript flow, it would lose subscribers. Elsevier began looking for ways to increase the visibility of *JCP*.

The usual methods of increasing the visibility of a title were judged to be of little use in this instance. *JCP* had increased its subject scope twice in its history, and was publishing in a limited research area. It was already being exhibited at the appropriate conferences, and was reaching its intended audience, so expanded exhibits coverage and direct mail were not the answer. Pressing the editorial board to solicit more manuscripts seemed unnecessary and perhaps risky under the circumstances, and a change in the cover or format would be as merely cosmetic.

The untraditional answer was to publish a newspaper edition of section A of the journal, intended for personnel subscribers and contributors, rather than for libraries. The possible advantages of this approach were: it placed the edition directly in the hands of the end-user; it was in a comfortable, familiar format (not electronic); it was easily manufactured once typesetting had been done for the archival version; it was easily distributed; and it would not be directly competitive with the archival format.

Possible disadvantages to this approach were that it flouted the tradition of scientific communications, the authors might perceive it as a down-graded product, and the risk to the archival product was unknown.

Elsevier decided to issue the newspaper edition on a trial basis. After deciding on the particulars of the newspaper edition, a cost for the first year of $52,000 was projected, which was considered to be a marketing expense and would not be charged back to subscribers. Elsevier allowed nine months to see an improved paper flow and fifteen months to monitor subscription levels; they also considered including advertising in the edition to offset costs. They limited circulation to scientists who had submitted articles to the journal or attended conferences in the subject area, and planned a reader survey after seven months to be sure there would be no adverse effect on its archival format.

The newspaper edition was launched April 1989. In December the reader survey was distributed, with response to the survey a condition of continuing to receive the newspaper edition. The responses were very positive.

The respondents found the newspaper very useful: 82 percent said they read the papers because they had a personal copies, and 73 percent found the format convenient for browsing; 80 percent of the respondents rated the papers as good or excellent, and 75 percent read selected abstracts and 2-3 articles in each issue. A majority of the readers retained the newspaper issues, and 13 percent forwarded selected issues to colleagues.

The newspaper edition's effects on the archival journal were neutral or positive. According to the survey, 37 percent of the respondents had regularly used the archival edition prior to the issuance of the newspaper, and 50 percent regularly used the archival edition after the newspaper edition. There was no substantial decline in subscriptions during the test period, which covered two renewal periods, and librarian response was neutral. Maintaining the same acceptance rate of 50 percent to 60 percent, the archival journal went from 12 to 18 articles a month, pulling manuscripts from more general science journals.

The survey provided valuable demographic data on *JCP*s readership. Elsevier found that a majority of the newspaper's readership were in academia, with smaller percentages in industry or government/military. The largest percentage of its readers, 44.1 percent, lived in Western Europe, with almost 27 percent in North America. Most of the authors (74 percent) who published in *JCP* published in a wide variety of journals, and most regularly consulted three to four specialty journals.

Based on survey response and the increase in papers, Elsevier concluded that the newspaper edition of section A succeeded in raising the visibility of its journal. For unknown reasons, the threat of a competitive journal never materialized, but publication of the newspaper edition has been continued. Elsevier has since launched a parallel newspaper edition of section B, with abstracts of papers and the full text of news and reviews. It is too soon to know if this will be equally successful.

Discussion after the presentation centered on what this case study suggests about scientific communication patterns, such as the need for browsable scientific publications. It was generally observed that mature journals are under terrific pressure, and that we will see further innovation to help them survive.

Case Study: A Society Journal Published by a Commercial Publisher

Jolanda L. von Hagen

Workshop Leader

Mary K. Castle

Recorder

This case study was one of four workshops sponsored by STM. Jolanda L. von Hagen, Managing Director, Springer-Verlag, Heidelberg, began the session with a brief description of factors that prompt a scholarly or professional society to seek a commercial publisher for the publishing of its journal.

Societies usually begin to publish using an in-house publishing office that handles the editorial and production aspects of the journal. In many instances, the staff may be volunteers or, in the case of academics, may be subsidized by the institution. When expenses repeatedly exceed the revenue from membership fees and educational programs are threatened, the society begins to look at its overall operations. The journal may be targeted as a money-losing operation. The society's aim is then to increase revenue to support educational programs by increasing journal sales. At this point the society seeks a commercial publisher.

In the specific case study posed by von Hagen, the fictional society enters into negotiations expecting that the publisher will in-

---

Mary K. Castle is Head, Acquisitions and Collection Development, University of Texas at Arlington, UTA Library, P.O. Box 19497, Arlington, TX 76019-0497.

crease the subscriber base outside the current membership, begin international distribution, improve promotion, increase advertisements, and give the society an upfront payment of royalties.

Increased membership from greater penetration in the open market would come from libraries, industry, and individuals within the field who might qualify as members. In most cases, these subscribers would be charged a higher rate for the journal, thereby allowing the society to maintain the current member subscription price.

Publishers have promotional programs, the sales force, and the marketing expertise to reach untapped sources of readers or potential members. International distribution by a reputable publisher results in better editorial status, wider interest, and greater prestige for the journal. Although advertisements are rare in academic journals, societies believe that it is easy for a commercial publisher to increase revenues by getting more advertisements.

In addition to these expectations, the society wants to maintain editorial and copyright control, select the editor-in-chief, determine the size, the format, the number of pages per year, and the quality of paper and binding.

Why can't the society accomplish these things and continue to publish its own journal? Through role-playing and discussion von Hagen led the group toward the discovery that the dominant reasons a society approaches a commercial publisher are the lack of manpower and the need for a full-blown distribution system.

Before entering into an agreement, the publisher determines whether or not he or she can meet the society's requirements through thorough investigation of the market and the scope and quality of the journal. Questions that should be asked of the society include: why don't you have more members? Are your membership requirements too strict? Do you offer the journal to others outside of the membership? Is the content of the journal still state-of-the-art?

The commercial publisher checks the market for potential subscribers outside of the country of publication, determines if there are competing journals, surveys subscribers and readers to determine their opinions/perceptions of the journal, and establishes the strengths and weaknesses in marketing. The journal is evaluated on the status and reputation of the editor, whether or not the contents reflect state-of-the-art research in the field and are within the scope of funding by various agencies, the origin and reputation of the authors, and the potential for international appeal.

If these findings are positive, the publisher agrees to publish the journal and then establishes marketing and promotion plans, production schedules, fulfillment services, and determines expenses to be incurred. The publisher sets goals for increasing the subscription base, reducing the production costs, and for profit sharing and royalty payments. The publisher is required to show commitment usually in the form of a cash payment or, in some cases, a contribution toward editorial office expenses.

The commercial publisher gains prestige by being the publisher of the official society publication, but a profit for both the society and publisher is necessary for a successful alliance.

Further discussion centered on questions concerning the role that each partner plays in the agreement, from control of advertising content and copyright to changes in frequency and number of pages per year.

Multiple Version Cataloging and Preservation Microfilming for Brittle Issues of Serials

Steve Savage
Mitch Turitz

Workshop Leaders

Geraldine F. Pionessa

Recorder

The purpose of this workshop was to give practical information about preservation microfilming to serials librarians, so that materials will be filmed correctly and the microfilm will last. According to Steve Savage, Head, Periodicals, Newspapers and Microforms Department, University of Kentucky Libraries, serials librarians must become involved in the preservation of serials, no matter what their primary duties, since they are the de facto guardians of serials.

Following the microfilming standards is essential for successful preservation microfilming. Standards written by the American National Standards Institute and the Association for Information and Image Management (ANSI/AIIM) and the guidelines published by the Research Libraries Group (RLG) cover the materials used, the process, the functionality of film, and its storage. An outline given to all workshop participants identified significant standards by number.

Preservation microfilming is an exacting process which Savage described in some depth, sharing practical information that he learned

---

Geraldine F. Pionessa is Microforms Librarian, University of Arizona Library, Tucson, AZ 85721.

during his involvement with the Kentucky Newspaper Project. He showed photographic slides of equipment, processes used during the project, and examples of brittle newspapers encountered. He compared rotary and planetary cameras, and defined important terms. Cameras vary in speed and resolution capability; the poorer the print quality on the original document, the more crucial the choice of camera. For microfilm preservation purposes, film is available in three degrees of permanence: archival quality, which, if produced and stored according to national standards, will last 500 years; long-term quality, which should last at least 100 years; and medium-term quality, which should last at least 10 years. Archival quality film must always be used for preservation microfilming.

Savage described the three generations of microforms called for by national standards and stressed that libraries performing original microfilming of serials must be sure to create a master negative film of archival quality, store it under optimum conditions, and use it only to produce a printing negative. The existence of archival master negative films is essential for serials preservation. Savage then gave an in-depth description of the actual filming process, including procedures, quality control, and newspaper filming. He also delved into specific technical matters such as information on ASA film speed, average gradient, film sizes, test charts, splicing, and identification for microforms using targets. Savage spoke briefly about microfiche and noted that the materials and procedures used to produce microfiche are basically the same as those for microfilm, although it is more difficult to correct errors in filming. He stressed the importance of proper storage conditions, enclosures, and containers in prolonging the life of microfilm.

Savage concluded by reiterating that serials in libraries are rapidly deteriorating, that problems in access and use will result from filming them as is, and that serials librarians must make preservation librarians aware of the unique factors that should be considered when filming serials.

Mitch Turitz, Serials Librarian, J. Paul Leonard Library, San Francisco State University, described two basic issues in microforms cataloging. The first issue concerns what to describe, i.e., the original or the reproduction; the rules have changed over the years. The second issue concerns how to describe items, i.e., in a separate bibliographic record for each format or in a single bibliographic record with attached records for various formats. There are advantages and disadvantages to each method.

Turitz defined the currently accepted cataloging standard as the revised Anglo-American Rules (AACR2) and then described some of the problems this standard causes for cataloging microform reproductions: cataloging bottlenecks, use of preservation monies for cataloging instead of actual filming, user confusion, and maintenance of numerous duplicate records.

Throughout the workshop, Turitz showed many examples of different record formats and examples of how these formats appear on OPAC browse screens and in brief displays, pointing out differences and similarities among the records, and indicating potential problems for users. He also noted that various groups have proposed solutions to the problems of cataloging microforms, but there has been little agreement among them.

The Association of Research Libraries (ARL) decided that a national standard was needed for bibliographic records for preservation microfilm masters. With input from the library community, ARL issued *Guidelines for Bibliographic Records for Preservation Microfilm Masters* in 1990, which allowed a record for the original publication to be "cloned" to form the basic of the microform record. This provided a way to catalog microform masters without causing a cataloging backlog, but did not alleviate the confusion and expense caused by separate bibliographic records for each version of a publication.

The Library of Congress (LC) coined the term "multiple versions" or "MULVER" to encompass all publications that are identical in content, but different in physical format, and an LC committee concluded that the display conventions of individual systems and bibliographic networks were the essence of the problem. The committee recommended the continued use of separate bibliographic records for related versions, but with links between related records. However, the fundamental question of the usefulness of these largely duplicate records and the expense of creating them was not addressed. The committee did give serious consideration to use of *USMARC Format for Holdings Data* for describing multiple versions.

CONSER also formed a task force to study the multiple versions problem, but never reached a consensus. Then in December 1989, a Multiple Versions Forum was held in Airlie House in Virginia, with representation from a variety of interested groups. The goal was to identify a technique for communicating bibliographic data about versions. Microreproductions were the most crucial category. The participants debated the pro's and con's of separate records, composite records, and two- and three-tiered hierarchical records. Finally they recommended a "two-tier" hierarchical technique, in other words, using the *USMARC Format for Holdings Data*.

Holdings records containing version information would be linked to a master bibliographic record. In the case of microreproductions, the full bibliographic record describes the original publication and each holdings record describes a reproduction. Turitz then summarized the many advantages to this approach. He concluded by saying that discussions on this topic continue. It is clear that change will not happen overnight and no official date for implementation has been set. In addition, the USMARC Format for Holdings Data itself has not yet been finalized.

The Impact of Electronic Journals on Traditional Library Services

Mary Beth Fecko
Linda Langschied

Workshop Leaders

Linda Hulbert

Recorder

Linda Langschied is Coordinator of Non-bibliographic Database and PC Services and Mary Beth Fecko is Special Formats Catalog Librarian, both of Rutgers University Libraries. Langschied began the workshop by commenting that their feelings range from feeling smug because they are familiar with non-traditional formats, to feeling responsible for the orphanage, to feeling like the garbage people — in all three cases getting what no one else wants to deal with. She defined e-journals, for the purposes of the workshop, as those without a print counterpart.

As to the value of e-journals, Langschied presented several conflicting predictions: (1) E-journals will reduce the proliferation of superfluous publishing; *or* they will enable scholars to publish more, faster. (2) E-journals will offset the costs of subscription fees; *or* they will break the back of libraries, because they will require new subscriptions rather than maintenance of existing subscriptions; (3) E-journals will be more widely available to users than print journals; *or* they will be inaccessible to most users and will become an "underclass" of journals.

Journals in print format have a number of disadvantages. Publication is slow. Restrictions on the length of articles limit the mate-

---

Linda Hulbert is Assistant Director for Technical Services, St. Louis University Medical Center Library, 1402 South Grand, St. Louis MO 63104.

© 1991 by The Haworth Press, Inc. All rights reserved.

rial (especially graphics) that can be included. The current proliferation of journals increases the scattering of related papers. And libraries and individual subscribers face ever-escalating subscription costs. E-journals might minimize some of these disadvantages.

Langschied discussed failed experiments with e-journals, including BLEND and EIES. The reasons for their failure included: computer illiteracy among authors and editors, unfriendly software, lack of standards, computer access and connect problems, unsatisfactory displays, unclear or nonexistent manuals, and readers unaccustomed to reading articles online. Articles were not published more quickly in the electronic format than in the print format; just the opposite proved to be true. Editors did not feel as pressured by invisible articles resting on their hard drives as they did by hard-copy articles sitting on their desks. Authors, editors, and readers preferred the print format, because it was familiar.

While many of the technical problems have been solved and the electronic format is becoming more familiar, standardization is still a problem. Some formal e-journals follow print conventions including ISSNs, volumes, issues, pages and dates, but any or all of these may be missing, which makes standard citation methods problematic.

Can e-journals solve print problems? The answer is still in dispute. Clearly, paper, distribution, and marketing costs are reduced or eliminated. Transmission of e-journals is very rapid. However, the peer review process will remain a bottleneck, no matter what the format. Other electronic communications such as e-mail, electronic newsletters, and pre-publication review systems have become popular; their success bodes well for the ultimate success of e-journals.

Langschied offered her own prediction. The younger researchers will lead the way until there is a critical mass of "e-publications" and the chicken/egg dilemma is solved. That is, no one will write for e-journals until they are a valued method of communication and they won't be valued until many people write for them.

Langschied pointed out that reference departments need to teach users how to use the new electronic formats, but ended her presentation with a difficult question: Is standard reference service a luxury libraries can no longer afford as we bring ourselves and our users into the electronic age?

Mary Beth Fecko discussed the librarian's responsibilities and suggested a cooperative effort between public and technical services to assure access to e-journals. She first discussed intellectual access to e-journals. How does the library perceive its responsibility to promote awareness of the e-journals? Will e-journal titles be included in the OPAC? Will they have full bibliographic information like print journals? Will they be included in the library's union list? Next she addressed technical access. What kinds of equipment are necessary? Will e-journals be available online? Training issues for patrons and staff will affect both intellectual and technical access.

Fecko also talked about the importance of archiving these journals. Who will be responsible for archiving? In what format will e-journal be preserved—paper, tape, CD-ROM? How will access be maintained as software and file formats become obsolete? Who will archive out-dated software to use with the journals or convert archived files to formats that can be used with current software.

Fecko recommended that catalogers handle e-journals as they would any other serial. She suggests using the 265 field for source of acquisition and for providing citation information. The 500 fields can be used for access notes and a 590 note can provide detailed commands and instructions for accessing the journal. Subject access should be provided and holdings information needs to be included in the union list.

The discussion at the end of the workshop included the following. We must provide access to e-journals and instructions on how to use them, just as we do with CD-ROMs. But in times of shrinking resources and increased demands libraries must carefully prioritize what type of intellectual and technical access they can provide. Some libraries are printing the e-journals to paper and handling them like other paper journals. In other libraries the e-journal is transmitted directly to the acquisitions department, transferred to a mainframe, and accessed by the patron through the OPAC. At present most publishers consider e-journals a financial risk, but as demand and technical capabilities increase publishing electronically will become more accepted. Librarians can't ignore e-journals just because electronic formats are unfamiliar; to do so will put libraries outside of the information loop.

Journal Contents Online: Patron Use and Implications for Reference Service

Melissa Bradley
Patricia Wallace

Workshop Leaders

Lisa A. Macklin

Recorder

Patricia Wallace, Head of the Serials Department at the University of Colorado Libraries at Boulder, began the workshop with a description of CARL (Colorado Alliance of Research Libraries). The CARL UnCover database provides article level access in an online periodical index. The database was created three years ago and now provides access to over 1.6 million articles, with approximately 3,000 articles added daily. The UnCover project is the first online database to index words in titles and to contain summaries from the table of contents of journal issues. The journals indexed include all periodicals subscribed to by participating Colorado libraries. This is accomplished at a central receiving area, which processes the journal issues within 24 hours. The UnCover database is now available for purchase by other libraries.

Melissa Bradley, Acquisitions Librarian at Denver Public Library, described the UnCover project in more detail. The database was started in June of 1988 with 67 periodical titles. It has grown to over 10,270 titles. The CARL staff maintains all serial records for each member library. Currently the staff checks issues into each

---

Lisa A. Macklin is Serials Records Librarian, University of North Texas Libraries, Box 5188, Denton, TX 76203.

© 1991 by The Haworth Press, Inc. All rights reserved.

participating library's database, but the article contents are entered only once for each issue. Document delivery of articles indexed in UnCover will be available in the summer of 1991.

Bradley and Wallace reported the results of their study that examined how a database such as UnCover is used. They looked at how searchers enter commands and what results are retrieved by their searches. They compared UnCover to other databases. Wallace pointed out that their study was not strictly scientific; instead, based on informed speculation, they drew conclusions by comparing searches and search results. The information gathered is of interest to serials and reference librarians, as well as system designers.

Wallace described the methodology of the study. Each library received a printout, or transaction log, from CARL of all the keystrokes entered into selected terminals for designated periods. The patrons and librarians were unaware that the terminals were being monitored. The printout recorded the terminal ID number, the date and time, and the search performed. The printout did not record the results of the search, but Bradley and Wallace were each able to replicate the results of the selected searches to provide a more detailed analysis.

Bradley briefly described the collections of the Denver Public Library, the only public library participating in CARL, and the training program used to acquaint staff with the UnCover database. The use of UnCover in the public library system allowed the branches to easily access the journal collection in the main library and also made professional reading easier for librarians. The use of journals (including interlibrary loan requests for journals) has increased since the implementation of UnCover. The CARL center has also noted an increase in requests for articles. However, the statistics of UnCover usage, gathered in this study, were relatively low. Possible explanations for this discrepancy include: (1) terminals were not monitored during peak periods; (2) the study did not monitor dial-up access to UnCover; (3) the terminals in the Reference area were not monitored; and (4) the number of terminals monitored may not have been statistically significant.

Bradley identified several areas for possible improvement in the use and design of UnCover. The help screen displays need to be modified, but there is no agreement among libraries on the best way to improve these screens. The patrons also need more information about the different search strategies and available databases. If the online session could begin with questions about the patron's research interests and needs, the system could automatically select the appropriate databases for the best search results. Also, the library must have a serious commitment to training. This is particularly true for public libraries, which, unlike university libraries, cannot require bibliographic instruction for patrons.

Wallace said that in over fifty percent of the cases searchers used only one search term, and did not modify their search unless the original strategy retrieved nothing. Also, the searches performed were relatively simple. These results support previous research that suggests patrons tend to use the simple search screens and learn only the minimum commands necessary to operate the system. For instance, a relatively new search feature, which displays, on command, the previous four searches input, was rarely used by the average patron. Patrons who did not use this feature often repeated earlier searches unnecessarily.

The study also monitored database switching on the CARL system. When patrons changed databases, they frequently applied incorrect search strategies to the new database or re-entered previously ineffective searches. Wallace concluded that changing databases is not only time consuming for patrons, but also often ineffective.

The difficulties patrons experienced searching the database were broken down into three categories. First, users need to know and understand system protocol to search effectively. Second, UnCover responds poorly to searches which retrieve large results. UnCover displays only the first 1,562 articles retrieved, arranged with the oldest article first, so more current articles will not be displayed in the large search results. Third, the patron may not understand how minor differences in search terms, for instance, alternate spellings or singular versus plural forms, can influence their search results.

The discussion which followed focused on the instruction needed to teach patrons to search effectively. One participant suggested that an automated reference interview may be an effective way to educate patrons. Bibliographic instruction is greatly needed in both the public library and the academic library, particularly since the introduction of the dial-up feature, where no interaction with library staff ever takes place.

An Introduction to the Structure of ANSI X12 and a Tutorial on X12 Mapping for Serials Related Transactions

Christopher Beckett
Fritz Schwartz
Sharon Cline McKay

Workshop Leaders

Joseph Barker

Recorder

Christopher Beckett, Product Manager, Blackwell's Periodicals Division, opened the workshop with an overview of the ANSI X12 standard. Its purpose is to facilitate EDI (electronic data interchange), the computer-to-computer exchange of structured business documents between an enterprise and its vendors, customers, and other trading partners. For serials librarians, EDI can provide a link between their serials control systems and the systems of serials agents; serials agents will use EDI in their transactions with libraries and publishers. EDI could handle ordering, status reporting, invoicing, price changes, claiming and claim responses, and address changes (as well as confirmation of each of these). EDI can eliminate much costly re-keying and evaluation of data. The ANSI X12 standard overcomes the variations in format or layout used by the systems of each partner in these interchanges. The X12 standard resembles a sequence of envelopes in successive sizes, each within

---

Joe Barker is Acquisitions Librarian, University of California at Berkeley, Berkeley, CA 94720.

another, with the possibility of more than one envelope of the same kind tucked into the next-larger envelope. The smallest unit is the "data element," that is, an ISSN, a title, an address, a price. Related data elements (perhaps an invoice line) are assembled in "data detail segments," surrounded by a header and a footer identifying and delineating each one for the receiving computer. Similar data detail segments are grouped together next in packets called "transaction sets," each with a header and footer. Like transaction sets are in turn grouped together in larger bundles called "functional groups," each with appropriate identifiers and delineating codes. One or more similar functional groups are enclosed in an even larger "interchange envelope," again with header and footer. Finally all the interchange envelopes to be transmitted at one time are enclosed in a "communications session," with a header and footer bearing "communications transport protocol" that describes vital information about the originating computer, such as the software, hardware, version of X12 used, and network and computer addresses. This information enables the receiving or "target" computer and the intermediary networks and software to perform the necessary conversions and adaptations to transmit, receive, process, and respond to the communication.

Fritz Schwartz, Manager, EDI Group, The Faxon Company, led the group in a mini-tutorial on mapping data into X12. He identified facts necessary before beginning mapping, including the purpose of the information to be interchanged, limitations of the source and target systems, the availability of machine-readable data from the sender and the desirability of machine-readable data for the receiver, and the version and release of X12 used at each end. To make X12 easier to understand, he compared its structures with the structures of human language: ASCII text used by computers corresponds to the characters within words of human language; data elements correspond to words; data segments to sentences; transaction sets to paragraphs; transaction envelopes to discussions; and the rules or syntax of X12 to the syntax of human language.

Four interchange standards exist within X12. The "data dictionary" standardizes terms used in X12. The "segment directory" is a vocabulary for describing and parsing headers, data, and footers within any data segments. "Transaction set" standards lay out the possible ID tags for all of the kinds of data within a transaction set (consisting of data segments and a header and footer). The transaction set represents an action to be taken, not an object, and can be compared to the verb in a sentence. Transaction sets can "loop" or repeat a set of actions on like data until it is all processed. "Transmission control standards" establish commonly understood communications on interchanges and systems. Schwartz distributed excerpts from the X12 standard, but time did not permit the group to go through the hands-on mapping of sample data into X12.

Sharon Cline McKay, Director of Library Services, Corporate Division, EBSCO Subscription Services, outlined general issues surrounding ANSI X12. She pointed out that X12 was developed with commerce in mind. It is market-driven and more practical than theoretical, because it has the economic purpose of facilitating commercial transactions. Compromises may be accepted in order to get transactions flowing, with the expectation that subsequent modifications can and will be allowed.

The committee (ASC X12) that developed the X12 standard is oriented primarily to U.S. commercial activity, but does not operate in a vacuum. It is fully accredited by ANSI (American National Standards Institute) and has over 150 sub-committees working on different aspects of the standard. This committee coordinates with ANSI/NISO (responsible for Z39 standards through BISAC and SISAC) and has loose ties with the International Committee for Electronic Data Interchange for Serials (ICEDIS), which is involved in standards for magnetic media transfer, and the British Book Industry Communication committee (BIC).

EDI communications require technological support from networks and translation software. Telecommunication is assumed, although magnetic media are sometimes used. Value-added networks (VANs) are almost always used in EDI. A VAN is used like a mailbox. Messages are sent to the VAN from the source computer and stored there until called for by the target computer. Between each computer and the VAN, translation software copes with variants caused by updates to X12 and harmonizes communications between the computers. VANs and translation software packages are significant cost factors for serials agents, other library materials vendors, libraries, and library systems vendors as each enters the EDI arena.

However, staff savings and increased speed are expected to offset these costs in a series of trade-offs.

Questions and answers focused on the potential for X12. Asked what library systems vendors are doing about X12, Fritz Schwartz answered that they are all becoming active in the X12 arena at different rates and to differing degrees. In response to a question about the relation between SISAC and X12, Schwartz said that SISAC never finalized a Z39 standard format for serials orders, claims, cancellations, etc., but some of the elements defined in that draft standard are being translated into the X12 formats. Since X12 is an inter-industry standard, the rate of development varies for different business sectors.

Job Descriptions Vis-à-Vis Job Applications: A Match Often Not Made in Heaven

Carole McIver
Lois N. Upham

Workshop Leaders

Rita Broadway

Recorder

Carole McIver, Administrative Services Librarian, University of North Carolina at Charlotte, analyzed serial related job advertisements, explaining the contents and interpreting terminology and formal language to show the importance of understanding the job advertisement for both the applicant and the search committee.

McIver examined the contents of several actual job advertisements. She stressed that the requirements of the job advertisement and the position announcement should be the same to expedite the work of the search committee and to prevent possible legal complications. Typical job advertisements include the working title of the position, who the position reports to, the name of the library or institution, description of the position, academic requirements, work and personal qualifications, length of appointment, starting date, academic expectations, application materials, application deadline, salary/benefits, and affirmative action statement.

Understanding each of these components can help the applicant become a serious candidate. The advertisement tells the candidate

---

Rita Broadway is Assistant Professor and head of Periodicals Department, Memphis State University, Memphis, TN 38152.

© 1991 by The Haworth Press, Inc. All rights reserved.

what application materials are essential and includes information on deadlines. Hiring deadlines are sometimes negotiable, but the application materials requested in the job announcement are not. Such statements as "send letter of application; resume; names, addresses, and telephone numbers of three current references" should be strictly adhered to. Not following specific instructions can cause qualified candidates to be dropped from consideration early in the application process. Also, the description of the job position allows the candidate to use job requirements to better prepare for the interview. Other information given in the job advertisement such as academic requirements, academic expectations, salary/benefits, and affirmative action goals can also be valuable during the interview.

Further, McIver emphasized that understanding the terminology used in job advertisements is helpful in a successful application. For instance, the statement "preferred experience in training or instructional design" shows that the search committee is emphasizing human resources. The statement "experience with creative leadership" indicates the committee is looking for a candidate with new ideas and concepts. "Demonstrated supervisory ability" means the search committee wants evidence that the candidate has supervisory experience. Terminology in job advertisements and announcements is important and may be taken literally. "Relevant experience" indicates the applicant's experience should be related to the prospective job. For example, monograph cataloging relates to serials cataloging, but reference experience might not. The word "required" means mandatory. The word "preferred" means a candidate having the preferred skills has an advantage over a candidate without the preferred skills.

Speaking as an academician, Lois N. Upham, Adjunct Assistant Professor, University of South Carolina, College of Library and Information Science, stressed the importance of letters of recommendation. Upham expressed concern about letters of recommendation written for recent graduates. Sometimes professors do not know their students well and write positive letters for students with weak credentials. Additionally, letters of reference for placement files written by teaching faculty are general letters that make no attempt to address specific job requirements, and may be of limited value, becoming dated rapidly. Letters in placement files lose value after about two years, especially if the applicant has gained work experience in the interim. Such letters may actually be harmful to the job candidate if areas of weakness mentioned in the letter have improved with work experience. Good letters of recommendation include the writer's relationship to the applicant, special strengths, skills and areas for improvement, assessment of interpersonal skills and recommended areas of employment.

In addition, Upham discussed the preparation of resumes. The resume should first list the applicant's name, address, and telephone number. The career objective, if used, should follow. The career objective should not be too narrow or too grandiose and should match the job description. Following the career objective, the applicant's educational history should be listed in chronological order with clearly visible dates. This history should include full name and location of the institution including name changes; full name of degree and date, including month, that the degree was awarded; for non-library degrees the major should be included; areas of concentration in the library degree; GPAs, honors and awards. Then the work history should be listed in reverse chronological order with clearly visible dates. References should include the individual's full title, name, address and telephone number. The resume should not include hobbies and personal information such as age, sex, marital status, religion, health, and ethnic group.

Upham emphasized the value of format and physical appearance to a good resume. The resume should be clear and succinct, but it does not necessarily have to be limited to one page, especially if such a limitation means leaving out important information. Unusual type faces, oddly-colored paper, and non-print formats should be avoided. White or pale gray paper and plain easy-to-read type are preferred. Unusual formats such as computer disks, fax machines, and electronic databases should not be used for submitting resumes.

Also, Upham discussed the application letter. This letter is used to judge communication skills; therefore, it should be typed, not handwritten. The letter should be legible, neat, with good grammar and correct spelling. The application letter should address all points of the job description and attempt to document possession of skills mentioned in the job announcement. The letter should state how the applicant learned about the job, indicating enclosed attachments and whether transcripts have been requested.

During the discussion period, diverse questions about employment were asked. (1) Can a successful applicant request that an employer not be contacted? Will the search committee contact the employer anyway? (2) Is it appropriate to discuss salary and benefits at the interview? (3) Is it legal to ask for a salary history? Will refusing to include such a history penalize the applicant? (4) How best can an applicant deal with the possibility of a bad reference from a current employer?

Serials Claims:
Three Perspectives,
Library/Publisher/Vendor

Gary Brown
Julia Gammon
Peter McKay

Workshop Leaders

Louise Diodato

Recorder

Julia Gammon, Head, Acquisitions Department, University of Akron Library, began with a definition of serials claiming. A claim is a complaint from the library to the serial vendor or publisher about non-receipt of a serial issue. Misleading orders, vendor error, inefficiencies in the publishers's office, postal errors, strikes, revolution, war, incorrect address, and poor check-in practices all make claiming necessary.

Gammon presented a "wish list" of actions for the publisher and vendor to help reduce the number of claims. Some of the items on her wish list for publishers include: Set realistic claiming periods. Print enough extra copies of the issues so that issues do not go out of print too soon. Don't print irregular supplements that are difficult for the library to predict. Don't ask for payment if there are no plans to publish. Please reply to claims courteously. Police those libraries that are heavy claimers. Do not change serial titles; do not merge

---

Louise Diodato is Coordinator of Access Services, Cardinal Stritch College Library, 8022 W. Glenbrook Rd., Milwaukee, WI 53223.

© 1991 by The Haworth Press, Inc. All rights reserved.

serial titles. Print frequency changes on the cover. Do not use cheap tissue paper wrappers for mailing. Please use correct addresses.

Some of the items on her wish list for vendors include: Police those libraries that are heavy claimers. Create a missing copy bank. Respond to claims quickly. Pass on information from publishers to the libraries. Support claiming standards. Please pay the publisher on time.

Gary Brown, Midwestern Regional Representative, The Faxon Company, presented a vendor's perspective of claiming, illustrated by a chart showing the claiming process. Distribution is one-way from the publisher to the library. Orders are one-way from the library, to the vendor and then to the publisher or from the library directly to the publisher. For claiming the vendor is in the middle, with claims passing back and forth between the library on one side and the publisher on the other side. breakdowns occur in this system.

Brown described a project at Faxon, which involved an audit of 100 claims to determine the need for the claim. The results showed that: 33 percent of the claims involved the publisher, Faxon, and the library; 8 percent involved Faxon and the library; 10 percent were library problems; 5 percent were publisher data-entry problems; 2 percent were defective issues; 5 percent were order problems; 4 percent were distribution problems; for 32 percent of the claims the problem could not be determined. Brown made some general observations: automation needs to better integrate information from the publisher and the vendor; libraries are claiming too early or too often, which annoys vendors; and 40 percent of repeat claims never receive a reply from the publisher. Brown believes that claiming offers opportunities. Claims should improve the exchange of data between the library, the publisher and the vendor. Vendors should adopt a continuous claim audit process. Adopting quality-based performance standards and analyzing claiming for patterns and frequency are two of Brown's recommendations.

Peter McKay, Sales and Marketing Director, Harcourt, Brace and Jovanovich, Ltd., presented the publisher viewpoint on serials claiming. He believes that all three groups should look on serials claiming as a welcome and necessary means of communication among the three groups. Without claims, the library has no means of evaluating the publisher's activities, and claiming also gives the publisher a means to stay in contact with the library. McKay explained that the serials publisher performs a task not performed by the monographic publisher. In addition to producing the item, the serials publisher is also the distributor of the item. Many mistakes can occur during the distribution of a serial issue that the publisher cannot control.

McKay explained that serial publishers deals with several groups of clients. The basic group includes the users of the journal and the authors of the journal articles. A second group includes the libraries that order serials and vendors who process subscription orders and payment.

For the publisher the claiming process consists of the following steps: verify the client's name; confirm the correct address; check the dispatch date; advise the client of the mailing date; enter claim in the database; and, at receipt of second claim, send replacement issue. If the clients address has changed then the publisher must be modify address records, redirect issues, and notify the client that the change has been processed. If the publisher finds no record of the order, then an invoice must be issued, along with a request for detail of payment.

Following the presentations, animated and friendly discussion on many topics dealing with claiming took place. Representative questions were: Should the library return duplicates to the publisher? McKay indicated that it is not the librarian's responsibility to do so; however, it is appreciated when they do. How does a publisher determine when a title change will occur? McKay answered that if the publisher has complete control, the title will change at the beginning of a new volume. The decision to change the title is made about a year in advance. Should the library notify the vendor if the publisher communicates important information to the library? Both Brown and McKay answered that the library should notify the vendor.

Acquiring and Cataloging the Elusive Latin American Serial

Nelly S. Gonzalez
Scott Van Jacob
Rosa Q. Mesa

Workshop Leaders

Lisa Peterson

Recorder

Nelly S. Gonzalez, Director, Latin American Library Services at the University of Illinois Library; Scott Van Jacob, Serials Librarian at Dickinson College; and Rosa Q. Mesa of the University of Florida Libraries' Latin American Collection presented this workshop on selecting, acquiring, pricing, and cataloging Latin American serials.

Nelly Gonzalez spoke on serials' importance as the primary means for communicating the intellectual, political, and social life of the Latin American region. Building and maintaining a good Latin American serials collection requires knowledge of appropriate information sources and continuous status checks on these titles. Important bibliographic sources include: *Hispanic American Periodicals Index* (HAPI); *Handbook of Latin American Studies* (HLAS); *Indexed Journals: A Guide to Latin American Serials; Bibliography of Latin American and Caribbean Bibliographies;* and *MLA Directory of Periodicals.*

Gonzalez also did a study of *Ulrich's International Periodicals Directory* on CD-ROM and found almost 7,000 titles listed for

---

Lisa Peterson is Head, Acquisitions Department, University of California at Riverside, Tomas Rivera Library, Riverside, CA 92517.

© 1991 by The Haworth Press, Inc. All rights reserved.

Latin America and the Caribbean, with the majority from Argentina, Brazil, and Mexico. Subject coverage was strongest in agriculture, business, history, literature, and political science.

International organizations and government agency publications form a major portion of the serial literature for Latin America. Some of these "official publications" are printed in limited quantities and are not always serviced by local serial jobbers. Lack of wide distribution causes special problems in acquiring these serials.

Gonzalez commented on gifts and exchange programs and said new technologies will aid resource sharing and cooperative acquisitions. Gonzalez sees the need for a union list of Latin American and Caribbean serials and for a *Current Contents*-style periodicals database for Latin American serials. The *Hispanic American Periodicals Index* is now available online via UCLA's ORION online catalog.

Scott Van Jacob presented a "Latin American Fact Sheet", which identified the influences on and problems in publishing Latin American periodicals, including: higher education, research and development, lack of financial resources, high inflation, high imported paper costs, lack of skilled labor in the publishing industry, and the drain of scholarly research to U.S. and European publications.

Van Jacob described his involvement in developing the *Periodicals Price Index for Latin America*. The index currently includes price information by subject (social sciences, humanities, sciences, general, law, and newspapers) for nine Latin American countries. Title and price information was gathered from the Faxon Company and Library of Congress subscription information.

The index covers 1985 through 1990 with more specific pricing information for the 1989/90 subscription year. Also included in the index are the number of holding libraries (taken from OCLC) and a weighted price based on cost to holding libraries. Van Jacob is still analyzing the data but hopes to publish the index in early 1992.

Rosa Mesa presented an overview of the challenges involved with cataloging Latin American serials. Inconsistencies in serial publishing result in many changes in the cataloged bibliographic record. Differences in serial terminology between AACR2 and publishing—in some Latin American countries "periodical" means "newspaper"—can cause confusion in both receipt and cataloging.

Between 20-30 percent of the Latin American serial cataloging at the University of Florida requires original cataloging. Some of the "challenges" in cataloging include: title changes, numerous publications with the same title ("memorias," "anuario"), changes in publication size, changes in publishers, frequencies that can't be taken at face value, double numbering, and numbering that may have different meanings in each country. Numerous title changes occur because the official publishers have no training in publishing and library science. Mesa further noted that there is a shortage of trained serial catalogers with language expertise.

Discussion after the presentations centered on difficulties in acquiring and cataloging. Presenters stressed corresponding in Spanish on letterhead (automated forms are often disregarded in Latin America); acknowledging receipt of material to ensure continued receipt; and ordering from country of origin vendors. The Seminar on the Acquisition of Latin American Library Materials (SALALM) provides information and assistance with managing Latin American serials.

Sixth Annual NASIG Conference Registrants, Trinity University, June 1991

Conference registrants   *Institutions*

Abston, Deborah	Arizona State University
Aiello, Helen M.	Wesleyan University
Aitchison, Jada A.	University of Arkansas
Alexander, Adrian W.	The Faxon Company
Alexander, Julie S.	University of Texas at Arlington
Algier-Baxter, Aimee	Santa Clara University
Amin, Mayur	Pergamon Press
Anderson, Alma	Marywood College
Anderson, Jan	Utah State University
Arcand, Janet	Iowa State University
Aro, Carlene	South Dakota State University
Asencio, Margarita Almada	Universidad Nacional Autonoma de Mexico
Astle, Deana	Clemson University
Aufdemberge, Karen	University of Toledo
Austin, Terry	Baker & Taylor Books
Bading, Kathryn	Trinity University
Bailey, Charles W., Jr.	University of Houston
Baker, Carol M.	CISTI
Baker, Mary Ellen	California Polytechnic University
Barker, Caroline J.	Florida International University
Barker, Joe	University of California, Berkeley
Barnes, Ilse E.	University of West Florida
Barnes, Roy	University of Toledo
Basch, Buzzy	Basch Associates
Bazirjian, Rosann	Syracuse University

© 1991 by The Haworth Press, Inc. All rights reserved.

Beckett, Chris — Blackwell's Periodicals
Bergholz, Donna C. — Duke University
Bernero, Cheryl — EBSCO Subscription Services
Blaes, Evelyn R. — The American University
Blatchley, Jeremy — Bryn Mawr College
Blixrud, Julia C. — National Serials Data Program, Library of Congress

Bonhomme, Mary — Chicago Public Library
Booker, Joan A. — Wayne State University
Born, Kathleen — EBSCO Subscription Services
Borsman, Mary Linn — Massachusetts General Hospital
Bottomley, Lucy — National Library of Canada
Bradley, Melissa B. — Denver Public Library
BrancheBrown, Lynne — Pennsylvania State University
Bray, Sandra — Arizona State University
Breithaupt, John — Allen Press
Brenner, Betty — New York City Technical College
Breton, Gabriel — National Library of Canada
Broadwater, Deborah H. — Vanderbilt Medical Library
Broadway, Rita — Memphis State University
Bross, Valerie — California Polytechnic University
Brown, Gary J. — The Faxon Company
Broxis, Peter F. — Assia-Bowker-Saur Ltd.
Buell, Vivian — Ballen Booksellers International
Bueter, Rita Van Assche — Blackwell North America
Bushell, Christiane D. — Michigan State University
Bustion, Marifran — Texas A & M University

Callaghan, Jean S. — Wheaton College
Canini, Tuula — University of Waterloo
Cap, Maria — Los Angeles County Law Library
Carlson, Barbara A. — Medical University of South Carolina
Carrington, Bradley Dean — University of Kentucky
Casetta, Prima — Getty Center for the History of Art and the Humanities
Castle, Mary — University of Texas at Arlington
Chadwick, Leroy — University of Washington

Champagne, Thomas	Ross & Hardies
Chatterton, Leigh A.	NELINET
Christiansen, Christine	University of Miami
Chung, Sejin	Michigan State University
Clack, Mary Elizabeth	Harvard College
Clay, Genevieve J.	Eastern Kentucky University
Cochenour, Donnice	Colorado State University
Coleman, Shirley	Purdue University
Compton, Bruce	Louisiana State University
Cook, Eleanor	Appalachian State University
Cooley, Elizabeth A.	University of Virginia
Couch, Sarah K.	University of Kansas
Courtney, Keith	Taylor and Francis
Cousineau, Marie	University of Ottawa
Cowan, Carol Ann	Moody Medical Library
Cox, Brian	Pergamon Press, Oxford
Cox, John E.	Blackwell's Periodicals
Coyle, Marian R.	Martinus Nijhoff International
Crinion, Jacquelyn	University of Texas at San Antonio
Cseh, Eugene F.	University of Connecticut
Curtis, Jerry	Springer-Verlag
Czech, Isabel	Institute for Scientific Information
Dabkowski, Charles	Niagara University
Dane, Stephen	Kluwer Academic Publishers
Dansker, George L.	New Orleans Public Library
Darling, Karen	University of Oregon
Davidson, Leanne B.	Ball State University
Davis, Susan	State University of New York/ Buffalo
Davis, Trisha L.	Ohio State University
Dawson, Julie Eng	Princeton Theological Seminary
Day, Nancy	Linda Hall Library
De Klerk, Ann	Bucknell University
DeBuse, Judy	Washington State University
Deeken, JoAnne	James Madison University
Degener, Christie T.	University of North Carolina at Chapel Hill

Delgado, Ana Leyba — Our Lady of the Lake University
Deurell, Anne — Phillips Research Library, Hanscomnb Air Force Base
Devlin, Mary — The Faxon Company
Dingley, Brenda — University of Missouri – Kansas City
Diodato, Louise — Cardinal Stritch College
Doi, Makiko — Central Washington University
Doran, Michael — University of Texas at Arlington
Douglass, Janet — Texas Christian University
Downing, Jeff — SSC Laboratory Library
Dunn, Pamela — Stanford University
Duranceau, Ellen Finnie — Massachusetts Institute of Technology
Durden, Iris — Georgia Southern University
Dyer, Susan K. — The FAXON Company

Echt, Rita — Michigan State University
Edelen, Joe — University of South Dakota
Edelman, Marla — University of North Carolina at Greensboro
Elliott, Maxine — Clemson University
Ertin, Donna — Kent State University
Ewalt, Roz — Dallas County Community College District

Fairley, Craig — Metro Toronto Reference Library
Farwell, Anne — CANEBSCO
Fecko, Mary Beth — Rutgers University
Feick, Tina — Blackwell's Periodicals
Ferley, Margaret — Concordia University
Field, Kenneth C. — Trent University
Fisher, Fran — North Dakota State University
Fisher, Janet — Massachusetts Institute of Technology Journals Press
Fitchett, Christine — Vassar College
Fleischmann, Janis D. — Ameritech Information Systems
Fletcher, Marilyn — University of New Mexico

Flint, Ruth Ellen	University of Kentucky
Folsom, Sandy L.	Central Michigan University
Foster, Constance L.	Western Kentucky University
Fugle, Mary	Elsevier Science Publishers
Galloway, Margaret E.	University of North Texas
Gammon, Julia	University of Akron
Garralda, John	CARL Systems
Gartrell, Joyce	Columbia University
Gearty, Tom	The Faxon Company
Gelenter, Win	National Agricultural Library
Geller, Marilyn	Massachusetts Institute of Technology
Gentz, William	Carnegie Mellon University
Germain, J. Charles	Gauthier-Villars North America
Gifford, Caroline	New York Public Library, Research
Gillespie, E. Gaele	University of Kansas
Gilmore, Peggy S.	Georgia Southern University
Gimmi, Robert D.	Shippensburg University of Pennsylvania
Goforth, Kathleen	Academic Book Center/Scholarly Book Center
Goldich, Terri J.	University of Connecticut
Gonzalez, Nelly S.	University of Illinois/Urbana Champaign
Gordon, Martin	Franklin and Marshall College
Gordon-Gilmore, Anit	Fort Hays State University
Gormley, Alice	Marquette University
Grande, Dolores	John Jay College
Grauer, Sally	Library Binding Institute
Greene, Philip E.N., III	EBSCO Subscription Services
Griffin, William H.	Southwest Texas State University
Gurshman, Sandra J.	Readmore
Haest, Ruth	University of New Mexico
Hamilton, Fred	Louisiana Tech University
Hardin, Barbara	Kennesaw State College

Harris, Jay	University of Alabama at Birmingham
Haverkamp, Dan	The Faxon Company
Hawks, Carol Pitts	Ohio State University
Hayes, Florence	Cornell University
Healy, Leigh Watson	The Faxon Company
Hedberg, Jane A.	Wellesley College
Helinsky, Zuzana	Bibliotekstjanst ab Swedish Library Service
Hepfer, Cindy	State University of New York/Buffalo; and, *Serials Review*
Herzog, Kate S.	State University of New York/Buffalo
Hill, Joan	National Research Council of Canada
Hinders, Thomas	Oberlin College
Hinger, Joseph P.	Case Western Reserve University
Hitchcock, Eloise R.	Tennessee Technological University
Holley, Beth	University of Alabama at Tuscaloosa
Holley, Sandra H.	University of Texas Health Science Center at Tyler
Holloway, Carson	EBSCO Subscription Services
Hord, Leveta J.	University of Texas at Arlington
Huesmann, James	University of Wisconsin—La Crosse
Hughes, Katherine	Loyola University of Chicago
Hulbert, Linda	St. Louis University
Hutto, Dena	Pennsylvania State University
Hyman, Barbara T.	United States Postal Service Library
Impellittiere, Agnes J.	Pergamon Press
Irvin, Judy	Louisiana Tech University
Ivins, October	Louisiana State University
Jaeger, Don	Alfred Jaeger, Inc.
James, David Willis	Johns Hopkins University
Jayes, Linda D.	Illinois Institute of Technology

Johnson, David L.	Princeton University
Johnson, Judy L.	University of Nebraska
Johnston, Judith A.	University of North Texas
Jones, Daniel H.	University of Texas Health Sciences Center at San Antonio
Joyce, Janet	Blackwell Publishing
Julian, Gail	University of South Carolina
Kalmerton, Phyllis	Palmer College of Chiropractic
Kanter, Dorothy A.	University of Wisconsin
Kasinec, Edward	New York Public Library
Kean, Gene	Allen Press
Keating, Lawrence R.	University of Houston
Keckley, Mary W.	University of Texas at El Paso
Kelley, Carol M.	University of Texas at El Paso
Kemp, Jan H.	Texas Tech University
Kennedy, Kit	Readmore Academic Services
Kenney, Brian J.	St. John's University
Kersey, Harriet F.	Georgia Institute of Technology
Ketcham, Lee C.	EBSCO Subscription Services
Khosh-Khui, Sam A.	Southwest Texas State University
King, Timothy B.	John Wiley & Sons
Kirkland, Kenneth L.	De Paul University
Knapp, Leslie C.	EBSCO Subscription Services
Kronick, David A.	University of Texas Health Science Center at San Antonio
Kropf, Blythe A.	New York Public Library
Kwan, Cecelia	University of California, Davis
Lamborn, Joan	University of Northern Colorado
Landesman, Betty	George Washington University
Lange, Janice	Sam Houston State University
Langschied, Linda	Rutgers University Libraries
Latyszewskyj, Maria A.	Environment Canada Atmospheric Environment Service
Lawrence, Jane	Academic Press, London
Lawton, Wesley	CRC Press

Leadem, Ellen	National Institute of Environmental Health Sciences
Leatham, Cecelia A.	University of Miami
Leazer, William V.	Majors Scientific Subscriptions
Leggett, Deborah	The Faxon Company
Lehman, Charlene	University of Iowa
Lennie, Mike	Dawson Subscription Service
Lesher, Marcella	St. Mary's University
Levin, Fran	Houston Public Library
Likness, Craig	Trinity University
Lin, Selina	University of Iowa
Linke, Erika	Carnegie Mellon University
Linzmayer, Fernie	University of Calgary
Lively, Donna	University of Texas at Arlington
Loafman, Kathryn	University of North Texas
Long, Maurice	British Medical Association
Lowry, Charles B.	University of Texas at Arlington
Lucas, John	Medical College of Ohio
Luce, Clarice	University of North Texas
Lutz, Linda	University of Western Ontario
MacAdam, Carol	Princeton University
MacArthur, Marit	Auraria Library
MacFarland, Scott	Turner Subscriptions
Macklin, Lisa A.	University of North Texas
MacLennan, Birdie	University of Vermont
Magenau, Carol	Dartmouth College
Malawski, Susan	John Wiley & Sons
Malinowski, Teresa	California State University, Fullerton
Malone, Debbie	Ursinus College
Mann, Rick	Ebsco Subscription Services
Markley, Susan	Villanova University
Martin, Sylvia	Vanderbilt University
Mathews, Earl D.	Indiana University
Mauch, John	Saginaw Valley State University
May, Charles	SOLINET
Mayhood, Gary W.	New Mexico State University

Mazuk, Melody	Southern Baptist Theological Seminary
McCafferty, Patrick	Case Western Reserve University
McCammon, Leslie V.	Florida International University
McCann, Kris K.	Dawson Subscription Service
McCawley, Christina	Westchester University
McClary, Maryon L.	University of Alberta-Edmonton
McCollough, Amy F.	Southwestern University
McDonough, Joyce G.	Columbia University
McGarry, Dorothy	University of California, Los Angeles
McGrath, Kathleen	University of British Columbia
McIver, Carole	University of North Carolina at Charlotte
McKay, Beatrice	Trinity University
McKay, Peter	Harcourt Brace Jovanovich, London
McKay, Sharon	EBSCO Subscription Services
McKee, Anne E.	Arizona State University
McKenney, Nancy	Eastern Kentucky University
McKinley, Margaret	University of California, Los Angeles
McMahon, Suzanne	Stanford University
McMillan, Gail	Virginia Polytechnic Institute and State University
McNee, Carolyn	United States Bureau of Reclamation Library
McReynolds, Rosalee	Loyola University, New Orleans
McShane, Kevin P.	National Library of Medicine
Meiseles, Linda	Brooklyn College
Melkin, Audrey	John Wiley & Sons
Mendoza, Rose Marie	Stanford University
Meneely, Kathleen	Cleveland Health Sciences Library
Mesa, Rosa Q.	University of Florida
Mesner, Lillian	University of Kentucky
Miller, David L.	Majors Scientific Subscriptions
Miller, Heather S.	State University of New York at Albany
Miller, Ruby	Trinity University

Miller, Stuart W.	NOTIS Systems
Moles, Jean Ann	University of Arkansas
Moody, Marilyn K.	Rensselaer Polytechnic Institute
Moore, Millie	Tulane University
Moore, Patricia L.	Michigan Tech University
Mouw, James	University of Chicago
Mrkich, Francie	Lehigh University
Mueller, Britt	University of Oregon
Murden, Steven H.	Virginia Commonwealth University
Murphy, Pency	Texas Instruments
Narin, Francis	CHI RESEARCH
Nelson, Carol L.	Baker & Taylor Continuations
Nelson, Catherine R.	Tulane University
Newsome, Nancy	University of North Carolina at Charlotte
Nordman, Alan	Dawson Subscription Service
O'Neil, Rosanna M.	Pennsylvania State University
O'Reilly, Sheila	Harcourt Brace Jovanovich
Oberg, Steven	University of Illinois, Urbana-Champaign Campus
Okerson, Ann	ARL
Osheroff, Sheila Keil	Oregon State University
Pabbruwe, Herman	Kluwer Academic Publishers
Parang, Elizabeth	University of Nevada, Las Vegas
Paredes, Providence F.	United States Postal Service Library
Parisi, Paul A.	Acme Bookbinding
Patrick, Carolyn	Texas Tech University
Pender, Maureen Jenkins	Faxon Canada
Perkins, John M.	Wake Forest Law Library
Persing, Robert	Boston College
Peterson, Candace A.	San Antonio College
Peterson, Lisa	University of California, Riverside
Phillips, Sharon	California State University, Hayward
Pidgeon, Sean	IOP Publishing
Pionessa, Gerry	University of Arizona

Piternick, Anne B.	University of British Columbia
Polson, Lin	Simon Fraser University
Postlethwaite, Bonnie	Tufts University
Presley, Roger L.	Georgia State University
Preslock, Karen	Bookquest/Serialsquest
Price, Margaret	University of British Columbia
Putney, Patricia	Brown University
Radulescu, Gabriela	Springer-Verlag
Raines, M. Diane	Dynix, Inc.
Ralston, M. Joan	Villanova University
Rankin, Juliann	California State University, Chico
Rast, Elaine K.	Northern Illinois University
Rauch, Theodore G.	Columbia University
Ravinder, Sarita	Princeton Theological Seminary
Redman, Betsy J.	Arizona State University
Reed, Joy	University Microfilms International
Reed, Virginia R.	Northeastern Illinois University
Reedy, Dianne	Houston Public Library
Revas, Robert	University of Utah
Rhodes, Sharon A.	University of Missouri – Columbia
Rice, Patricia Ohl	Pennsylvania State University
Riddick, John F.	Central Michigan University
Riding, Ed	Dynix, Inc.
Riley, Cheryl	Central Missouri State University
River, Sandra	Texas Tech University
Roach, Sandra	Trinity University
Robillard, Jane A.	Veteran's Administration
Robinson, Helen	University of Colorado at Colorado Springs
Robischon, Rose	United States Military Academy
Roepke, Gregory A.	University of Maryland at Baltimore
Roesemann, Douglas N.	Springer-Verlag
Rogers, Marilyn L.	University of Arkansas
Romaniuk, Elena	University of Victoria
Rossignol, Lucien R.	Smithsonian Institution
Roth, Dana	Caltech

Salk, Judy	R.R. Bowker
Salomon, Patricia H.	Bowling Green State University
Santosuosso, Joe	The Faxon Company
Sarazin, Georges	Faxon Canada
Savage, Steve	University of Kentucky
Saxe, Minna C.	City University of New York
Scanlon, Kaval	George Washington University
Scarry, Patricia	University of Chicago Press
Schaafsma, Carol A.	University of Hawaii
Schack, Cathy	University of Texas at Dallas, Southwestern Medical Center
Schierling, Ingrid	University of Colorado at Colorado Springs
Schimizzi, Anthony J.	University of Alabama at Birmingham
Schingeck, Candace	University Microfilms International
Schipul, Elizabeth V.	Incarnate Word College
Schmidt, Sandra	NOTIS Systems
Schmidt, Vincent	EBSCO Subscription Services
Schmidt, Kathy Wodrich	Indiana University
Schwartz, Frederick	The Faxon Company
Schweitzberger, Kathleen	University of Missouri—Kansas City
Scott, Sharon K.	University of Nevada, Reno
Scullin, Jan	Massachusetts General Hospital
Sederstrom, Gene	University of South Dakota
Shaffer, Barbara A.	University of Toledo
Shaw, Deborah L.	Oklahoma State University
Shelton, Judith M.	Georgia State University
Shen, Emily C.	University of Texas at Arlington
Sherer, Ree	EBSCO Subscription Services
Showalter, Madeleine	Abilene Christian University
Shropshire, Sandra	Idaho State University
Shroyer, Andrew	University of California, Santa Barbara
Sievers, Arlene Moore	Case Western Reserve University
Sleep, Esther L.	Brock University

Smink, Marjorie M.	College of Physicians of Philadelphia
Smith, Beth	Trinity University
Smith, Sue	B.H. Blackwell
Sommer, Deborah	University of California, Berkeley
Soupiset, Kathryn	Trinity University
Sowa, Kathryn A.	New Mexico State University
Steele, Heather	B.H. Blackwell
Stephens, Joan Luke	Georgia State University
Stewart, Silvia	University of Texas at Austin
Stillman, Garry	St. Mary's University
Su, Julie	Indiana University/Purdue University
Sullivan, Patricia	California State University, Chico
Sutherland, Laurie	University of Washington
Swetman, Barbara	Hamilton College
Tagler, John	Elsevier Science Publishers
Talley, Kaye M.	University of Central Arkansas
Teague, Elaine E.	Burroughs Wellcome Company
Teaster-Woods, Gale	Winthrop College
Teel, Katherine	Columbia University
Tenney, Joyce	University of Maryland at Baltimore
Tento, Nancy	Academic Book Center
Terry, Nancy	Grand Valley State University
Thomas, Evelyne B.	Davidson College
Thompson, Sherry	Majors Scientific Subscriptions
Thomson, Mary Beth	University of Houston
Thorn, Sue	PION Limited
Thornberry, Pat	University of South Florida
Thorne, Kathleen	San Jose State University
Thornton, Christopher P.	Case Western Reserve University
Tijerino, Cathy	University of New Orleans
Timberlake, Phoebe	University of New Orleans
Tirados, Marie Jo	Schering Plough Research
Tong, Dieu Van	University of Alabama at Birmingham
Tonkery, Dan	Readmore

Tribit, Donald	Millersville University
Turitz, Mitch	San Francisco State University
Turner, Lillie	St. Phillip's College
Tusa, Sarah D.	Lamar University
Unver, Amira	George Washington University
Upham, Lois N.	University of South Carolina
Urka, Mary Ann	George Washington University
Van Avery, Annalisa R.	State University of New York at Albany
Van Goethem, Jeri	Duke University
Van Jacob, Scott	Dickinson College
Van Velzen, Antoon	SWETS Subscription Service
Vanderhoof, Audrey	Texas Christian University
Varga, Terese M.	Arizona State University
Vent, Marilyn	University of Nevada, Las Vegas
Vidor, Ann B.	Emory University
Von Hagen, Jolanda L.	Springer-Verlag
Walker, Elaine	Cornell University
Wall, Colleen	3M Technical Library
Wallace, Patricia M.	University of Colorado
Walters, Mitchel	University of Texas at Dallas, Southwestern Medical Center
Wan, William	Texas Women's University
Ward, Jeannette	University of Central Florida
Waring, Jonathan	Collets Subscription Service
Warren, Louise	Emory University
Weaver, Sandra	Innovative Interfaces
Weed, Merry	Springer-Verlag
Weng, Cathy	Temple University
Wesley, Dianne	University Microfilm International
West, Kathleen	University of Kansas
Wetzel, Bonnie	New Mexico State University
Whittaker, Brenda	National Library of Medicine
Whittaker, Martha	CARL Systems
Wilkinson, Frances C.	University of New Mexico
Williams, Geraldine	Northern Kentucky University

Williams, Sue	University of Colorado, Boulder
Winchester, David	Washburn University
Winjum, Roberta	University of Missouri-Columbia
Wirtz, Theresa M.	Yankee Book Peddler
Wolfe, Garry R.	Faxon Canada
Woodward, Hazel	UK Serials Group
Wright, Bernice	Stephen F. Austin State University
Yuster, Leigh C.	R.R. Bowker
Ziegler, Roy	Southeast Missouri State University
Zook, Ruth Ann	United States Bureau of Reclamation Library
Zubal, John T.	USBE

Index

Abrahams Magazine Service, 166
Abstracting and indexing services, 8,11-13
Access-based paradigm for libraries, 120-121,133-134
Access vs. ownership
  representation in bibliographic records, 103-104
  representation in serials control systems, 88
ADONIS project, 8,27,135
Advertisements for journals, 143-145
AIIM. *See* Association for Information and Image Management
All-Union Bookchamber, Moscow, 65
Alley, Brian, 92
American Chemical Society, 24
American Library Association, 126
  Committee on Accreditation, 127
American Mathematical Society, 19
ANSI, 181
ANSI X12, 93,193-196
ARL. *See* Association of Research Libraries
Artificial intelligence, 91-93
ASC X12 (committee), 195
ASCII files, 9,99
Association for Information and Image Management, 181
Association of American Publishers, 126
Association of Research Libraries, 119
  Guidelines for Bibliographic Records for Preservation Microfilm Masters, 183

Authorship, online, 23
Automation, effects on organizations, 121-126
Aveney, Brian, 92

Back issues. *See* Replacement issues
Bailey, Charles, 19
Baker & Taylor, 93
Baratz, Allan, 113
Basch, Buzzy, 169,171
Bazirjian, Rosann, 149-150
Beckett, Christopher, 193-194
BIBLAT, 80
Bibliographic records
  representation of access in, 103-104
  serials control system links to, 162
  use in serials record conversion, 154
Bibliometric research, 34-36,81-82
BIBLIOTECH system, 157-160
BIC. *See* British Book Industry Communication committee
Bindery system, 159-160
Birmingham Loughborough Electronic Network Development. *See* BLEND
Bitnet, 107
BLEND, 22-23,26,186
Border controls, European Community, 46-47
Bradley, Melissa, 189-191
BrancheBrown, Lynne, 157-160
Breithaupt, John, 169-170
British Book Industry Communication committee, 195

© 1991 by The Haworth Press, Inc. All rights reserved.

Brown, Gary, 202
Brownrigg, Ed, 94
BT LINK, 93

c. elgans project, 10
Cameras for preservation microfilming, 182
Campus information systems, 95, 102-103
CARL system, 191
CARL UnCover database, 12,135, 136,147
   use study, 189-191
CARL UnCover document delivery service, 12,190
   use of electronic storage technology, 9
Carrington, Bradley Dean, 147-148
CAUSE, 119
CD-ROM databases, 135
   use in Latin American libraries, 80
CD-ROM format, choice to publish in, 113
CEC. *See* Commission of the European Communities
Censorship, breakdown of, in Eastern bloc countries, 63
Chamberlain, Carol, 89,92,93
Chemical Abstracts, 166
CHI Research, 36
CICH. *See* Universidad Nacional Autonoma de Mexico
Citation(s)
   counts, 27
   indexes, 11
   in U.S. patents, 41-44
CLASE, 80
Coalition for Networked Information, 119
   document delivery service, 9
Coauthorship data, 41,42 (chart)
Cockfield, Lord, 45-46
Cole, F.J., 34-36
Collaboration
   role of telecommunication networks in, 11,13
   within organizations, 123-126
Collection development, artificial intelligence applications in, 92
Collection management workstations, 93
Colorado Alliance of Research Libraries. *See* CARL
Commission of the European Communities, 36
Communication
   between public and technical services staff, 152
   between publisher, vendor, and library, 162,170
Computer conferences. *See* Electronic conferences
Computer Human Factors, 22
Computer use by humanities and social science scholars, 30
Computer-mediated communication, human factors in, 29
Computing platforms, 134-135
CONSER, 103,184
Contracts with system vendors, 163
Copyright, 120,137
Cornish, Graham, 27
Current awareness services, 12
Current Contents, 8
Custom publishing, 8

Data Disc Man Electronic Book, 110,113
Data transmission across international borders, 24-25
Davis, Trisha L., 161-164
Delgado, H., 83
Delors, Jacques, 45,54
Denver Public Library, 189-191
Desmarais, Norman, 92
Direct mail marketing to libraries, 143-144
   effect of library staff cuts on, 145

Directory of Back-Issue Dealers, 166
Directory of Electronic Journals, Newsletters, and Digests, 119
Display quality, electronic, 12
Document delivery, 8-9,11,136
  role of libraries and vendors, 12
DocuTech copier, 8,9
Dostroika, 63-67
Drexler Technology Corporation, 110
Drucker, Peter, 121,126
Duplicates
  exchange lists, 166
  in Eastern bloc libraries, 61
  returning to publisher, 203

Eales, Nellie B., 34-36
Eastern bloc countries, 59-67. *See also* U.S.S.R.
  area studies in United States, 66
  cost of publications, 65-66
  integration with West, 63-67
  libraries
    automation, 65
    commercialization, 62-63
    contact with other countries, 61
    lack of resources, 63
  library collections in United States on, 60
  government funding for, 67
  services to immigrants, 66
  use by private enterprise, 66-67
  publication and collection of emigre literature, 64
EBSCONET, 157-160
EC-92, 45-57
  effect on serials industry, 51-56
  German participation in, 50,54
  Japanese influence, 55
  publishing costs and, 51-52
  removal of border restrictions, 46-47
  technical standardization, 48

  telecommunications, 52-53,55
EDI, 193-196
EDUCOM, 119
EFTA. *See* European Free Trade Association
EIES, 21-22,186
  exclusion of British authors, 21-22,24-25
  informal communication features, 21
Electronic bulletin boards
  for electronic journal access, 100
  informal scholarly communication on, 6-7
  reviewed articles on, 7
Electronic conferences, 7,12,17-18
Electronic Data Interchange. *See* EDI
Electronic Information Exchange System. *See* EIES
Electronic journals. *See also* specific titles
  access, 97,100-102
    bibliographic, 103-104,187
    international, 25
    online vs. printouts, 26,98,187
    via campus information systems, 95
    via Internet, 119
  archiving, 12,97,187
  as solution to journal crisis, 15-31
  benefits to libraries, 97
  graphics in, 99
  holdings statements, 104
  human factors, 16-17,24-27,28
  impact on library services, 185-187
  production costs, 23
  publishers' attitudes about, 187
  refereed, 7,119
  reference service for, 105,186
  selection, 106-107
  serial treatment, 98-99
  staff training issues, 106,187
  standardization, 186

storage, 97,99,100-102,108
technical processing, 94-95, 104-105,107
value, 185-186
without print versions, 10
Electronic mail, 115
  human factors, 16
  notices from publishers via, 104
  scholarly communication using, 17-18
  submission of journal articles via, 12
  use in Latin America, 84
Electronic media
  abstracting and indexing, 25
  access, 119
    bibliographic, 25
    in less developed countries, 24
  author's control of text in, 26
  citation standards, 25-26
  economic censorship, 27
  human factors, 24
  libraries' support of, 136
  output formats, 26
  permanence, 26-27
  replacing local collections, 119
Electronic networks. *See* Telecommunication networks
Electronic newsletters, 18. *See also* specific titles
  use for informal scholarly information, 7,12
Electronic publications. *See also* specific titles
  as archival versions, 10
  ROM versions, 119
  replacement issues, 167
Elsevier, 52,94,173-176
Emigre literature in Eastern bloc countries, 64
Etzioni, Amiati, 126,128-129
European Community
  banking system, 49
  development cycle, 39-40
  economic relations with other countries, 54-55
  Internal Market. *See* EC-92
  technological growth (chart), 37
European Free Trade Association, 50
European Monetary System, 48-49
Expert systems, 91-93

FAX, 15-16
Faxon Company, 9,93,202,206
  document delivery service, 12
Faxon Institute, 133
Faxon SC-10 system, 153-155
Fecko, Mary Beth, 185-187
Fee-based services in Eastern bloc libraries, 62-63
Feick, Tina, 169,171-172
File transfer, 115
  for graphics, 99
Format, choice of, 113-119,114 (chart)
Fortress Europe, 45,53,54-55
Frame, J. Davidson, 36
Freedom to Read (ALA-AAP joint statement), 126

Gammon, Julia, 201-202
GATT. *See* General Agreement on Trades and Tariffs
Geac system, 90,150
General Agreement on Trades and Tariffs, 49-50
  negotiations, 54,56
Geological Society of America, 20
Georgia State University, 153-154, 156
Germany, reunification of, 50
Gifts and exchange programs for Latin American publications, 206
Gonzalez, Nelly S., 205-206
Graphics
  electronic transmission of, 7,99

in electronic media, 115,119,135
Gray literature, 17
Gross Domestic Product (GDP), 36-38
Gross National Product (GNP), 36
Guidelines for Bibliographic Records for Preservation Microfilm Masters, 183

H. W. Wilson, 166
Help screens
  for electronic journals, 103-104
  for holdings data, 152
HERTZBERG CONNECTION, 159-160
Hierarchical organizations, effect of information technology on, 122-123
High definition television, 115
High technology light industry, library as, 109
Hispanic American Periodicals Index, 206
Holley, Beth, 165-166
Houghton, Jean, 89-90
Huesmann, James L., 161-164
Hughes, Katharine, 157,159-160
Human Genome Project, 7,10
Humanities scholars, computer use, 30
Hypertext, 26

ICEDIS. *See* International Committee for Electronic Data Interchange for Serials
Incomplete volumes, alternatives to binding, 165-166
Index Medicus, 135
Informated organizations, 121-126
  vs. hierarchical organizations, 123-126
Information exchange between North and South America, 83
Information Store, 135

Information technology
  as medium for relationships, 111, 124
  impact on librarianship, 109-132
  impact on library organizations, 121-126
  use by Latin American journal publishers, 83
Information UK 2000, 6
Information-seeking behavior, 112
INNOVACQ system, 94-95
Innovations, human factors in adoption of, 28
Innovative Interfaces, 88,90
Institute of Czech Literature, 63
Institute of Scholarly Information in the Social Sciences, 65
Institutional coauthorship, 41
Integrated file access to contents, 147-148
Integrated library systems, 123
Intellectual property rights, 137
Interfaces, library system, 93-94, 159-160
Interlibrary loan
  as source of replacement issues, 166
  impact of CARL UnCover document delivery service on, 190
International Committee for Electronic Data Interchange for Serials, 195
Internet, 107
  electronic journals on, 119
Invisible college, 17
Iowa State University, 92

Japan
  development cycle, 39
  technological growth, 33-34
Job advertisements, serials related, 197-198
Job applications, 198-200
John Wiley & Sons, 94

Johns Hopkins University, 7,10
Journal of Applied Mathematics, 24
*Journal of Photochemistry and
    Photobiology,* 173-176
*Journal of the American Society of
    Information Science,* 23
Journal of the History of Sexuality,
    143-145
Journals. *See also* Serials and
        specific titles
    articles
        electronic storage, 8-10,12
        online catalog access, 147-148
        retrospective conversion to
            electronic format, 13
        submission via
            telecommunication networks,
            7
    articles, electronic
        on-demand printing, 103
        retention, 27
    future of print format, 133,
        185-186
    marketing, 143-146,173-176
    new titles, 139-141,145-146
    publicity, 174
    publishing
        costs, 140-141
        in Latin America, 81
    review process, 7
    sales, 177
    simultaneous publication in
        electronic and print formats,
        9-10
    variable pricing, 75
Journals, scientific
    alternatives to, 19-21
    browsability, 175-176
    citations in U.S. patents, 41-44
Journals, social science, 143-146
Journals, society-based, 177-179
Journals, women's studies, 143-145

Kartashov, N.S., 61
Katzen, May, 28

Kentucky Newspaper Project, 182
Kluwer, 94
Knowledge
    industry, 126-129
    vs. information, 111
    workers
        librarians as, 109-111
        skill levels, 121-123
Kraus Periodicals, 166
Kuhn, T.S., 120

Langschied, Linda, 185-187
Latin America
    effect of economic and political
        policies on information flow,
        84
    scholarly information in, 69-85
    scholars, 81
    serials
        bibliographic sources, 205-206
        cataloging, 206-207
        importance to Latin American
            collections, 205
        indexes, 80-81
        publications
            by universities, 81
            official, 206
        publishing industry, 81,83
        vendors, 207
Lenin Library, 60-61,65
Letters of recommendation, 198-199
Librarians
    professional status in Eastern bloc
        countries, 62
    role in research process, 126
    standardization of credentials in
        European Community, 53
Librarianship
    as a "semi-profession", 132
    increasing professionalization of,
        128-129
Libraries
    collections, cost of, 134
    cooperation, 128
    education, 137

Index   231

curriculum revision, 131
impact of information
    technology on, 127
relationship to knowledge
    industry, 126-129
staff training, 127
users, growing expectations of,
    133-134
Library of Congress, 206
    Exchange and Gifts Division, 166
    MARC Standards Office, 148
    study of multiple versions
        cataloging, 183
Library of the Academy of Sciences,
    61
Local area networks
    effect on library organizations,
        123
    for electronic journal access, 100
Loyola University of Chicago
    Medical Center Library, 157,
    159-160
Lynden, Fred, 93

Malawski, Susan, 167-168
MARBI, 148
MARC records for contents access,
    147-178
Martell, Charles, 120
Mathematical Offprint Service, 19
McGraw-Hill/Donnelly, 8
McIver, Carole, 197-198
McKay, Peter, 202-203
McKay, Sharon Cline, 195-196
McLuhan, Marshall, 113
Megaword, 110
Mental Workload, 21,25
Mergers, impact of EC-92 on, 52-53
Mesa, Rosa Q., 205-207
Microcomputers
    human factors, 112
    impact on libraries, 110
Microfilm, 181-182
Microform
    cataloging, 182-184

publication, 20
Miniprint publication, 20
Monetary policy, European
    Community, 49
Moscow-San Francisco Teleport, 65
Motion simulation in scholarly
    publications, 10
Multi-media
    file transfer, 115
    publications, 11-12,13
Multiple Database Access System,
    147
Multiple versions
    cataloging, 183-184
    serials control, 88
Multiple Versions Forum, 184
Murden, Stephen H., 153,155-156

National development cycles, 38-40
National Library of Medicine,
    Williams and Wilkins vs.,
    137
National scientific size, 36
National University of Mexico. *See*
    Universidad Nacional
    Autonoma de Mexico
Negotiation
    between libraries and vendors,
        171
    between vendors, 158
New Jersey Institute of Technology,
    21
Newsletter on Serials Pricing Issues,
    94
NISO, 195
NOTIS system, 149-150
NREN, 115-116; 116 (chart)
NSFNET, 115-116; 116 (chart)

OCLC serials subsystem, 155
Ohio State University, 161-164
    processing of electronic journals,
        94-95
OhioLINK, 88

Okerson, Ann, 10
Online catalogs
  access to contents, 147-148
  search protocols, 148
Optical mass-storage media, 110
Optical media cards, 110,113
Organizations, effects of automation on, 121-126
ORION (online catalog), 206

PACS-L, 18
PACS Review, 25,26
Parallel computing, 115
Patents
  as measure of technological performance, 34,36,37
  globalization of, 33-44
  national trends, 41-43
Pergamon Press, 52,94
PERIODICA, 80
Periodicals Price Index for Latin America, 206
Polson, Lin, 149-152
Position announcements, serial-related, 197-198
PostScript files, 9,99
Preservation microfilming, 181-182
Price, Derek de Solla, 36
Primis system, 8
Print runs, planning of, 167
Print vs. electronic media, 6
Print-outs of electronic media, 133
Profiles, 92,162-163
Public Access Computer Systems News, 18
Publication counts as measure of technological performance, 34-36
Publication patterns
  database, 95
  migration to new serials control systems, 91
Publishers
  decision-making processes, 139-141
  inventory control, 167-168
Publishers, commercial
  ownership of copyright, 120
  publication of society-based journals, 177-179
Publishers, society-based, 169-170
Publishing in Latin America, 206

Quality, judgment of, as part of information service, 126-127

Radulescu, Gabriela, 139-141
Rasstroika, 60-63
Raytheon Equipment Division Technical Information Center, 157-160
Replacement issues, 165-168
Research, globalization of, 33-44, 134
Research Libraries Group, 181
Resumes, 199
Retrospective collection building and replacement issues, 166-167
Retrospective searching of journal literature, 11
RLG. *See* Research Libraries Group
Royal Chemical Society, 94
Russell, J.M., 83

SALALM. *See* Seminar on the Acquisition of Latin American Library Materials
Saltykov-Shchedrin, 61
Savage, Steve, 181-182
Scanning, electronic, of texts, 13
Scarry, Patricia, 143-146
Scholarly communication, 5-13
  informal, 6-7,12
Scholarly Communications Project, 97-98
Scholarly information
  current awareness, 8-10
  globalization, 33-44

Scholarly publishing crisis, 120-121
Scholars' use of electronic formats, 136-137
Schrage, Michael, 111,124
Schwartz, Fritz, 194-195
Science and technology, relationship between, 41-44; 43 (chart)
Science Citation Index, 41
　coverage of Latin American journals, 81
　Japanese papers in, 39; 39 (table)
Science Indicators, 36
Scientific cooperation, international, 40-41
Search protocols, 148
Seminar on the Acquisition of Latin American Library Materials, 207
Separate file indexes on online catalogs
Separates, dissemination of, 19-20
Serials. *See also* Journals and specific titles
　acquisitions in Latin America, 70, 75,80
　analytics, 147-148
　catalogers, 207
　check-in
　　back-log, 155-156
　　space requirements, 150
　　staffing, 149-152
　claiming, 201-203
　holdings statements
　　availability of, 149-152
　　for electronic journals, 104
　　online displays, 152
　prices, 89
　　for Latin American libraries, 70,75,79-80; 76 (chart)
　selection in Latin American libraries, 79
　transportation in Latin America, 75
　vendors in Latin America, 79
Serials, nonperiodical
　conversion of, 153-156
　manual check-in, 155
Serials control systems, 87-96
　adaptation to local needs, 164
　artificial intelligence applications, 91-93
　conversion to, 154-156,161-164
　evaluation, 162
　hardware, 163
　indexing, 162
　local data, 163
　management reports generated by, 88,89-90
　standardization, 91
　test databases, 162,163
　user's groups, 162
Serials functions, integration of, 150-151
Serials industry, effect of EC-92 on, 51-56
Serials of Illinois Online, 159
Serials Quest, 93
Signs, 143-145
SILO. *See* Serials of Illinois Online
Simon Fraser University, 149-152
Single Administrative Document (European Commission, 1988), 46
SISAC
　barcode, 94
　relationship with ANSI X12, 196
Smartbook, 110,113
Smith, Eldred, 119
Social science scholars, computer use, 30
Society of Automotive Engineers, 19
Software for text preparation, 24
Sony Corporation, 110,113
Sound in scholarly publications, 10
Southeast Asia development cycle, 40
Special Library Association, 133, 137
Springer-Verlag, 139,141,177
Staff training, 164

Stephens, Joan Luke, 153-154,156
Stock reduction plans, publishers', 168
Subject electronic databases, 10
  as scholarly publications, 13
  conversion of retrospective literature to electronic format for, 11
  reviewed articles in, 7
Subscription
  agencies. *See* Vendors
  data, 158
  maintenance, 95
SULIRS system, 149
Synopses, publication of, 20
Swets & Zeitlinger, 166
Syracuse University, 149-152

Tagler, John, 173-176
Task Force on the Electronic Journal (Virginia Polytechnic Institute and State University), 98
Taylor & Francis, 94
TCP/IP, 107
Technological change in libraries, 87-88
Technological development, polarization of, 34
Technology, affordability of, 134
Technology and science, relationship between, 41-44; 43 (chart)
Telecommunication networks
  as low-cost access to electronic media, 113
  data capacity, 113,115-116,119; 116 (chart)
  graphics transmission, 9
  higher education and 115; 118 (chart)
  libraries and, 110
  low-cost access to electronic media, 113
  publishers' access to, 12
  publishing and library applications, 115,118-119; 117,118 (charts)
  reliability, 25
  user interfaces for, 115
Telecommunications, 135
  tariffs, 30
  use for acquisitions by Latin American libraries, 80
Text, electronic storage of, 8-9
Text Pack, 110
Thor decision, 167
Title changes, 203
Transmission/Control Protocol/Internet Protocol. *See* TCP/IP
Turitz, Mitch, 182-184

Ulrich's International Periodicals Directory, 205-206
Ulrich's Plus, 93
UMI, 8
  photocopy service, 166
UNAM. *See* Universidad Nacional Autonoma de Mexico
Uncitedness, 27,31
Union lists, 94
  covering Latin American serials, 206
United Kingdom development cycle, 38
United States
  development cycle, 40
  international economic interests, 55
United States Book Exchange/Universal Serials & Book Exchange, 166-167
Universidad Nacional de Mexico, 69-85
  bibliometric studies, 81-82
  document delivery services, 81
  journal indexes published by, 80-81; 82 (chart)
  scholars' publications, 83
  serials acquisitions, 77-79

budget, 70; 71 (chart)
check-in, 78
serials subscriptions, 70; 72-74 (charts)
staffing, 75,77
University of Arizona at Tucson, 10
University of Calgary, 23
University of California-Los Angeles, 206
University of Chicago Press, 143-146
University of Colorado at Boulder, 189-191
University of Florida, 207
University of Kentucky, 147-148, 181-182
Upham, Lois N., 198-200
USBE. *See* United States Book Exchange/Universal Serials & Book Exchange
USMARC Format for Holdings Data, 91
  use for cataloging multiple versions, 183-184
U.S. patent system, Japanese patents in, 39; 39 (chart)
U.S.S.R. *See also* Eastern bloc countries
U.S.S.R. Ministry of Culture, 60

Value Added Network (VAN), 195
Value Added Tax (VAT), 47,51
Van Jacob, Scott, 205-206
Vendor system interfaces, 157-159
Vendors, 169-172
  fees to libraries, 171,172
  performance statistics, 95
  publishers' discounts to, 169-170
  role in claiming process, 202
  selection of, 172

support of electronic formats, 136
use in Latin America, 75
Video, 10,119
  conferences, 7,115
Virginia Commonwealth University, 153,155-156
Virginia Polytechnic Institute and State University, 97-108
Virtual library
  effect on library organizations, 121
  role of librarian in, 129
Visualization, super computer, 115
Volik, A.P., 61
von Hagen, Jolanda L., 177-179
VTLS system, 65,101

Wallace, Patricia, 189-191
Walter J. Johnson, 166
White Paper (European Commission, 1985), 46,55
William Dawson, 166
Williams and Wilkins vs. National Library of Medicine, 137
Wilson, Patrick, 126
Workstations, electronic, 135
  for collaborative research, 13
  for collection management, 93
  for journal editors, 7
  for scholars, 8-9

X12. *See* ANSI X12; ASC X12 (committee)
Xerox Corporation, 8

Zager, Pam, 92
Zastroika, 59-60
Zubal, John T., 166-167
Zuboff, Shoshana, 121-122

For Product Safety Concerns and Information please contact our EU
representative GPSR@taylorandfrancis.com
Taylor & Francis Verlag GmbH, Kaufingerstraße 24, 80331 München, Germany

www.ingramcontent.com/pod-product-compliance
Lightning Source LLC
Chambersburg PA
CBHW070723020526
44116CB00031B/1474